Hiking South Carolina

HELP US KEEP THIS GUIDE UP TO DATE

Every effort has been made by the author and editors to make this guide as accurate and useful as possible. However, many things can change after a guide is published—trails are rerouted, regulations change, techniques evolve, facilities come under new management, and so on.

We would appreciate hearing from you concerning your experiences with this guide and how you feel it could be improved and kept up to date. While we may not be able to respond to all comments and suggestions, we'll take them to heart, and we'll also make certain to share them with the author. Please send your comments and suggestions to the following address:

Globe Pequot Press
Reader Response/Editorial Department
PO Box 480
Guilford, CT 06437

Or you may e-mail us at: editorial@GlobePequot.com

Thanks for your input, and happy trails!

Hiking
South Carolina

A Guide to the State's
Greatest Hiking Adventures

Joshua Kinser

FALCONGUIDES

GUILFORD, CONNECTICUT
HELENA, MONTANA
AN IMPRINT OF GLOBE PEQUOT PRESS

I would like to dedicate this book to Jessica Nile. Thank you so much for all the love, support, and hard work on this book. I could not have done it without you.

FALCONGUIDES®

FalconGuides is an imprint of Globe Pequot Press.
Falcon, FalconGuides, and Outfit Your Mind are registered trademarks of Morris Book Publishing, LLC.

All interior photos by Joshua Kinser
Maps: Daniel Lloyd © Morris Book Publishing, LLC
Text design: Sheryl P. Kober
Layout: Sue Murray
Project editor: Julie Marsh

Library of Congress Cataloging-in-Publication Data

Kinser, Joshua.
  Hiking South Carolina : a guide to the state's greatest hikes / Joshua Kinser.
      pages cm. – (State hiking guides series)
  Summary: "Hiking South Carolina covers the best hiking throughout the entire state."– Provided by publisher.
  ISBN 978-0-7627-8307-6 (pbk.)
  1. Hiking–South Carolina–Guidebooks. 2. Trails–South Carolina–Guidebooks. 3. South Carolina–Guidebooks. I. Title.
  GV199.42.S58K58 2013
  796.5109757–dc23
                              2013030999

Printed in the United States of America
10 9 8 7 6 5 4 3 2 1

Contents

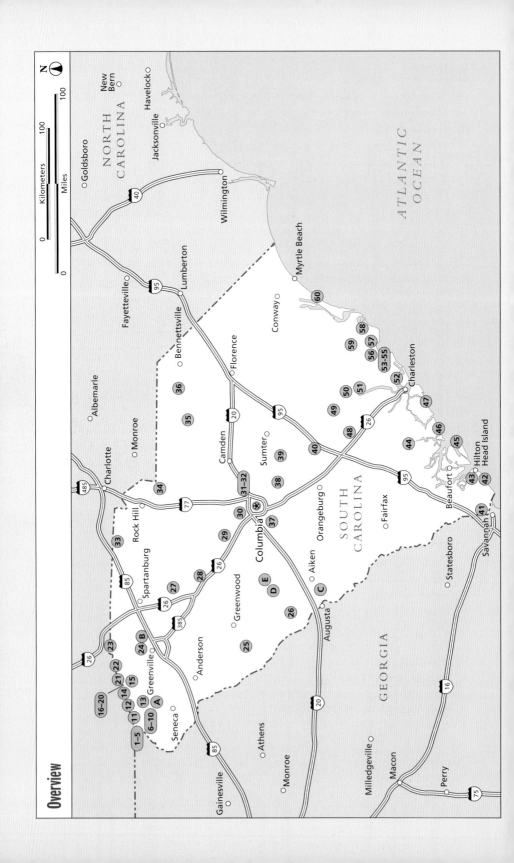

Overview

N

Kilometers
0   100

Miles
0   100

ACKNOWLEDGMENTS

Thank you to Imee Curiel for making this project possible and for giving me this wonderful opportunity to spend more than four months doing nothing but trekking around the mountains, midlands, and coastal gems of South Carolina. I would also like to thank the trail crews, volunteers, park and government employees, visionaries, and various citizenry of the great state of South Carolina who have fought and worked tirelessly to build and maintain the trails that we enjoy. We are lucky that they had the foresight to protect the beautiful forests, beaches, marshes, wetlands, lakes, rivers, ponds, and creeks that are such an integral part of the wonderful culture and experience of the Palmetto State. And I extend my most sincere gratitude to all of the State Park employees, Game and Wildlife Officials, and National Park rangers who helped me so much as I was working on this book. South Carolina has got some boss government staff who are passionate, knowledgeable, and dedicated to supporting and conserving the stunning landscape of this outstanding state.

Rhododendron along the Gum Gap segment of the Foothills Trail (hike 14).

INTRODUCTION

Let's explore South Carolina's extensive network of trails, from the rugged and incomparably scenic mountain lands in the northwest all the way to the sandy beaches, serene marshlands, and maritime forests on the Atlantic Coast. If you are a visitor to the great state of South Carolina, this collection of hiking trails will serve as a valuable tool in becoming familiar with the great diversity of excellent hiking opportunities throughout the state. My hope is that the book will bring you such fulfilling outdoor adventures and experiences within the vastly diverse ecosystems found in the Palmetto State that you will keep returning to our state's trails time and time again. If you are a longtime resident of South Carolina, this book will hopefully stretch the boundaries of your already intimate knowledge of a landscape you know well and love more; taking you to new adventures and discoveries in the lesser known corners of this dynamic hiker's heaven.

My goals in writing this book were simple. I aim to provide accurate and easy-to-understand maps, information, and directions to a diverse collection of trails in South Carolina. I focus on the trails that I consider to be the best trails in the state and also highlight the superior trails nearest to the areas where the greatest populations are located in South Carolina. I want as many people to enjoy the trails in this book as possible. In this inclusive spirit, I have selected trails from every part of the state while still making sure to include those trails widely considered to be superior in their scenic and historical significance and those trails that trek through rare and uniquely special ecosystems or otherwise offer the finest opportunities for wildlife viewing. The book also highlights trails nearest to the population centers of the state, putting a special focus on select trails around Charleston, Spartanburg, Columbia, Greenville, Myrtle Beach, Hilton Head, and Florence. Visitors to the state will find trails in the most popular resort areas such as Kiawah Island, Hilton Head, Edisto Beach, Beaufort, Lake Marion, and the vast network of trails around the stunning mountains surrounding Table Rock and Caesars Head State Park. This book is by no means meant to serve as a compendium of the "best" trails in the state, a term that I find unbearably vague, tired, and hackneyed. This book will serve as a diverse collection of trails of varying difficulty that offers a wide range of experiences suitable for hikers and walkers with a wide-ranging level of hiking and navigation abilities. However, long-distance backpackers and extreme outdoor adventurists should not cringe at this mainstream approach of inclusiveness. This book includes long-distance backpacking trips on the Foothills Trails and Palmetto Trails through rugged gorges and calf-sculpting mountain landscapes difficult enough to make you cry every time you see a set of steep rock steps. It also offers short, easy walks around scenic lakes on flat, paved paths for those looking for opportunities to experience the beauty, solitude, and serenity of the outdoors in a less challenging way.

A hiker takes a moment to cool off at Station Cave Creek along the Station Cave Falls spur trail (hike 8).

My ultimate goal for this book is that it will encourage those who use it to further explore and discover the gift of South Carolina's outstanding trails and outdoors. This book is intended as an introduction to the state and I encourage you to run away from the couch and voyage into a landscape filled with adventure, curiosities, and unparalleled beauty. If you embrace the trails of South Carolina and explore the state's mountains, marshes, and beaches, they often lead you to a life-long love affair with this diverse and spectacular landscape. Just be careful: This is one of the few states where you can encounter bears, poisonous snakes, and gators all in one hike, and I know this all too well. However, there is no other state where you can spend the morning hiking through spectacularly scenic and challenging mountains, the afternoon in the midlands exploring the rolling hills around a stun-ningly beautiful lake, and the evening watching the sun sink behind the Atlantic Ocean on a relaxing barefoot stroll along the beach with the sound of waves rolling onto shore. Then you can cap it all off with the best dinner you've ever had in your life at 39 Rue de Jean in Charleston's charming and historic downtown. Only in a day hiker's daydream. Only in an outdoor enthusiast's perfect paradise. Only in the great state of South Carolina.

Weather

South Carolina has some of the best weather for hiking in the entire country, and most of the trails in this book can be hiked year-round. Winters are mild and gener-ally last from mid-November through mid-February. Summers are extremely hot in the southern and coastal regions of the state and last from May through August. However, these months are a great time to beat the heat and drive to the mountains in the northwest part of the state. The best time of the year to hike anywhere in South Carolina is during the spring (March through May) and fall (September through November). Spring offers spectacular displays of blossoming wildflowers, and in the fall hikers flock to the forests to witness the colorful autumn leaves.

Summer is unarguably the hottest time of the year. It's not just the high tempera-tures but also the intense humidity that creates some very uncomfortable hiking during the summer months in the southern areas of the state. However, the trails often follow along bodies of water where hikers can cool off, and summer afternoon thunderstorms offer some relief from the heat for hikers. The hottest temperatures are found in the midlands, where the average temperatures range between 91°F and 70°. The coast, with its sea breezes, is only slightly, and I mean slightly, cooler, with summer temperatures averaging between 88° and 70°. The mountains are the best bet for summer hiking, with an average high temperature of 84° and an average low of a cool 64°.

The best times to hike on the coastal plain are during the winter, early spring, and late fall. Apart from the welcome colder temperatures, which average between 61° and 49° on the coast, hiking in this area during the winter is more enjoyable because you encounter fewer insects, gators, and snakes that can ruin your fun on the trail, plus there are excellent opportunities for bird watching during these months.

The state receives a moderate amount of rainfall (around 49 inches a year). The rain is for the most part distributed pretty evenly throughout the different seasons and regions of the state. In the midlands and coastal regions, hikers will receive slightly more rain in the summer when those spectacular and somewhat dangerous afternoon thunderstorms that occur around 2 p.m. each day bring a healthy dose of rain and lightning to the regions.

Flora and Fauna

Similar to the landscape and ecosystems of South Carolina, the wildlife is extremely diverse throughout the state. In the mountains you will find species such as black bears and peregrine falcons. In the swamps and the southern end of the state, you find subtropical species such as alligators and a wide variety of birds. On the coast you will also find dolphins and sea turtles in the Atlantic Ocean. In the midlands are large populations of deer and wild turkeys. Throughout the state you will find mammals including beavers, raccoons, foxes, bobcats, feral hogs, and river otters. The bald eagle has made an exciting recovery in South Carolina in recent years. And preservationists continue to fight for the conservation of habitat to protect the threatened red-cockaded woodpecker and the fascinating gopher tortoise, which is considered a keystone species and which builds extensive burrows that provide habitat for hundreds of species of other reptiles, insects, and small mammals.

South Carolina is also a spectacular attraction for birding enthusiasts. The most popular sites are Huntington Beach State Park and the Savannah National Wildlife Refuge, where more than 350 species of birds have been identified. The wetlands along the coast are generally the best areas for spotting birds. They are popular year-round with wading birds like herons, egrets, and ibises and they provide essential wintering grounds for ducks. A wide variety of birds pass through the state during their spring and fall migrations to and from the north. You will find various birds of prey patrolling the skies, including ospreys and bald eagles. Throughout the year songbirds and woodpeckers can be found within the forests.

Take extra precautions when hiking the trails in South Carolina to watch for poisonous snakes including eastern diamondback rattlesnakes, timber rattlesnakes, copperheads, cottonmouths (aka moccasins), and even coral snakes. Then again, encountering poisonous snakes along the trail is fairly rare. Don't let their presence keep you from enjoying the outdoors. For the most part, if you leave them alone, they won't bother you.

Alligators are another concern in South Carolina. Attacks have occurred, including one in 2007 when 59-year-old Bill Hedden of Summerville was snorkeling in Lake Moultrie and a 12-foot alligator attacked him, ripping off his arm. Attacks are rare, but it goes without saying that even though alligators may appear extremely docile and alarmingly apathetic, they are extremely dangerous and capable of easily killing a human. They are also surprisingly fast when moving over short distances. Alligators are seldom a threat to hikers. However, alligators are known to enjoy feasting on pets. So keep your Yorkshire terrier from becoming gator bait by keeping your dog restrained on a leash while trekking through gator country.

The trees and plants of South Carolina are widely diverse as well. In the mountains you find forests dominated by oak and hickory, mountain laurel, and rhododendron. Spring is an especially nice time to be in the mountains when the rhododendron, wildflowers, mountain laurel, and azaleas are in full bloom. The scents and sights are wonderful. The rest of the state is mostly covered forests dominated by oaks and pines. In the maritime forests on the coast, you will find vegetation and trees resistant to the constant salt spray and intense wind brought in from the Atlantic Ocean. In this region you find trees such as Carolina palmetto, laurel oak, live oaks draped in Spanish moss, slash and loblolly pines, as well as hollies, dwarf palmetto, wax myrtle, red bay, and red cedar.

In the wetlands along the coastal plain, there are excellent and mostly level trails that traverse through serene swamps with dark tea-colored water where bald-cypress and tupelo trees thrive. Many of the marshlands are reclaimed agricultural growing operations where rice and other crops were grown throughout the 1700s. These areas are often managed as waterfowl and migrating bird habitat and are exceptionally beautiful, especially in the spring when the spider lilies and wildflowers are blossoming.

Wilderness Restrictions/Regulations

The hiking trails in this book traverse through lands that are controlled and managed by various public and private groups. Each group has its own rules and regulations that must be respected and adhered to at all times while hiking on these lands. Most of the trails in this book traverse through national forests and state parks. However, there are several hikes within National Wildlife Refuges and one in Congaree National Park that tend to have stricter rules and regulations in regard to recreation and land-use restrictions.

When day hiking, permits are generally not required to enjoy any of the trails in this book. However, when embarking on long-distance hiking trips, you will often need to call the managing office of the area through which you are hiking to secure a backcountry permit for that area. Occasionally you will also be required to reserve campsites for each night that you will be camping along the trail, especially in the Congaree National Park. National forest lands are less strict in regard to camping and generally allow dispersed, primitive camping along the trails as long as you are not within a particular distance from waterways, the trail, roads, and other areas of importance or historical significance. Before embarking on a hiking trip, check for camping restrictions on the websites or with the offices of the managing bodies of the lands you will be traversing. Rules and regulations are always changing and it is important to be up to date on the current rules to avoid expensive tickets and fees that may be issued to hikers.

A view of the Gum Gap segment of the Foothills Trail in winter.

How to Use This Guide

Each regional section begins with an introduction that gives you a sweeping look at the lay of the land. After this general overview, specific hikes within that region are described. You'll learn about the terrain and what surprises each route has to offer.

To aid in quick decision making, each hike chapter begins with a hike summary. These short summaries give you a taste of the hiking adventure to follow. You'll learn about the trail terrain and what the route has to offer. Next, you'll find the quick, nitty-gritty details of the hike: where the trailhead is located, total hike length, approximate hiking time, difficulty rating, type of trail terrain, best hiking season, what other trail users you may encounter, trail schedules, whether a fee is required, and trail contacts (for updates on trail conditions). The "Finding the Trailhead" section gives you dependable directions from a nearby city or town right down to where you'll want to park your car. The hike description is the meat of the chapter, where you'll get a detailed and honest personally researched impression of the trail. In "Miles and Directions," mileage cues identify all turns and trail name changes, as well as points of interest. The "Hike Information" section at the end of each hike is a hodgepodge of information. In it, you'll find such things as local information resources through which you can learn more about the area, where to stay, where to eat, and what else to see while you're hiking in the area.

Route maps show all of the accessible roads and trails, points of interest, water, towns, landmarks, and geographical features along the hike. They also distinguish trails from roads. The selected route is highlighted, and directional arrows point the way.

Trail Finder

Best Hikes for Backpackers
1 Foothills Trail: Chattooga Valley Segment
2 Foothills Trail, Fork Mountain Trail, Chattooga Trail Loop
11 Lower Whitewater Falls and Coon Branch Natural Area
12 Foothills Trail: Jocassee Gorges
14 Foothills Trail: Sassafras Mountain Segment
49 Palmetto Trail: Lake Moultrie Passage
50 Palmetto Trail: Swamp Fox Passage
56 Palmetto Trail: Awendaw Passage

Best Hikes for Waterfalls
1 Foothills Trail: Chattooga Valley Segment
2 Foothills Trail, Fork Mountain Trail, Chattooga Trail Loop
4 Big Bend and King Creek Falls
6 Oconee State Park
7 Hidden Falls Trail
10 Lee Falls
12 Foothills Trail: Jocassee Gorges
17 Raven Cliff Falls
19 Rainbow Falls
20 Rim of the Gap Trail
21 Falls Creek and Hospital Rock Trails

Best Day Hikes
7 Hidden Falls Trail
15 Table Rock State Park
17 Raven Cliff Falls
19 Rainbow Falls
20 Rim of the Gap Trail
24 Paris Mountain State Park
31 Sesquicentennial State Park Sandhills Trail
33 Kings Mountain National Park Battlefield Trail
34 Landsford Canal State Historic Site
38 Congaree National Park
39 Poinsett State Park Coquina Trail
42 Sea Pines Forest Preserve
45 Edisto Beach State Park
46 Hunting Island State Park
47 Kiawah Island; Marsh Island Park

A beautiful horse pasture on the way to Jones Gap State Park

Best Hikes for Beach/Coast Lovers

Map Legend

Municipal

≡(20)≡   Interstate Highway

≡(178)≡   US Highway

≡(107)≡   State Road

≡[263]≡   Local/County Road

≡[FR 356]≡   Forest Road

≡ ≡ ≡ ≡   Unpaved Road

┠──┼──┼──   Railroad

── ·· ──   State Boundary

Trails

------   Featured Trail

------   Trail

──────   Paved Trail

Water Features

Body of Water

Marsh

River/Creek

Intermittent Stream

Waterfall

Spring

Land Management

National Park/Forest

National Monument/Wilderness Area

State/County Park

Symbols

Bench

Bridge

Backcountry Campground

Boardwalk/Steps

Boat Launch

Building/Point of Interest

Campground

Cliff

Gate

Lighthouse

Parking

Pass

Peak/Elevation

Picnic Area

Ranger Station/Park Office

Restroom

Scenic View

Tower

Town

Trailhead

Visitor/Information Center

There are plenty of great views of the Catawba River along the Nature and Canal Trails (hike 34).

Mountains and Northern Region

T he highlights of the mountain region are the numerous waterfalls, creeks, and rivers found in this rugged and challenging terrain. In South Carolina the piedmont and the mountain area is often called the Upcountry. However, in this book we have divided the state into three sections, and the mountain section refers to the Upcountry tourism district that includes the most mountainous areas in the northern part of the state. Twenty-four of the trails in this book are found scattered above and around the Blue Ridge Escarpment, which is often referred to as the Blue Wall. South Carolina's mountains are at the southern end of the Blue Mountain Range. Here the mountains often drop off in spectacular, scenic, and dramatically steep bluffs and slopes that range from 1,000 to 2,000 feet. This is the coolest part of the state, which makes for exceptionally comfortable hiking during the spring, summer, and fall seasons. Summer brings a higher amount of rain to the mountains of South Carolina, which are among the rainiest places in North America.

A large portion of the hikes in the mountains are within the Mountain Bridge Wilderness Area, considered the crown jewel of South Carolina hiking, which is now managed by the State Park Service; the Andrews Pickens District of Sumter National Forest; and the Jocassee Gorges Wilderness, now managed by the South Carolina Department of Natural Resources. It is worth noting that although the name misleadingly implies it, the Mountain Bridge Wilderness is not a federally designated wilderness area. Another highlight of the mountain area is the Wild and Scenic Chattooga River, which can be enjoyed by hiking various trails in this book, most notably the Chattooga Valley Segment of the Foothills Trail and otherwise along the Foothills Trail, Fork Mountain Trail, and Chattooga Trail Loop, which I highly recommend for backpacking in the mountain region. Around the Chattooga River you will enjoy views of the stunningly beautiful river gorges that funnel powerful and scenic rivers into Lake Jocassee.

Station Cove Falls is considered one of the most impressive waterfalls in the state (hike 8).

1 Foothills Trail: Chattooga Valley Segment

Discover several of the best waterfalls in South Carolina and scenic views of the Chattooga River and surrounding mountain landscape along this moderately challenging three-day backpacking trip. You traverse through the lush Chattooga River watershed, onto high bluffs, and over mountains on a sparsely used trail that often offers hikers welcome solitude. This is a top-pick trail in South Carolina for backpacking and one you don't want to miss if you like to combine fishing with your backcountry explorations.

Start: From the trailhead in Oconee State Park
Distance: 29.4-mile shuttle
Hiking time: About 2–3 days
Difficulty: Moderate to strenuous due to length and elevation gains
Trail surface: Forested trail, gravel path, dirt road
Best seasons: Spring (Mar–May) for wildflower displays; fall (Sept–Nov) for fall foliage
Other trail users: Hikers only
Canine compatibility: Dogs permitted

Fees and permits: None
Schedule: Open year-round
Maps: TOPO! CD: North Carolina–South Carolina; USGS maps: Tamassee, Satolah, and Cashiers, South Carolina; USFS maps: Andrew Pickens and Sumter National Forest Trail Guides
Trail contacts: Foothills Trail Conference, PO Box 3041, Greenville, SC 29602; (864) 467-9537; info@foothillstrail.org: foothillstrail.org

Finding the trailhead: *From I-85 northbound:* Take exit 1 at the Georgia/South Carolina state line onto SC 11. Drive for 26 miles and turn left onto Oconee Station Road. Drive for 2 miles and look for the Oconee State Park entrance. Follow the Foothills Trail signs to the parking area.

From I-85 southbound: Take exit 19B onto SC 28 toward Clemson. Drive 26 miles, take the ramp toward Tamassee/Salem, and merge onto SC 11; drive 6 miles. Turn left onto Oconee Station Road. Drive for 2 miles and look for the Oconee State Park entrance. Follow the Foothills Trail signs to the parking area. GPS: N34 51.835'/W83 05.916'

The Hike

This hike is described from west to east, starting at the trailhead in Oconee State Park. Be sure to register your vehicle at the park office before embarking on an overnight hike. After-hours registration is also available at the park office. There are great campsites and cabins available at the state park if you want to spend the night at the park and then hit the trail early the next morning. There are ample opportunities to filter water along most sections of this trail so there is no need to take more than two liters on the trail at any given time, granted you are bringing a water filter. The beginning of the Foothills Trail is clearly marked.

A highlight of this trail is the many waterfalls along the route. You arrive at your first opportunity to hike to a waterfall just 1.1 miles into the trail. A short spur trail leads to Hidden Falls, a 50-foot waterfall tucked into a tight mountain gap. The side trip is worth the hike, and if you are a waterfall lover, the extra 2 miles total to see this wonderful waterfall is a must. Don't worry, though, if you want to make some progress today. You will have plenty of chances to see waterfalls along this route. During this next section of the trail, you traverse through a forest of mostly pine and oak and pass into the Sumter National Forest. The red slashes on trees along the trail mark the national-forest boundary. After passing through an area of young white pines, you reach another opportunity for a side trip on the spur trail that leads to the fire tower on Long Mountain. From the intersection with the spur trail, you will cross three bridges and several old logging roads before reaching the parking area and trailhead at Jumping Branch. The trail does not cross SC 107 here but instead continues

Chattooga Valley segment of the Foothills Trail

to the left and then enters back into the forest. The trail crosses 107 about a mile from this point.

Just after reaching Pig Pen Creek and Pigpen Falls, you arrive at the junction with the Chattooga River. The trail turns sharply to the right and joins the Chattooga Trail, which follows parallel to the Chattooga River for nearly 8 miles before turning east toward the Bad Creek Trailhead. During this section you have the opportunity to camp at many campsites atop small bluffs and at picturesque sandy beaches along the Chattooga. Farther down the trail you will reach the primitive campground at Burrells Ford. You also pass Big Bend Falls and a spur trail that leads to Kings Falls before reaching the parking lot at Burrells Ford Road.

The trail turns sharply to the east and ascends toward the peak of Medlin Mountain, then reaches the parking lot at the Walhalla Fish Hatchery. The trail continues on the other side of Fish Hatchery Road, running parallel to the East Fork of the

Chattooga River before descending to Sloan Bridge and SC 107. You cross SC 107 at the Sloan Bridge Picnic Area.

Along this next section of trail, you cross into North Carolina and enter the Nantahala National Forest. Before reaching Round Mountain, a spur trail to the left leads toward NC 281. There are several excellent campsites along this spur trail if you're looking for a spot to camp for the night. Over the next 3 miles, you have many opportunities for excellent views of the surrounding piedmont, Table Rock Mountain, Lake Jocassee, and Paris Mountain. There are several benches along the way. Give yourself plenty of time along this section to stop and enjoy the wonderful views. This spectacular section of trail leads to an overlook with breathtaking views of the 400-foot Upper Whitewater Falls. The trail climbs to the overlook parking lot, where you will find restrooms.

From here the trail descends steeply, following a series of switchbacks to a 60-foot bridge that spans the Whitewater River. You cross Corbin Creek over a bridge and then traverse through a thick area of rhododendron before beginning a very steep section of trail that descends sets of stairs and bridges to the South Carolina / North Carolina state line. You pass back into South Carolina and then cross the Whitewater River before arriving at the junction with the Bad Creek Access Spur Trail, which leads to the Bad Creek Access parking area and the end of this hike.

Miles and Directions

0.0 Start from the trailhead at Oconee State Park.

0.5 Arrive at a junction with the Tamassee Knob Spur Trail on your right. Stay straight and continue on the Foothills Trail toward Hidden Falls.

1.1 Arrive at the trail junction with the Hidden Falls Spur Trail on the right. The falls are 1 mile from the trail junction. Stay straight on the Foothills Trail or enjoy a short side hike to the falls.

1.6 Reach the trail junction with the spur trail to the Long Mountain Fire Tower on your left. Stay straight on the Foothills Trail.

1.7 Cross Old Ridge Road.

2.1 Cross the large footbridge over the ravine.

2.4 Reach the junction with an old logging road. Veer to the right.

2.5 Cross the old logging road.

2.8 Cross the wooden bridge over the small stream.

4.4 Reach the Jumping Branch Trailhead.

5.2 Arrive at Cheohee Road. The trail passes the parking area along the road and then follows along the unpaved road toward SC 107.

5.6 Cross SC 107.

6.4 Reach the trail junction with the spur trail to Thrift Lake on left. Stay straight on the Foothills Trail.

7.2 Arrive at the end of the parking lot and trailhead at the end of Nicholson Ford Road.

7.8 Reach Pigpen Falls.

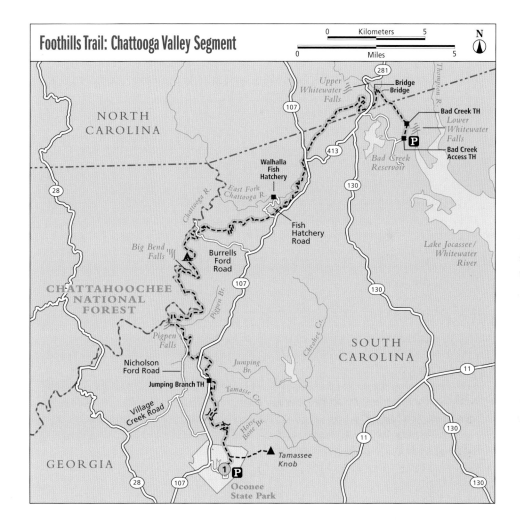

Foothills Trail: Chattooga Valley Segment

0 — Kilometers — 5

0 — Miles — 5

N

NORTH CAROLINA

281

Upper Whitewater Falls

107

Bridge Bridge

Bad Creek TH

Lower Whitewater Falls

Bad Creek Access TH

413

Walhalla Fish Hatchery

East Fork Chattooga R.

Bad Creek Reservoir

28

Chattooga R.

130

Fish Hatchery Road

Lake Jocassee / Whitewater River

Big Bend Falls

Burrells Ford Road

CHATTAHOOCHEE NATIONAL FOREST

Pigpen Br.

107

130

Pigpen Falls

Chicohee Cr.

SOUTH CAROLINA

Nicholson Ford Road

Jumping Br.

Jumping Branch TH

11

Tamassee Cr.

Village Creek Road

Horse Bone Br.

Tamassee Knob

130

GEORGIA

1

Oconee State Park

28

107

11

130

7.9 Reach the trail junction with Chattooga River. Turn right, staying on the Foothills Trail, which joins the Chattooga River Trail.

11.7 A steep spur trail to the left leads down to a view of Big Bend Falls along the Chattooga River.

12.1 The Big Bend Trail is to your right and leads to the Cherry Hill Recreation Area Campground and SC 107. Stay straight and follow alongside the Chattooga River.

12.9 Arrive at a recommended campsite along the river, with excellent views.

13.8 The trail splits. The Foothills Trail stays to the left. The Chattooga Trail splits to the right toward Burrells Ford Campground.

14.7 Cross Burrells Ford Road.

15.6 The trail splits. To the left a spur to the Chattooga River Trail leads past Spoonauger Falls. Stay to the right and continue on the Foothills Trail.

18.9 Cross Fish Hatchery Road.

22.2 Arrive at the trailhead at the Sloan Bridge Picnic Area. The trail crosses SC 107.

24.3 Reach a trail junction. The Round Mountain Loop Trail is to your left. Stay straight on the Foothills Trail.

24.8 The trail splits. To the left is the spur trail that leads to Upper Whitewater Falls. Veer to the right and stay on the Foothills Trail toward SC 281.

26.3 Cross SC 281.

26.5 Arrive at the junction with a spur trail that leads to a parking lot on 281.

26.9 The spur trail to the Upper Whitewater Falls Observation Deck is straight ahead. Veer sharply to the right and continue on the Foothills Trail toward the Whitewater River.

27.4 Cross the metal bridge spanning the Whitewater River.

27.6 Cross the wooden bridge spanning Corbin Creek.

29.0 Arrive at the trail junction with the Bad Creek Spur Trail to the Bad Creek Trailhead. The Foothills Trail is to the left. Turn right and follow the Bad Creek Spur Trail to the Bad Creek Trailhead.

29.4 Reach the parking lot at the Bad Creek Trailhead and the end of the Chattooga section of the Foothills Trail.

Hike Information

Local Information: Mountain Lakes CVB, 105 W. South Broad St., Walhalla, SC 29691; (877) 685-2537; scmountainlakes.com

Local Events/Attractions: Carolina Foothills Heritage Fair, 1220 Highway 59, Fair Play; carolina foothillsheritagefair.org

Oconee Heritage Center, 123 Browns Square Dr., Walhalla; (864) 638-2224; oconeeheritage center.org. Open Thurs–Fri noon to 6 p.m., Sat 10 a.m. to 3 p.m.

Lodging: Cabins at Oconee State Park, 624 State Park Rd., Mountain Rest; (864) 638-5353. Cabins include fireplace, screened porch, and a grill.

Mountain Rest Cabins, 175 Homeland Dr., Mountain Rest; (864) 718-0333; mountain restcabins.com. Fully furnished cabins.

Walhalla Liberty Lodge B&B, 105 Liberty Ln., Walhalla; (864) 638-8239; walhallaliberty lodge.com

Restaurants: Tommy's on Main Italian Restaurant, 124 E. Main St., Walhalla, (864) 638-5005

The Steak House Cafeteria, 316 E. Main St., Walhalla; (864) 638-3311; thesteakhouse cafeteria.com

Dakota Grill, 2911 Highlands Hwy., Walhalla; (864) 718-0553; dakotagrillsc.com

Organizations: Foothills Trails Conference, PO Box 3041, Greenville, SC 29602; (864) 467-9537; foothillstrail.org

KINSER'S TROPHY-TROUT TASTER

Serves 4–6

  1¼ cups bread crumbs

  1 clove minced garlic

  2 tablespoons chopped parsley

  2 tablespoons chopped fresh oregano leaves

  Dash of crushed red pepper flakes

  Sea salt

  1 zested lemon

  3 juiced lemons

  ½ cup Dijon mustard

  4 fresh trout, belly flap removed, rinsed and patted dry

    (Optional: Remove the heads and tails.)

  Olive oil

  4 tablespoons (½ stick) butter

1. Preheat the oven to 250°F.

2. In a large, flat plate, combine the bread crumbs, garlic, parsley, oregano, red pepper flakes, salt, and zest of one lemon to your taste.

3. In a small mixing bowl, stir together the juice of one lemon and the Dijon mustard. Using a brush, coat both sides of the trout with the lemon juice and mustard, then cover the entire fish with the bread crumb mixture. Press the bread crumbs firmly against the fish so the crumbs stick to the trout.

4. Pour about ¼ inch of olive oil into a large skillet. Bring the pan up to a medium-high temperature. Place the fish in the skillet with the skin side down. Cook the fish just three-quarters of the way. This takes 7 to 10 minutes. Flip the trout over and cook the other side until the trout is thoroughly cooked and the fish appears brown and crispy. This takes around 3 to 4 minutes. Take the trout out of the pan using a spatula and place the trout on paper towels so that the oil may drain from the fish. After the oil is drained, place the fish on the warm oven rack until the remaining fish are finished cooking.

5. After all of the trout have been cooked, pour the remaining oil from the pan into a small bowl. Pour the butter and the rest of the lemon juice into the bowl with the oil and stir the mixture well. Season with a little salt to taste, and pour the mixture back into the skillet and reduce the sauce to around half. Plate the trout and drizzle a little lemon sauce onto the fish.

2 Foothills Trail, Fork Mountain Trail, Chattooga Trail Loop

This moderately difficult overnight backpack combines sections of the Foothills Trail, Chattooga Trail, and the Fork Mountain Trail. You will traverse through scenic river and mountainous habitat as the trail makes its way through the Ellicott Wilderness Area and Sumter National Forest.

Start: From the parking lot for Burrells Ford Campground
Distance: 17.7-mile loop
Hiking time: About 2–3 days
Difficulty: Moderate to strenuous due to length and elevation gains
Trail surface: Forested trail, gravel path, dirt road
Best seasons: Spring (Mar–May) for wildflower displays; fall (Sept–Nov) for fall foliage
Other trail users: Hikers only

Canine compatibility: Dogs permitted
Fees and permits: None
Schedule: Open year-round
Maps: TOPO! CD: North Carolina–South Carolina; USGS maps: Tamassee, Satolah, and Cashiers, and South Carolina; USFS maps: Andrew Pickens and Sumter National Forest Trail Guides
Trail contacts: Sumter National Forest, Andrew Pickens Ranger District, 112 Andrew Pickens Circle, Mountain Rest, SC 29664; (864) 638-9568

Finding the trailhead: From Walhalla drive northwest on SC 28 for 7.5 miles and bear right onto SC 107. Drive approximately 10 miles and turn left onto Burrells Ford Road (FS 708). The parking area is 3 miles ahead on the left. The trailhead is at the northeast corner of the parking area behind a large brown signboard. GPS: N34 58.305' / W83 06.902'

The Hike

This hike is mapped to start along the Foothills Trail from the Burrells Ford Campground parking lot and starts out with a challenging climb in the beginning of the trail. However, for an easier route, you can go north on the Chattooga River Trail and enjoy a more leisurely hike along the scenic Chattooga River. To follow the route described here, start along the Foothills Trail by crossing the unpaved Burrells Ford Road and hike toward the Walhalla Fish Hatchery. You climb up to an elevation of nearly 3,000 feet along a 0.7-mile section of switchbacks that take you out of the Chattooga Gorge and onto Medlin Mountain. The climb eases and you descend slightly to Fish Hatchery Road. To the left the road leads to the fish hatchery along the East Fork of the Chattooga River. Cross Fish Hatchery Road and continue on the Foothills Trail toward Sloan Bridge.

At Sloan Bridge there are picnic shelters, restrooms, and water. From here you will go north, following SC 107 for a short distance to the Fork Mountain Trailhead, then head west toward Ellicott Rock Wilderness. This section of the trail is mostly surrounded by a dense understory of rhododendron and mountain laurel, which is exceptionally beautiful in the spring when these varieties are blossoming in displays of wonderful flowers. Note also that this trail is often less well maintained than the other two trails along this route. You will often find sections where you may need to cross logs and do a little bushwhacking from time to time in order to get around small blowdowns or other obstacles along the trail. Please consider this before you hike this section of the trail, and keep your eyes open for the red blazes that mark the trail to ensure that you keep on the path.

The Fork Mountain section is more than 6 miles long and stays primarily along the northern side of Fork Mountain, dipping in and out of sometimes steep mountain gaps and ravines as the trail descends toward the Chattooga River. The elevation changes along this trail make this section of the route particularly challenging. Occasionally you encounter areas along the trail that offer rewarding views of the surrounding mountains and gorges.

You mostly explore the 9,012-acre Ellicott Rock Wilderness along this section of the trail. The wilderness was named after Andrew Ellicott, who was the first to survey the thirty-fifth paral-

Spoonauger Falls

lel and the border of North Carolina and Georgia. Ellicott Rock along the Chattooga Trail was the exact point where he believed the North Carolina, South Carolina, and Georgia borders met. However, he was off by just a few feet as the true spot where the borders meet was determined to be at Commissioner's Rock to the south.

At the junction with the Chattooga River Trail, turn toward the south and hike along the Chattooga River back toward the Burrells Ford Bridge and the campground parking lot where you started your hike. There are several excellent campsites along this section of trail atop the small bluffs and small sandy beaches beside the river. Before reaching Burrells Ford Bridge, I highly recommend that you take the short spur trail to the beautiful 40-foot Spoonauger Falls. Once you reach Burrells Ford Road, turn left and follow the road back to the parking lot where you started to complete this excellent backpacking adventure.

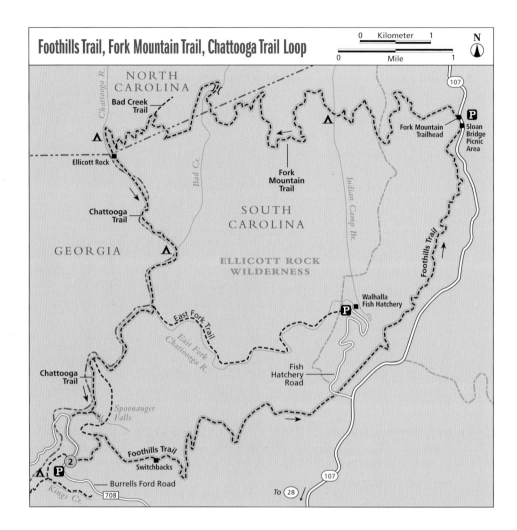

Foothills Trail, Fork Mountain Trail, Chattooga Trail Loop

Miles and Directions

0.0 Start from the parking lot for the Burrells Ford Campground just off Burrells Ford Road. Cross Burrells Ford Road and turn right to walk along the gravel Burrells Ford Road for approximately 90 feet. Turn left at the Foothills trail sign. Leave the gravel road and head north on the Foothills Trail toward Sloan Bridge.

0.6 Arrive at a split in the trail. A connector trail that connects to the Chattooga River Trail is to the left. Stay to your right and continue on the Foothills Trail.

1.2 Begin a steep climb on switchbacks to the top of a peak.

3.8 Cross Fish Hatchery Road. Over the next 0.5 mile, the trail crosses the road several times. Simply stay on the Foothills Trail.

6.7 Reach the Sloan Bridge Picnic Area parking lot and the end of the Foothills Trail section of this hike. Walk to 107 and turn left (north). Follow the road for 450 feet until you reach the trailhead for the Fork Mountain Trail.

6.8 Arrive at the trailhead to the Fork Mountain Trail on the left side of the road.

7.4 A wooden sign marks the beginning of the Ellicott Rock Wilderness. Continue on the Fork Mountain Trail.

9.0 Reach a great campsite. Here you will find a fire pit and access to the creek for water.

11.7 Cross Bad Creek.

12.7 Arrive at a trail junction. The Bad Creek Trail is to the right. Stay straight on Fork Mountain Trail toward the Chattooga Trail.

13.8 Arrive at a campsite on the Chattooga River and the start of the Chattooga Trail. Follow the Chattooga Trail south to the left.

14.1 Arrive at Ellicott Rock.

15.0 Reach a nice campsite on the Chattooga River.

15.7 Reach a trail junction. The East Fork Trail is to the left. Continue straight and continue on the Chattooga Trail across the bridge toward the Burrells Ford Bridge.

16.7 Reach a split in the trail. A connector trail that leads to the Foothills Trail is to the left. Continue straight on the Chattooga Trail toward the Burrells Ford Bridge.

17.0 Arrive at a spur trail to the left that leads down to Spoonauger Falls. The hike is worth it.

17.1 Arrive at Spoonauger Falls. After enjoying the falls, turn around and head back to the Chattooga Trail. Turn left toward the Burrells Ford Bridge.

17.4 Reach Burrells Ford Road. Turn left and follow the road back to the Burrells Ford Campground parking lot where you started.

17.7 Arrive at Burrells Ford Campground Parking Lot and the end of the hike.

Hike Information

Local Information: Mountain Lakes CVB, 105 W. South Broad St., Walhalla, SC 29691; (877) 685-2537; scmountainlakes.com

Local Events/Attractions: Carolina Foothills Heritage Fair, 1220 Highway 59, Fair Play; carolinafoothillsheritagefair.org

Oconee Heritage Center, 123 Browns Square Dr., Walhalla; (864) 638-2224; oconeeheritagecenter.org. Open Thurs–Fri noon to 6 p.m., Sat 10 a.m. to 3 p.m.

Lodging: Cabins at Oconee State Park, 624 State Park Rd., Mountain Rest; (864) 638-5353. Cabins include fireplace, screened porch, and a grill.

Mountain Rest Cabins, 175 Homeland Dr., Mountain Rest; (864) 718-0333; mountainrestcabins.com. Fully furnished cabins.

Walhalla Liberty Lodge B&B, 105 Liberty Ln., Walhalla; (864) 638-8239; walhallalibertylodge.com

Restaurants: Tommy's on Main Italian Restaurant, 124 E. Main St., Walhalla; (864) 638-5005

The Steak House Cafeteria, 316 E. Main St., Walhalla; (864) 638-3311; thesteakhousecafeteria.com

Dakota Grill, 2911 Highlands Hwy., Walhalla; (864) 718-0553; dakotagrillsc.com

3 East Fork Trail

This great choice for a short day hike takes you down to the Chattooga River and is a popular way to access the Ellicott Wilderness Area. Starting from the Walhalla Fish Hatchery parking lot, this trail follows along the bank of the East Fork of the Chattooga River for most of the route. The dense forest that surrounds the trail is scenic and lush. When you reach the Chattooga River, you arrive at a junction with the Chattooga River Trail and have the option to extend this hike to a spur trail that leads to Spoonauger Falls.

Start: Walhalla Fish Hatchery parking lot
Distance: 4.6-mile out and back
Hiking time: About 2.5 hours
Difficulty: Easy to moderate due to length and elevation gains
Trail surface: Boardwalk, paved trail, forested trail
Best seasons: Spring (Mar–May) for wildflower displays; fall (Sept–Nov) for fall foliage
Other trail users: Hikers only
Canine compatibility: Dogs permitted
Fees and permits: None

Schedule: Open year-round
Maps: TOPO! CD: North Carolina–South Carolina; USGS maps: Tamassee and South Carolina; USFS map: Ellicott Rock Wilderness, available at district offices and at the forest supervisor's office. Closest office is the Andrew Pickens Ranger District in Mountain Rest.
Trail contacts: Sumter National Forest, Andrew Pickens Ranger District, 112 Andrew Pickens Circle, Mountain Rest, SC 29664; (864) 638-9568

Finding the trailhead: From Walhalla drive north on SC 28 for 7.5 miles and veer right onto SC 107. Drive 12 miles and turn left onto Fish Hatchery Road (Oconee County S-37-325). The east trailhead is at a bridge just past the Walhalla Fish Hatchery and picnic area. GPS: N34 59.120' / W83 04.320'

The Hike

The East Fork Trail has two trailheads. There is one at the Burrells Ford Campground parking lot on the west end of the trail and another at the Walhalla Fish Hatchery. This route starts from the parking lot at the Walhalla Fish Hatchery. There are restrooms and drinking water available at the trailhead. From the kiosk at the back of the parking lot, follow the elevated, wooden boardwalk that follows alongside the East Fork. There are many junctions along the first 0.1 mile of the trail, and the easiest way to stay on the East Fork Trail is to stay to the left. This area is used mainly as a picnic area. There are several picnic tables along the bank of the East Fork and there is also an impressive picnic pavilion at the end of the picnic area along the trail that

A rock wall along the East Fork Trail ▶

has a fire pit. This is a great spot to reserve for a gathering of friends or family in the cooler spring and fall months.

Along this section of the trail, you are likely to see a lot of families and people exploring the boardwalk part of the trail. However, don't let the crowds near the hatchery and in the picnic area dissuade you from hiking on the trail. Once you pass the picnic pavilion and get onto the wilderness portion of the trail, the number of people on the trail decreases precipitously.

At the first junction on the trail, you reach a spur trail to the right that leads to a bridge that crosses the East Fork and leads to the hatchery office. Stay to the left and pass the picnic tables on the right side of the trail on the bank of the East Fork. Cross the wooden bridge that spans the small stream that feeds into the East Fork. Then, when you reach the next junction, stay to the left again toward the large picnic pavilion. The trail follows around the front of the picnic pavilion and then enters into the forest.

You cross another wooden bridge that crosses a small stream and then cross a third bridge that spans the East Fork. After this bridge the trail ascends over the next 0.25 mile. The trail then begins a gradual decent over the next mile. Along this section you cross a steep slab of rock that would be dangerous and difficult to cross if it were not for an innovative trail crew that placed concrete steps directly on top of the slick, bare rock. It's impressive and creative and makes life easier for all of us.

Most of this trail is within the Ellicott Wilderness Area, a 9,012-acre preserve that is closed to logging, vehicles, and other activities that would disturb the natural state of the area. The Ellicott is also the only wilderness area that straddles three states. It is named after Ellicott Rock, where George Ellicott chiseled a mark on a boulder in 1811 that defined the border between North Carolina and Georgia. Over the next 0.85 mile, you climb over three small hills and follow the East Fork as it curves to the northwest toward the Chattooga River. At the most dramatic curve along the East Fork, you reach an impressive rock wall on the right side of the trail. Continue on the East Fork Trail until you reach the junction at the Chattooga River with the Chattooga River Trail, which is poorly marked, like many of the trails in the Ellicott Wilderness. You will know you are at the end of the East Fork Trail when you reach a T junction with the Chattooga River Trail and see a large wooden bridge that crosses the East Fork to the left and the Chattooga River Trail continuing straight ahead.

From here, you can turn around and retrace your steps back to the parking lot at the Walhalla Fish Hatchery, turn left and follow the Chattooga Trail to the spur trail that leads to Spoonauger Falls, or stay straight and follow the Chattooga River Trail to Ellicott Rock.

Miles and Directions

0.0   Start from the parking lot at Walhalla Fish Hatchery.

0.1   After passing the picnic pavilion, cross the wooden bridge that spans a small stream.

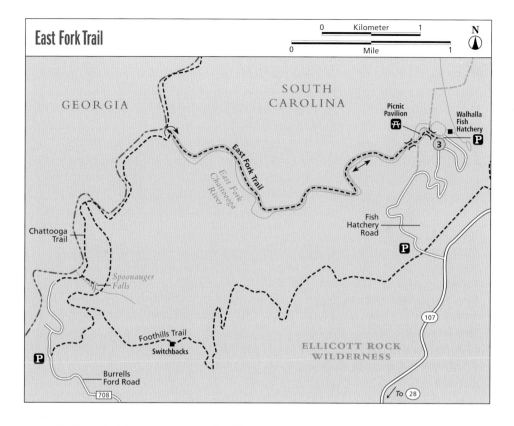

East Fork Trail

0.5 Cross the bridge that spans the East Fork.

1.5 After the trail curves to the right and follows the contour of the East Fork, you reach a sheer wall of rock on the right side of the trail.

2.3 At the junction with the Chattooga Trail, turn around and retrace your steps. (**Option:** Turn left here, cross the East Fork Chattooga River, and follow the Chattooga Trail to a spur trail that leads to Spoonauger Falls.)

4.6 Arrive back at the trailhead.

Hike Information

Local Information: Mountain Lakes CVB, 105 W. South Broad St., Walhalla, SC 29691; (877) 685-2537; scmountainlakes.com

Local Events/Attractions: Oconee Heritage Center, 123 Browns Square Dr., Walhalla; (864) 638-2224; oconeeheritagecenter.org. Open Thurs–Fri noon to 6 p.m., Sat 10 a.m. to 3 p.m.

Lodging: Mountain Rest Cabins, 175 Homeland Dr., Mountain Rest; (864) 718-0333; mountainrestcabins.com

Walhalla Liberty Lodge B&B, 105 Liberty Ln.; (864) 638.8239; walhallalibertylodge.com

Restaurants: Tommy's on Main Italian Restaurant, 124 E. Main St., Walhalla; (864) 638-5005

The Steak House Cafeteria, 316 E. Main St., Walhalla; (864) 638-3311; thesteakhousecafeteria.com

4 Big Bend and King Creek Falls

Along this moderately challenging trail, you'll hike through the forest surrounding the Burrells Ford Campground before descending to the 70-foot-high Kings Creek Falls. Somehow, when you arrive at the falls, they look much higher than just 70 feet. From the falls the trail gently descends to the Chattooga River. You'll follow alongside the river until you arrive at Big Bend Falls, which is more accurately described as a steep rapid in the Chattooga River. Rock outcroppings along the riverbank make excellent viewing spots for the small falls and the winding river. They are also a great spot to rest before you turn around and head back to the trailhead.

Start: Burrells Ford Campground parking lot
Distance: 6.2-mile out and back
Hiking time: About 3 hours
Difficulty: Easy to moderate due to length and some slightly challenging elevation
Trail surface: Gravel road, forested trail
Best season: Mar–Nov
Other trail users: Hikers only
Canine compatibility: Dogs permitted
Fees and permits: None

Schedule: Open year-round
Maps: TOPO! CD: North Carolina–South Carolina; USGS maps: Tamassee and North Carolina; USFS maps: Sumter National Forest, available at park office in Mountain Rest
Trail contacts: Sumter National Forest, Andrew Pickens Ranger District, 112 Andrew Pickens Circle, Mountain Rest, SC 29664; (864) 638-9568

Finding the trailhead: From Walhalla drive northwest on SC 28 for approximately 8 miles and bear right (north) onto SC 107. Drive 10.4 miles and turn left onto Burrells Ford Road (FS 708, paved for first 0.3 mile). Drive approximately 3 miles to the gravel parking area on the left. GPS: N34 58.297' / W83 06.897'

The Hike

Start from the gravel parking lot at Burrells Ford Campground, where you will find restrooms. At the back of the parking lot, a metal gate blocks the road. This is the start of the Burrells Ford Campground Trail. Follow the wide gravel road for 2.8 miles down a gentle slope to the Burrells Ford Campground, which is marked with a kiosk on the right side of the trail. Camping is available year-round at the campground and there is no charge to camp, which hands-down makes this the best deal on a campsite in all of South Carolina.

Continue on the trail for about 50 feet until you reach the junction with the Kings Creek Falls Trail to the left. The junction is well marked with a sign. Turn left and follow the Kings Creek Falls Trail through a dense forest of mountain laurel and rhododendron. You cross Kings Creek and then reach a junction with the Foothills Trail. Turn left, then ascend up to the base of Kings Creek Falls. There is a small beach and a swimming hole at the base of the falls. This is definitely a welcome sight on a hot summer day.

A view of Big Bend Falls from the Chattooga River Trail

After exploring the falls and enjoying the view, turn around and head back to the junction with Chattooga River Trail. Instead of heading back to the parking lot, turn left and head toward the Chattooga River. The trail continues to descend along the gravel road and crosses over Kings Creek again before you reach a large campsite on the bank of the river. This is the junction with the Chattooga River Trail. The junction is not marked at all, and the campsite obscures the path along the riverbank. The best way to find the trail is to walk down to the river, turn left (south), and walk along the riverbank until you can see the trail form as you get a short distance from the campsite.

The Chattooga River was designated a Wild and Scenic River in 1974 and is protected along a 15,432-acre corridor. This is one of the last remaining free-running rivers in the Southeast. If you hike this section in the late spring, you will see the white and pink blossoms of the mountain laurel that line the river. This river is also the site where many scenes were filmed for the classic movie *Deliverance*. Also, in January of 2012 the US Forest Service made a decision that restored boating to the upper headwaters of the Chattooga River when the conditions and water heights are suitable.

The trail follows along the scenic river for 1.5 miles, occasionally leaving sight of the river and traversing over small hills in the surrounding forest until you reach a trail junction with the Chattooga River Trail High Water Trail. This is an alternative route that you can take if the water level in the river is too high to skirt the edge of the river on the next section of trail. If the water is low enough, I recommend that you stick to the more scenic route and follow the edge of the river, simply following

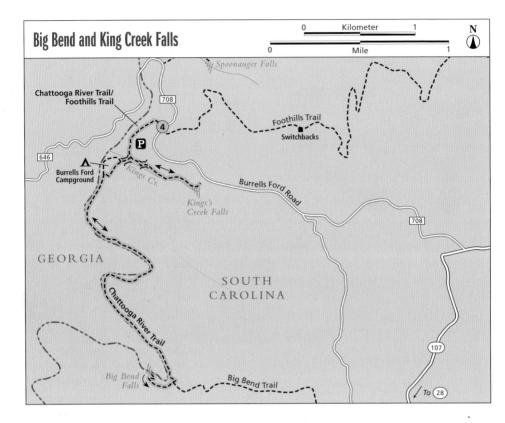

Big Bend and King Creek Falls

the blazes that are painted on the rocks. After passing the junction with the Big Bend Trail, you continue to the Big Bend Falls. You will hear the falls before you see them. At first the trail passes above the falls and you get a nice view of them from above. Then the trail descends to a very short spur trail that leads down to the riverbank, where you are able to enjoy a view of the small falls in the Chattooga River from the rock outcroppings on the river's edge. From here turn around and retrace your steps back to the Burrells Ford Campground parking lot.

Miles and Directions

0.0 Start from Burrells Ford Campground parking lot. Follow the Chattooga River Trail down to the campground via the wide gravel road.

0.3 Reach Burrells Ford Campground on the right. A kiosk marks the spur trail that leads back to campsites. Continue 50 more feet on the Chattooga River Trail until you reach the junction with the Kings Falls Trail on the left. Turn left onto the Kings Falls Trail.

0.5 Cross the wooden bridge over Kings Creek. About 300 feet from the bridge, you'll reach a junction with the Foothills Trail. Turn left and ascend the wooden steps and continue toward King Creek Falls.

0.8 Reach King Creek Falls. From here turn around and retrace your steps back to the Chattooga River Trail. On the way back, after you cross the wooden bridge over Kings Creek, it is easy to stay straight. However, on the other side of the bridge, you want to veer left and follow the Kings Creek Falls Trail, which stays alongside the creek bank and continues back to the Chattooga River Trail.

1.3 Once you reach the Chattooga River Trail again, turn left and continue to follow the trail downhill toward the Chattooga River, crossing the large bridge over Kings Creek just 200 feet from the junction with the Kings Creek Falls Trail. After another 200 feet from the bridge, you will reach a junction where the road splits to the right and is blocked with wooden posts. Stay to the left.

1.5 Arrive at a large campsite on the bank of the Chattooga River. Look for the bear cables on the left side of the campsite. Walk toward the bear cables and follow the trail that runs to the south and alongside the riverbank. This is the Chattooga River Trail.

3.0 The trail splits. To the left is an alternative route of the Chattooga River Trail that follows along higher ground. If the water level is not too high, stay straight and follow the blazes that are painted directly onto the exposed rocks on the edge of the river.

3.4 Reach a trail junction with the Big Bend Trail on the left. This trail connects the Chattooga River Trail with Winding Stairs Trail and the Cherry Hill Recreation Area to the east. Stay straight on the Chattooga River Trail and continue toward Big Bend Falls.

3.6 Reach a very short spur trail that leads down to the rock outcroppings on the edge of the river, where you can get a great view of the falls on the stretch of river behind you. From here turn around and retrace your steps.

3.8 Stay straight at the junction with the Big Bend Trail on your right.

4.2 Continue straight at the junction with the Chattooga River High Water Trail to the right.

5.7 Turn right at the junction with the Chattooga River Trail, marked by the large campsite with bear cables alongside the Chattooga River.

5.9 When you reach the Kings Creek Falls Trail, stay straight unless you want to add the extra mile to go and see the falls again.

6.2 Arrive at the Burrells Ford Campground trailhead and parking lot where you started your hike.

Hike Information

Local Information: Mountain Lakes CVB, 105 W. South Broad St., Walhalla, SC 29691; (877) 685-2537; scmountainlakes.com

Local Events/Attractions: Oconee Heritage Center, 123 Browns Square Dr., Walhalla; (864) 638-2224; oconeeheritagecenter.org. Open Thurs–Fri noon to 6 p.m., Sat 10 a.m. to 3 p.m.

Lodging: Cabins at Oconee State Park, 624 State Park Rd., Mountain Rest; (864) 638-5353. Cabins include fireplace, screened porch, and a grill.

Mountain Rest Cabins, 175 Homeland Dr., Mountain Rest; (864) 718-0333; mountain restcabins.com

Walhalla Liberty Lodge B&B, 105 Liberty Ln., Walhalla; (864) 638-8239; walhallaliberty lodge.com

Restaurants: Tommy's on Main Italian Restaurant, 124 E. Main St., Walhalla; (864) 638-5005

The Steak House Cafeteria, 316 E. Main St., Walhalla; (864) 638-3311; thesteakhouse cafeteria.com

Dakota Grill, 2911 Highlands Hwy., Walhalla; (864) 718-0553; dakotagrillsc.com

SOUTH CAROLINA FACTS

The Palmetto State, the best-known of several nicknames for South Carolina, refers to the state tree, the sabal palmetto, or cabbage palmetto, a small palm tree. When the state seceded from the Union in 1861, the palmetto was depicted on the new "national" flag. Today it graces the state flag, the state quarter, and the state seal and is part of the salute to the flag of South Carolina:

I salute the flag of South Carolina and pledge to the Palmetto State love, loyalty and faith.

The palmetto represents the defeat of the British fleet in 1776 at Fort Moultrie on Sullivan's Island. The fort was built of palmetto logs, which absorbed the impact of the cannonballs.

South Carolina was the eighth state to join the new United States in 1788. It's the fortieth in geographic size among all the states, and its 2012 population was 4.7 million.

Other South Carolina nicknames:

- The Rice State, due to the production of rice in the state
- The Swamp State, as the area is well known for the swamps and marshes where rice is grown. Notice all the boardwalks in this book's featured hikes that enable hikers to find continuous routes despite all the swamps.
- Keystone of the South Atlantic Seaboard, because of the state's wedge shape
- The Iodine State, because iodine is found in large amounts in the state's vegetation

Other South Carolina symbols:

- State animal: White-tail Deer
- State bird: Carolina Wren
- State flower: Yellow Jessamine
- State fruit: Peach
- State snack: Boiled Peanuts
- State wildflower: Goldenrod

5 Winding Stairs Trail

This is the perfect trail if you are looking for a short, easy day hike that will take you to a beautiful waterfall. The hardest part of this route is getting a good view of Miuka Falls, which is best viewed from directly beside the creek and is reached by climbing down the steep creek bank. However, you can still get a glimpse of the waterfall from along the trail if you don't want to climb down the spur trail. This trail is very popular with folks camping at Cherry Hill Recreation Area and is highly recommended for people who may not be able to handle the harder hikes in this mountainous region or a hike on the entire Winding Stairs Trail, which descends 1,100 feet over 3.5 miles.

Start: The gravel parking lot on the east side of SC 107 near the Cherry Hill Recreation Area

Distance: 2.2-mile out and back

Hiking time: About 1.5 hours

Difficulty: Easy due to length and gently sloping elevation profile

Trail surface: Forested trail

Best seasons: Spring (Mar–May) for wildflower displays; fall (Sept–Nov) for fall foliage

Other trail users: Hikers only

Canine compatibility: Dogs permitted

Fees and permits: None

Schedule: Open year-round

Maps: TOPO! CD: North Carolina–South Carolina; USGS maps: Tamassee and South Carolina; USFS maps: Andrew Pickens Ranger District Trail Guide, available at the National Forest Office in Mountain Rest.

Trail contacts: Sumter National Forest, Andrew Pickens Ranger District, 112 Andrew Pickens Circle, Mountain Rest, SC 29664; (864) 638-9568

Finding the trailhead: To the northern trailhead: From Walhalla drive west on SC 28 for 7.5 miles and bear right onto SC 107. Drive 8.8 miles to Cherry Hill Recreation Area on the right. The trailhead is on the right (east) side of the highway, just 100 feet north of Cherry Hill Road. From the north the trailhead parking lot is just 100 feet south of the entrance to the Cherry Hill Recreation Area. GPS: N34 56.473' / W83 05.397'

The Hike

This route traverses more than one-third of the entire Winding Stairs Trail and makes the hike more suitable for those looking for an exceptionally easy hike. However, you can always take the option of following the Winding Stairs Trail the entire 3.5 miles to the southern trailhead at Tamassee Road. Along the trail, you'll traverse through a hardwood forest of oaks, poplars, white cedars, hickories, white pines, and several dense areas of rhododendron and mountain laurel. The forest understory is filled with blueberries, buckberry, and a variety of shrubs and wildflowers. You may see wild pigs, deer, and black bears, as well as many birds, including warblers and thrushes.

Miuka Falls

From the parking lot near the Cherry Hill Recreation Area, the only signage marking the trailhead is a thin brown metal post with the trail name written on it. The trail ascends for the first 0.1 mile and then you start your easy descent down to Miuka Falls. The trail is very popular with campers at Cherry Hill Recreation Area, where you can find a twenty-nine-site campground with flush toilets and hot showers. Reservations are not necessary at the campground, and Cherry Hill is a perfect location and affordable spot to set up a base camp and explore many of the trails in this book and in the surrounding forests. The trails surrounding Chattooga River are easily accessible from this campground, as well as the trails at the Walhalla State Fish Hatchery, Ellicott Rock Wilderness Area, and Oconee State Park. I highly recommend the Cherry Hill Recreation Area.

After 0.2 mile you reach a junction with a spur trail to your left that leads to the Cherry Hill Recreation Area. Turn right and continue the easy descent, which follows several switchbacks that only make the trail that much easier to walk. Continue toward Tamassee Road. Just 0.4 mile farther you will start to hear the roar of the falls, but it isn't until you are right next to the falls that you will get your first peek of the

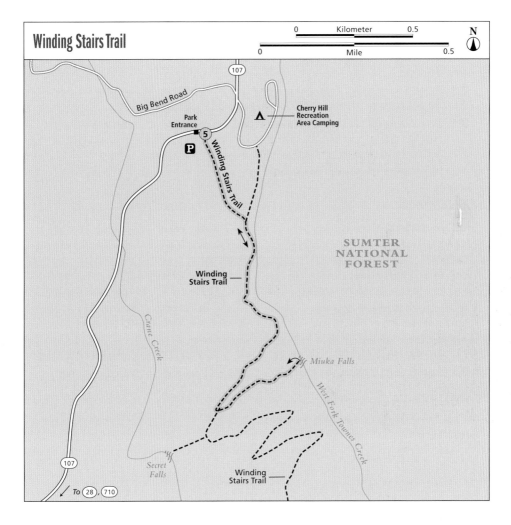

impressive Miuka Falls. A spur trail leads off the trail to a small clearing where you can see the falls through the trees. The view is much better in late fall or in the winter after the trees have lost their leaves and are no longer obscuring the view. If you are capable and willing to work a little more, you can climb down the spur trail that leads to the base of the falls and the bank of West Fork Creek. The climb down is steep and it is often easy to slip on the loose dirt and leaves on the creek bank. Make sure you are wearing shoes with good grips if you are going to climb down the creek bank to get a better view of the falls, and keep low to the ground to avoid a big fall.

From here, you can turn around and retrace your steps, or continue on the Winding Stairs Trail to the parking lot and trailhead at Tamassee Road. However, Miuka Falls are the most impressive feature along this trail and I would recommend exploring some of the other trails in this area, described elsewhere in this book, instead of walking the rest of this trail.

Miles and Directions

0.0 Start from the gravel parking lot 100 feet south of the Cherry Hill Recreation Area off SC 107.

0.2 Reach a trail junction. A spur trail to the right leads to the Cherry Hill Recreation Area. Turn left and continue on the Winding Stairs Trail toward Tamassee Road.

1.1 Reach Miuka Falls. A spur trail leads down the steep creek bank to a better view at the base of the falls. From here turn around and retrace your steps back to the parking lot on 107, or continue on the Winding Stairs Trail to the trailhead at Tamassee Road.

2.2 Arrive back at the parking lot trailhead.

Hike Information

Local Information: Mountain Lakes CVB, 105 W. South Broad St., Walhalla, SC 29691; (877) 685-2537; scmountainlakes.com

Local Events/Attractions: Oconee Heritage Center, 123 Browns Square Dr., Walhalla; (864) 638-2224; oconeeheritagecenter.org. Open Thurs–Fri noon to 6 p.m., Sat 10 a.m. to 3 p.m.

Lodging: Cabins at Oconee State Park, 624 State Park Rd., Mountain Rest; (864) 638-5353. Cabins include fireplace, screened porch, and a grill.

Mountain Rest Cabins, 175 Homeland Dr., Mountain Rest; (864) 718-0333; mountainrestcabins.com

Walhalla Liberty Lodge B&B, 105 Liberty Ln., Walhalla; (864) 638-8239; walhallalibertylodge.com

Restaurants: Tommy's on Main Italian Restaurant, 124 E. Main St., Walhalla; (864) 638-5005

The Steak House Cafeteria, 316 E. Main St., Walhalla; (864) 638-3311; thesteakhousecafeteria.com

Dakota Grill, 2911 Highlands Hwy., Walhalla; (864) 718-0553; dakotagrillsc.com

6 Oconee State Park

This route combines the Oconee Trail and the Old Waterwheel Trail in Oconee State Park to create a nearly 4-mile-long hike that almost forms a complete loop. Whether you start from the Old Waterwheel side of the route or start your hike from the trailhead for the Oconee Trail, you can easily hike along the park road to return to your cabin, campsite, or car. The hike passes one of the mountain lakes found in the park, crosses several picturesque creeks, and visits the Historic Waterwheel Site.

Start: Parking lot near the campground amphitheater, behind the trading post

Distance: 3.4-mile shuttle

Hiking time: About 2 hours

Difficulty: Moderate due to rolling hills

Trail surface: Dirt trail

Best seasons: Spring (Mar–May) for wildflower displays; fall (Sept–Nov) for fall foliage

Other trail users: Joggers

Canine compatibility: Leashed dogs permitted. Dogs not permitted in cabins or cabin areas.

Fees and permits: Free for kids under age 16; small fee for ages 16 and over; senior discount available

Schedule: Sun–Thurs 7 a.m. to 7 p.m., Fri–Sat 7 a.m. to 9 p.m. (extended to 7 a.m. to 9 p.m. daily during daylight saving time)

Maps: TOPO! CD: North Carolina–South Carolina; USGS maps: Tamassee and Walhalla, South Carolina; USFS maps: Trail Guide, Andrew Pickens Ranger District, available at the National Forest Office in Mountain Rest

Trail contacts: Oconee State Park, 624 State Park Rd., Mountain Rest, SC 29664; (864) 638-5353; www.southcarolinaparks.com/oconee

Other: Fishing is allowed in the lake along this trail. A South Carolina fishing license is required.

Finding the trailhead: From I-85, take exit 1 to SC 11 toward Walhalla. From SC 11 take SC 28. Travel through Walhalla and continue for approximately 10 miles. Turn right onto SC 107 and the park is 2 miles farther on the right. GPS: N34 51.829' / W83 06.39'

The Hike

This hike is fun and moderately challenging. The changing landscapes and historical features along the trail make this a great path for older children who are up for the long hike. There is enough of interest to keep their attention for the length of the trail.

Pick up a map at the park office and then drive toward the campground area of the park. If you have two cars, you may want to drop one of them off at the trailhead on the east side of the park that serves as the end of this hike and the trailhead for the Foothills Trail and the Hidden Falls Trail. Just behind the trading post, turn right onto the gravel road that leads to a small parking lot. Follow the dirt path through the outdoor amphitheater to a kiosk that marks the beginning of the trail. The Oconee Trail is marked with white and green diamond-shaped markers. Like most of the trails in this park, the Oconee Trail is not very well marked, but it is easy enough to follow. The path descends to a bridge that crosses a boggy area and a small stream that leads

to the lake. A short climb takes you to the top of a hill where you can see views of the lake through the trees.

Oconee State Park contains three mountain lakes. The largest of the three, which is not along this route and is closer to the park entrance, is the most popular site for paddling and fishing. However, the lake along this trail is stocked with bream and bass. Many small spur trails along this route lead down to decent fishing spots along the lakeshore. The abundance of footpaths created by fishing enthusiasts combined with a lack of trail blazes can make this trail challenging to follow. Most of the time, if you simply stay on the larger trail, you will find your way along this route.

Once you get close to the lake, you will have ample opportunities to take small spur trails down to the lakeshore for fishing or just a little relaxing by the lake.

Descend to the lakeshore and cross the soil berm that runs adjacent to the lake. At the eastern edge of the lake, there is a junction with a spur trail. This junction is unmarked and can be confusing. Straight ahead is a spur trail that leads up to three exceptionally nice backcountry campsites. Each site has a gravel tent pad, picnic table, a small grill, and a fire ring. However, turn right and stay on the Oconee Trail; head away from the lake and enter the forest. Along this next section of the trail, there are several impressively large white pine trees.

After 0.3 mile you'll reach a beautiful creek with mossy banks that curves through the forest in a particularly picturesque way. On the other side of the creek, you'll enter into a part of the forest with a dominant understory of mountain laurel. If you're hiking the trail in spring, these mountain laurels bordering the trail may be in bloom and displaying thousands of white and pink blossoms that eventually fall from the trees and carpet the trail with flowers. Over the next section of trail, you will climb over rolling hills of hardwood forest until you reach the junction with the Waterwheel Trail, which is blazed with white and orange plaques and marked much more frequently than the Oconee Trail. Follow the trail downhill to the spur trail that leads down to the Waterwheel Site and the relics of the pumphouse built by the Civilian Conservation Corps (CCC) in the 1930s. Down at the Waterwheel Site, you can imagine the large overshot waterwheel that once pumped water up to a tank near what is now called Cabin #7. After returning to the Waterwheel Trail, you'll follow along the left side of the creek. Keep your eyes out for wild turkeys along this next section of trail. This is a common spot to see lots of wild-turkey activity.

You'll cross a log bridge that spans the creek, and then you might want to stop and make sure your boots are laced up tight because this next section of trail is exceptionally hilly. Over the next 0.8 mile, you will climb over rolling hills and ascend nearly 400 feet. The trail ends at a trailhead shared with the Foothills Trail and Hidden Falls Trail. You can hike along the road and get back to the trailhead where you started, which is only 0.3 mile away.

◄ *A view of the lake along the Oconee Trail*

Oconee State Park

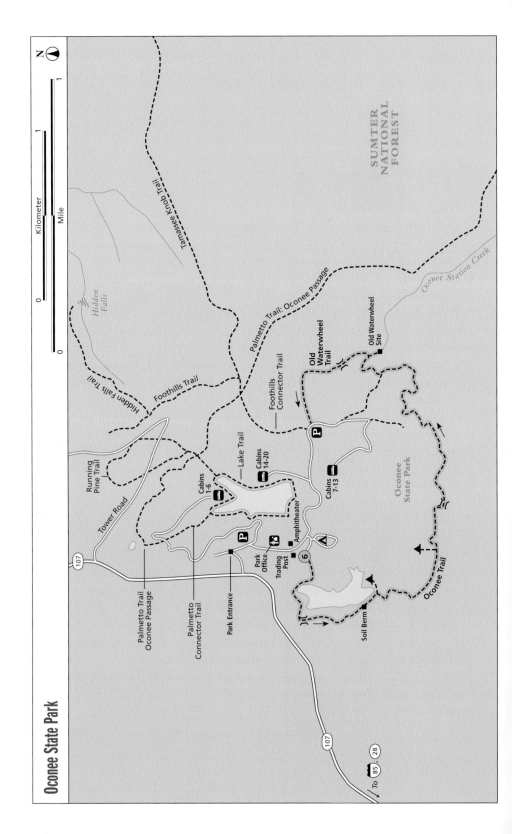

Miles and Directions

0.0 Start from the gravel parking lot near the campground amphitheater. The parking lot is found behind the campground trading post.

0.2 Cross the wooden bridge spanning a boggy area and a small stream that flows down toward the lake. Climb up the hill toward the lake.

0.3 A spur trail leads down to the left. This is the first opportunity of many to take a spur trail that leads down to the lake. Stay straight on the Oconee Trail.

0.6 Reach a T junction with an old roadbed. Turn left to stay on the Oconee Trail. In about 250 feet, descend to the lakeshore and follow the trail across the soil berm that runs adjacent to the lakeshore.

0.7 At the end of the lakeshore, arrive at an unmarked junction. Turn sharply right at the end of the lakeshore. A spur trail continues straight and leads to a very nice backcountry campsite near the lakeshore.

1.0 Stay straight at this four-way junction. A spur trail on the left leads to a backcountry campground.

1.2 Cross a beautiful winding creek via a short wooden bridge.

2.2 At this trail junction with the Waterwheel Trail, turn right and head downhill.

2.3 Turn right and take the spur trail down to the old Waterwheel Site along the creek. Turn around and hike the spur trail back to the Waterwheel Trail. Once you reach the Waterwheel Trail, turn right and continue hiking east on the Waterwheel Trail.

2.5 Cross the creek via a 5-foot-long log bridge.

3.4 The trail ends at the park road. This is also the trailhead for the Foothills Trail and the Hidden Falls Trail. From here you can turn right and follow the paved road back to the parking lot and campground where you started, or turn left and follow the road back to the cabins if you are staying in one of them.

Hike Information

Local Information: Mountain Lakes CVB, 105 W. South Broad St., Walhalla, SC 29691; (877) 685-2537; scmountainlakes.com

Local Events/Attractions: Oconee Heritage Center, 123 Browns Square Dr., Walhalla; (864) 638-2224; oconeeheritagecenter.org. Open Thurs–Fri noon to 6 p.m., Sat 10 a.m. to 3 p.m.

Friday Night Square Dancing, 624 State Park Rd., Mountain Rest. Fri 8 to 10 p.m. from Memorial Day to Labor Day. Small fee; discount for children.

Lodging: Cabins at Oconee State Park, 624 State Park Rd., Mountain Rest; (864) 638-5353. Cabins include fireplace, screened porch, and a grill.

Mountain Rest Cabins, 175 Homeland Dr., Mountain Rest; (864) 718-0333; mountainrestcabins.com. Fully furnished cabins.

Walhalla Liberty Lodge B&B, 105 Liberty Ln., Walhalla; (864) 638-8239, walhallalibertylodge.com

Restaurants: Tommy's on Main Italian Restaurant, 124 E. Main St., Walhalla; (864) 638-5005

The Steak House Cafeteria, 316 E. Main St., Walhalla; (864) 638-3311; thesteakhousecafeteria.com

Dakota Grill, 2911 Highlands Hwy., Walhalla; (864) 718-0553; dakotagrillsc.com

7 Hidden Falls Trail

Hike along the Foothills Trail from Oconee State Park through a forest of hardwood and conifer trees to the Hidden Falls Spur Trail, which leads back to a picturesque 60-foot waterfall tucked away in a lush forested cove filled with rhododendrons and ferns. At the base of the falls are several large, flat boulders that are perfect for relaxing and taking in the view.

Start: Foothills Trail parking lot in Oconee State Park
Distance: 4.8-mile out and back
Hiking time: About 2.5 hours
Difficulty: Easy to moderate due to length and elevation gains
Trail surface: Forested path
Best seasons: Spring (Mar–May) for wildflower displays; fall (Sept–Nov) for fall foliage
Other trail users: Hikers only
Canine compatibility: Leashed dogs permitted
Fees and permits: Free for kids under age 16; small fee for age 16 and over; senior discount available

Schedule: Sun–Thurs 7 a.m. to 7 p.m., Fri–Sat 7 a.m. to 9 p.m. (extended to 7 a.m. to 9 p.m. daily during daylight saving time)
Maps: TOPO! CD: North Carolina–South Carolina; USGS maps: Tamassee and Walhalla, South Carolina; USFS maps: Trail Guide, Andrew Pickens Ranger District, available at the National Forest Office in Mountain Rest
Trail contacts: Oconee State Park, 624 State Park Rd., Mountain Rest, SC 29664; (864) 638-5353; www.southcarolinaparks .com/oconee

Finding the trailhead: From Walhalla drive northwest on SC 28 for approximately 8.4 miles and bear right onto SC 107. Continue on SC 107 to Oconee State Park and enter the park. After the fee station turn right and drive to a small parking area on the right, just beyond the entrance to Cabin Area 14–20. The trailhead is on the left at the Foothills Trail sign. GPS: N34 51.808' / W83 05.887'

The Hike

The falls may be called "hidden," but you are going to discover one of the best hikes and waterfalls in Oconee State Park on this trail. The path is well marked and very easy to follow, and it is just a gradual descent down to the base of the beautiful falls. There are two sections of this trail with moderately steep descents, but these are relatively short sections and nothing to be too concerned with.

Due to construction, the parking situation is fluid. When you arrive at the park, stop at the park office and inquire about parking and its location relative to the Foothills Trail trailhead.

A large sign marks the start of the Foothills Trail and you immediately come to a split in the trail. Stay to the left and follow the Foothills Trail toward Hidden Falls. The first 1.3 miles of the trail is fairly level and easy walking, and along this section

The trailhead for the Foothills Trail at Oconee State Park

you'll cross and join an old logging road for a short distance and then enter back onto a forested trail. You'll traverse through a forest of oaks and conifers before reaching the junction with the Hidden Falls Trail and beginning your descent toward the falls. As you descend toward the falls, the trail begins to follow along Tamassee Creek. The creek is never too far away from the trail, and you can hear the sounds of the rocky creek tumbling in the distance. However, for most of the trail, the creek is obscured by the dense understory of the forest until you arrive at Hidden Falls.

As you get closer to the falls, you will begin to notice that the forest subtly changes and more rhododendrons and ferns appear in the understory. The trail turns sharply to the south and drops into a densely forested cove. If the water is high, you will hear the roar of the falls long before you ever see it. The falls live up to their name and stay hidden by the forest until you are only 50 feet from the base of the falls. At times of low water, you may only have a trickle of water running over the 60-foot drop, but even then the falls are still beautiful and worth the hike.

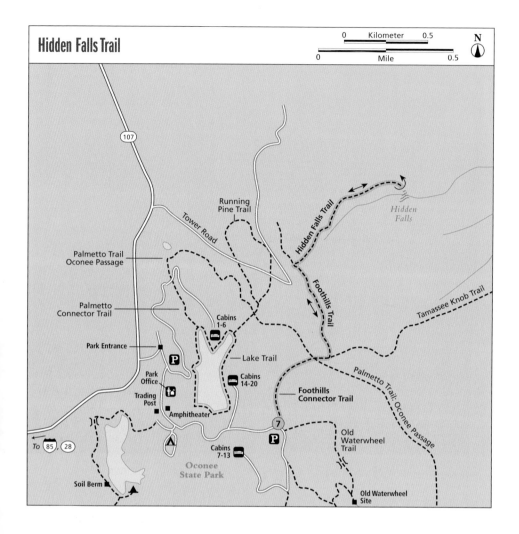

There are several undesignated trails running up the steep, forested bank beside the falls. If you choose to explore these undesignated trails up the sides of the falls, please be careful. Do not try to climb up the slick rocks of the falls, and do not attempt to wade across the stream above the falls. People who try to wade in streams directly above falls occasionally lose their footing and die when they are swept over the waterfall. In 2009 a 20-year-old man was killed at Hidden Falls. Three hikers climbed up the left side of the falls and then decided to cross Tamassee Creek at the top of the falls. One hiker made it safely across. Unfortunately, the second hiker slipped on a rock and lost his footing while trying to cross the creek. He attempted to grab onto a loose rock, but the current swept him over the top of the falls, and the 60-foot drop killed him. Waterfalls are beautiful, but they can also be deadly.

After enjoying the view of the falls from the flat rocks around the base of the falls, turn around and retrace your steps back to the Foothills Trail parking lot where you started.

Miles and Directions

0.0 Start from the Foothills Trailhead at Oconee State Park. The trail splits at Foothills Trail. Stay to the left toward Hidden Falls.

0.4 Cross an old logging road. You'll reach a T junction 50 feet from the road crossing. The Tamassee Knob Trail is to the left. Turn right and stay on the Foothills Trail toward the Hidden Falls Trail.

1.2 Reach an old logging road. Follow the wooden steps down to the road. The logging road has been barricaded by a metal gate to the left and the Foothills Trail continues straight. Turn right onto the Hidden Falls Trail, follow the logging road for 300 feet, then veer left, following the Hidden Falls Trail back into the forest. From here you will begin the descent down to Hidden Falls.

2.4 Reach Hidden Falls. Turn around and retrace your steps back to the Foothills Trail parking lot.

4.8 Arrive back at the trailhead.

Hike Information

Local Information: Mountain Lakes CVB, 105 W. South Broad St., Walhalla, SC 29691; (877) 685-2537; scmountainlakes.com

Local Events/Attractions: Oconee Heritage Center, 123 Browns Square Dr., Walhalla; (864) 638-2224; oconeeheritagecenter.org. Open Thurs–Fri noon to 6 p.m., Sat 10 a.m. to 3 p.m.

Friday Night Square Dancing, 624 State Park Rd., Mountain Rest. Takes place Fri 8 to 10 p.m. from Memorial Day to Labor Day. Small fee; discount for children

Lodging: Cabins at Oconee State Park, 624 State Park Rd., Mountain Rest; (864) 638-5353. Cabins include fireplace, screened porch, and a grill

Mountain Rest Cabins, 175 Homeland Dr., Mountain Rest; (864) 718-0333; mountainrestcabins.com. Fully furnished cabins

Walhalla Liberty Lodge B&B, 105 Liberty Ln., Walhalla; (864) 638-8239; walhallalibertylodge.com

Restaurants: Tommy's on Main Italian Restaurant, 124 E. Main St., Walhalla; (864) 638-5005

The Steak House Cafeteria, 316 E. Main St., Walhalla; (864) 638-3311; thesteakhousecafeteria.com

Dakota Grill, 2911 Highlands Hwy., Walhalla; (864) 718-0553; dakotagrillsc.com

8 Palmetto Trail: Oconee Passage

Start from Oconee State Park at the trailhead, which also serves as the northern terminus of the Palmetto Trail. Hike over challenging rolling hills to the entrance of the Oconee Station State Historical Site. Along the way take a spur trail to the beautiful 60-foot-high Station Cove Falls, the highlight of the trail. Part of this route follows an old roadbed that is lined with impressive ferns.

Start: Chestnut Trailhead parking lot at Oconee State Park

Distance: 8.2-mile out and back

Hiking time: About 4 hours

Difficulty: Moderate due to length and elevation gains

Trail surface: Forested trail, old roadbed

Best seasons: Spring (Mar–May) for wildflower displays; fall (Sept–Nov) for fall foliage

Other trail users: Mountain bikers

Canine compatibility: Leashed dogs permitted

Fees and permits: Free for kids; small fee for ages 16 and over; senior discount available

Schedule: Sun–Thurs 7 a.m. to 7 p.m., Fri–Sat 7 a.m. to 9 p.m. (extended to 7 a.m. to 9 p.m. daily during daylight saving time)

Maps: TOPO! CD: North Carolina-South Carolina; USGS maps: Tamassee and Walhalla, South Carolina; USFS maps: Trail Guide, Andrew Pickens Ranger District, available at the National Forest Office in Mountain Rest

Trail contacts: Oconee State Park, 624 State Park Rd., Mountain Rest, SC 29664; (864) 638-5353; www.southcarolinaparks .com/oconee

Finding the trailhead: From Walhalla drive northwest on SC 28 for 8.4 miles and bear right onto SC 107. Continue on SC 107 to Oconee State Park and enter the park. From the park office drive toward cabins 1–6. Before reaching the cabins, the road curves sharply to the southeast. Just before this curve you will find the trailhead parking lot on the left side of the road. It's easy to miss, so look for the stone columns on the edge of the parking lot. Stone steps lead down to a kiosk and the trailhead. GPS: N34 52.309' / W83 06.331'

The Hike

While Oconee State Park is not conspicuously mountainous, the rolling hills that you encounter along this trail are a surprising challenge. Once the Palmetto Trail is finally completed, this hike will officially be the northern terminus for the mountains-to-sea trail that runs the entire length of the state. Don't be confused by the fact that this trail has more than one name. The state park map lists this trail as the "Palmetto Trail to Oconee Station," while the Palmetto Trail Association calls this path the "Oconee Passage." No matter what the trail is called, this route is a moderately challenging and enjoyable way to hike to Station Cove Falls. The trail does traverse all the way to the Oconee Station State Historic Site, but after you see the stunning waterfall near the end of the trail, somehow hiking uphill to a road at the end of the trail is unarguably anticlimactic. Unless you want to add the hike around the lake at the Oconee

Station Site, which is also included in this book, I would suggest simply hiking to the falls and back. The waterfall, Station Cove Falls, is alone worth the hike. It isn't just a trickle of water over a couple of rocks. This is a full-on, 60-foot-high waterfall, the kind that nature photographers dream about.

The hike begins in Oconee State Park near a group of rustic cabins built by the Civilian Conservation Corps (CCC). The cabins are definitely worth seeing and highly recommended for an overnight visit. Each cabin has that artful stone-and-wood construction that is a hallmark of CCC work; and they're priced to be some of the best deals for cabin rental in South Carolina. The trailhead is at the Chestnut Trailhead parking lot. The trail gently descends through a dense forest to a small creek that is obstructed by an old dam. You cross the creek by walking across the top of the dam. On the other side of the creek is a picnic table near the creek bank. Even if you don't want to hike all the way down to the falls and

Crossing the old dam near the beginning of the Oconee Passage Trail

back, pack a picnic and enjoy this secluded picnic spot right near the creek bank.

The route starts out relatively flat, but don't let the fact that you start the hike atop the ridge fool you: This trail gets harder. In the spring and summer, you will hike along this high ridge through a dense hardwood forest. However, if you hike the trail in the late fall or winter, you will enjoy remarkable views of the surrounding Blue Ridge foothills, not to mention the much cooler temperatures. You join the Palmetto Trail from here and follow this relatively flat section of the trail for the next 1.8 miles. Enjoy it, because you then leave the ridge in a dramatic way. Over the next 1.4 miles, you descend nearly 1,000 feet and reach the base of Station Cove Falls. The trail isn't so tough on the way down, but remember, this is not a loop trail. You're going to have to turn around at the end of the trail and hike back up the massive hill to climb back onto the ridge.

At the end of the trail you reach SC 95. This is also the trailhead of the Historic Site Trail. You can simply cross the road and start the Historic Site Trail, which circles a picturesque lake and is blazed with blue markers.

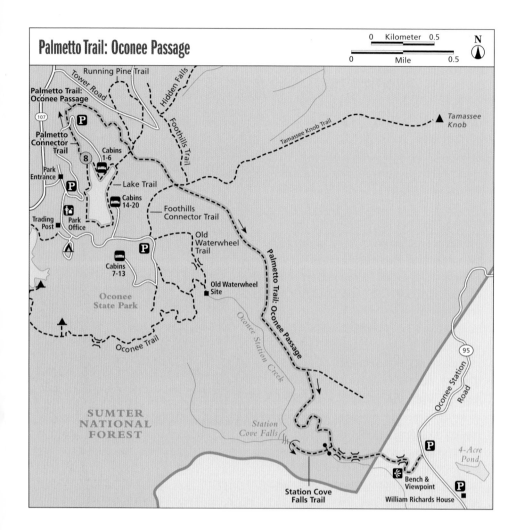

Palmetto Trail: Oconee Passage

Miles and Directions

0.0 Start from the Chestnut Trailhead. Stone steps lead up to a kiosk. The trail splits at the kiosk. Follow the Palmetto Connector Trail to the right.

0.1 Cross the remains of an old dam spanning a small creek. In about 50 feet you will find a picnic table at a split in the trail. Stay straight and join the Palmetto Trail.

0.5 Cross the wooden bridge spanning the stream.

0.9 Turn right onto the old road and continue to follow the yellow-blazed Palmetto Trail.

1.1 Stay straight at the four-way junction. To the left the Foothills Trail leads toward Hidden Falls. To the right you can hike 0.4 mile back to the trailhead for the Foothills Trail and a parking lot in the state park.

3.1 Reach a trail junction. Take the Station Cove Falls Trail sharply to the right and pass through the wooden gate that restricts the trail to only foot traffic.

3.3 Follow the stone steps down to Station Cove Creek and cross the creek, following the stone steps back up the other side of the bank. Follow the trail alongside the creek.

3.4 The spur trail ends at the base of the 60-foot-high Station Creek Falls. After enjoying the falls, turn around and hike back to the junction with the Palmetto Trail. Continue straight on the Palmetto Trail toward Oconee Station.

3.6 Cross the wooden bridge and continue on the Palmetto Trail.

3.7 Cross the small creek via another wooden bridge.

3.8 Reach a small stream that has cut an 8-foot-deep gully into the landscape. Cross the stream via the small wooden bridge.

3.9 Take in the views of the creek below from the wooden bench at this viewpoint.

4.1 Reach the end of the trail marked by a wooden kiosk. From here you can continue straight and hike the Oconee Station Trail, or turn around and walk back the way you came to return to Oconee State Park.

8.2 Arrive back at the Chestnut Trailhead.

Hike Information

Local Information: Mountain Lakes CVB, 105 W. South Broad St., Walhalla, SC 29691; (877) 685-2537; scmountainlakes.com

Local Events/Attractions: Oconee Heritage Center, 123 Browns Square Dr., Walhalla; (864) 638-2224; oconeeheritagecenter.org. Open Thurs–Fri noon to 6 p.m., Sat 10 a.m. to 3 p.m.

Friday Night Square Dancing, 624 State Park Rd., Mountain Rest. Fri 8 to 10 p.m. from Memorial Day to Labor Day. Small fee; discount for children

Lodging: Cabins at Oconee State Park, 624 State Park Rd., Mountain Rest; (864) 638-5353. Cabins include fireplace, screened porch, and a grill.

Mountain Rest Cabins, 175 Homeland Dr., Mountain Rest; (864) 718-0333; mountainrestcabins.com. Fully furnished cabins

Walhalla Liberty Lodge B&B, 105 Liberty Ln., Walhalla; (864) 638-8239; walhallaliberty lodge.com

Restaurants: Tommy's on Main Italian Restaurant, 124 E. Main St., Walhalla; (864) 638-5005

The Steak House Cafeteria, 316 E. Main St., Walhalla; (864) 638-3311; thesteakhouse cafeteria.com

Dakota Grill, 2911 Highlands Hwy., Walhalla; (864) 718-0553; dakotagrillsc.com

Organizations: Palmetto Conservation Foundation, 722 King St., Columbia, SC 29205; (803) 771-0870; palmettoconservation.org

⑨ Oconee Station Historical Trail

This hike is located in the 210-acre Oconee Station State Historic Site and circles a picturesque 4-acre pond. The route is a pleasant and short day hike that follows a mostly level dirt path around the perimeter of the pond and passes through upcountry forest. In spring the wildflowers along this trail and throughout the park are particularly impressive. If you're into fishing, make sure to bring your pole for a little leisurely casting in the pond for bluegill and largemouth bass.

Start: Gravel parking lot north of the park entrance

Distance: 1.1-mile lollipop

Hiking time: About half an hour

Difficulty: Easy to moderate due to a few rolling hills along the route

Trail surface: Forested trail

Best seasons: Spring (Mar–May) for wildflower displays; fall (Sept–Nov) for fall foliage

Other trail users: Joggers

Canine compatibility: Leashed dogs permitted

Fees and permits: None

Schedule: Mar 1 to Nov 30 daily 9 a.m. to 6 p.m.; Dec 1 to Feb 28 Fri–Sun only, 9 a.m. to 6 p.m.

Maps: TOPO! CD: North Carolina–South Carolina; USGS maps: Tamassee and Walhalla, South Carolina; USFS maps: Trail Guide, Andrew Pickens Ranger District, available at the National Forest Office in Mountain Rest

Trail contacts: Oconee Station State Historic Site, 500 Oconee Station Rd., Walhalla, SC 29691; (864) 638-0079; southcarolinaparks .com/oconeestation

Finding the trailhead: *From I-85 northbound:* Take exit 1 at the Georgia / South Carolina state line onto SC 11. Drive for 26 miles and turn left onto Oconee Station Road. Drive for 2 miles to the park entrance then drive about 0.2 mile more to the gravel parking lot on the left side of the road. The trailhead is across the street.

From I-85 southbound: Take exit 19B onto SC 28 toward Clemson. Drive 26 miles and take the ramp toward Tamassee/Salem. Merge onto SC 11 and drive 6 miles. Turn left onto Oconee Station Road. Drive for 2 miles and look for the park entrance. GPS: N34 50.943' / W83 04.462'

The Hike

If you're hiking from Oconee State Park along the Palmetto Trail, you can add another 1.1 mile to your adventure by crossing SC 95 and following this path around a 4-acre pond. Once you cross SC 95, you enter onto the Oconee Station State Historic Site property. The Oconee Station Site brochures call this route an interpretive trail, but don't be fooled: Whether as the result of complete neglect or because of some change-of-heart, you will not find a single interpretive sign or plaque anywhere along this hike. What you will find is a beautiful pond that is regularly stocked with bluegill and largemouth bass and surrounded by a fine example of upland forests.

The Oconee Station Trail circles a 4-acre pond stocked with largemouth bass and bluegill.

Be forewarned though: This trail is not well marked. There is nearly a complete lack of trail markers and blazes, and the ubiquitous footpaths likely made from those fishing in the pond can make staying on the actual trail quite the difficult task. Luckily, the goal of following the main path around the perimeter of the pond is easy enough to achieve if you simply follow the directions below, and when in doubt follow the largest-size path around the pond.

You start from a parking lot north of the park entrance. This parking lot and trailhead are also shared by the Palmetto Trail, which leads west to the impressively beautiful 60-foot-high Station Cove Falls. This is one of the most remarkable falls in the entire state, and from this parking lot the falls are only 1 mile away. So, do yourself a favor and add another mile to your day and hike down to this waterfall too. However, to get to the pond along the Oconee Station Trail, you are going to have to cross I-95 and follow the small path into the forest. The trail descends immediately down a moderately steep hill toward the lakeshore. You cross a soil berm along the pond shore and then continue to follow the trail around the pond until you complete a loop and then return to the parking lot where you began.

Oconee Station Historical Trail

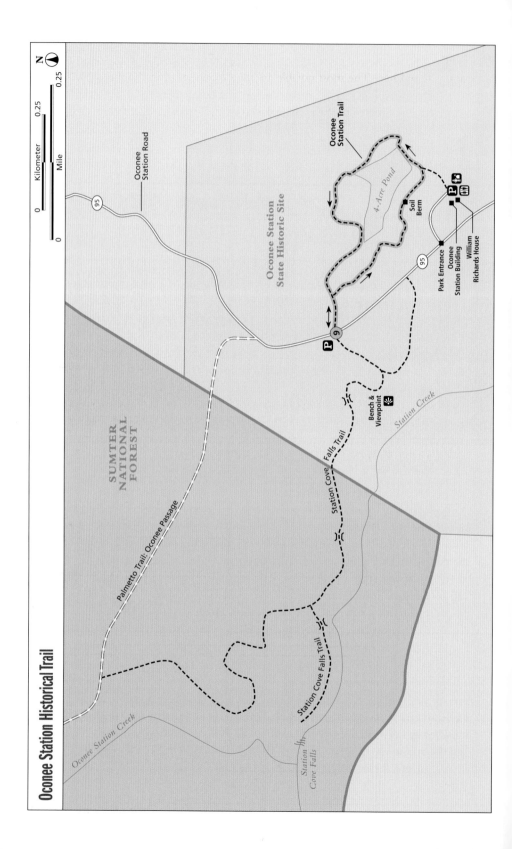

N

0   0.25   Kilometer
0   0.25   Mile

SUMTER
NATIONAL
FOREST

Oconee Station Creek

Palmetto Trail: Oconee Passage

Station Cove Falls Trail

Station Cove Falls Trail

Station
Cove Falls

Oconee Station Road

95

Oconee Station
State Historic Site

Oconee Station Trail

4-Acre Pond

Soil
Berm

9   P

95

Bench &
Viewpoint

Station Creek

Park Entrance

Oconee
Station Building

William
Richards House

P

While you are in the park, you can also visit many of the historical structures and features found here. The most notable are the Oconee Station Building and the William Richards House. Both of these sites are located near the park office and ranger station. At the entrance to the park, make an immediate right and follow this road to a parking lot, where you can explore these historical buildings, which are listed on the National Register of Historic Places. The stone blockhouse was built in 1792 by the South Carolina State Militia. During that time the area was considered the western frontier of South Carolina, and the Oconee Station Building was built to protect settlers from the persistent raids of Creek Indians. The William Richards House was used as the main residence for the namesake Irish immigrant from 1805 all the way into the 1970s when it was used as a summer home.

Miles and Directions

0.0 Start from the gravel parking lot north of the entrance to Oconee Station Historic Site. Driving from the park entrance, the parking lot is on the left (west) side of the road. A kiosk marks the trailhead. From the parking lot, cross SC 95 and follow the blue-blazed Oconee Station Trail. From here you can also take the Station Cove Falls Trail, which starts from the parking lot, leads west to Station Falls, and after 4 miles ends at Oconee State Park.

0.1 After you descend down the trail toward the 4-acre pond, turn right onto the 2-foot-wide dirt path.

0.4 Turn left toward the lake at this trail junction. (The spur trail to the right leads to another parking lot and trailhead for this hike.) Follow along the soil berm that runs adjacent to the lakeshore. Follow the trail along the lakeshore.

1.0 Turn right at the end of the loop and hike back toward SC 95.

1.1 Reach the end of the trail at the gravel parking lot where you started.

Hike Information

Local Information: Mountain Lakes CVB, 105 W. South Broad St., Walhalla, SC 29691; (877) 685-2537; scmountainlakes.com

Local Events/Attractions: Oconee Heritage Center, 123 Browns Square Dr., Walhalla; (864) 638-2224; oconeeheritagecenter.org. Thurs–Fri noon to 6 p.m., Sat 10 a.m. to 3 p.m.

Lodging: Cabins at Oconee State Park, 624 State Park Rd., Mountain Rest; (864) 638-5353. Cabins include fireplace, screened porch, and a grill

Mountain Rest Cabins, 175 Homeland Dr., Mountain Rest; (864) 718-0333; mountainrestcabins.com. Fully furnished cabins

Walhalla Liberty Lodge B&B, 105 Liberty Ln., Walhalla; (864) 638-8239; walhallalibertylodge.com

Restaurants: Tommy's on Main Italian Restaurant, 124 E. Main St., Walhalla; (864) 638-5005

The Steak House Cafeteria, 316 E. Main St., Walhalla; (864) 638-3311; thesteakhousecafeteria.com

Dakota Grill, 2911 Highlands Hwy., Walhalla; (864) 718-0553; dakotagrillsc.com

10 Lee Falls

This short day hike may seem like an easy way to get back to a waterfall, but don't be fooled. Nearly nonexistent trail markings and extremely light traffic make this trail considerably difficult to follow. Along the hike you will pass through four experimental agriculture fields that are maintained by the Forest Service, cross Tamassee Creek three times, and visit the barely accessible Lee Falls. The falls are not the most impressive in the state. However, the adventure of following the trail and the solitude you usually find along this route warrant the trail's inclusion in this book.

Start: Large dirt parking lot off FR 715A
Distance: 2.6-mile out and back
Hiking time: About 2.5 hours
Difficulty: Moderate due to the difficulty of following the trail and elevation gains
Trail surface: Forested trail, dirt path
Best seasons: Spring (Mar–May) for wildflower displays; fall (Sept–Nov) for fall foliage
Other trail users: Hikers only
Canine compatibility: Dogs permitted
Fees and permits: None

Schedule: Open year-round
Maps: TOPO! CD: North Carolina–South Carolina; USGS maps: Tamassee, South Carolina; USFS maps: Trail Guide, Andrew Pickens Ranger District, available at the National Forest Office in Mountain Rest
Trail contacts: Sumter National Forest, Andrew Pickens Ranger District, 112 Andrew Pickens Circle, Mountain Rest, SC 29664; (864) 638-9568

Finding the trailhead: The trailhead can be very difficult to find, and it is definitely recommended that you do yourself a favor and simply drive to Walhalla and follow the directions below to the trailhead. Unless you are extremely familiar with this area, the way that Cheohee Valley Road and Jumping Branch Road intersect will send you on a wild goose chase that will likely end up costing you more money in gas than you wanted to spend. From the intersection of SC 11 (Cherokee Foothills Scenic Highway) and SC 28 at Walhalla, drive north on SC 11 for 8.3 miles and turn left (west) onto Cheohee Valley Road (Oconee County S-37-375). Drive 2.3 miles and turn left onto Tamassee Knob Road (S-37-95). Drive 0.5 mile and turn right (northwest) onto Jumping Branch Road. Drive 1.5 miles and turn left (northwest) onto FS 715A, which is gravel. Drive 0.7 mile to a large unpaved parking area on the right, which is just before a small bridge over Tamassee Creek. Once you find the parking lot, feel free to park anywhere, and look for the metal gate at the back of the lot that blocks the entrance to a large field. The trail starts from this metal gate at the back of the parking lot. GPS: N34 53.628' / W83 04.899'

The Hike

If you are in training for the television show *Survivor* or simply want to go on a rugged trail where you might be able to put your navigation skills to the test, then this is the trail for you. This is also one of the best trails in this book for finding the solitude you have been looking for.

The trailhead to the Lee Falls Trail

There is a reason that Lee Falls is one of the least visited waterfalls in the entire state: The trail is nearly impossible to follow at many points along the route. The Lee Falls Trail starts out as a very clear path that cuts through four experimental growing fields managed by the USDA Forest Service. A small dirt path cuts through a field of wildflowers and goldenrod where you are likely to find all sorts of insects buzzing around including large bumblebees and honeybees.

Tamassee Creek flows to the left side of the fields, and it is common to see turkeys wandering around the edges of the fields. There are several unbridged crossings of Tamassee Creek along this section of the trail. The creek is usually easily crossed by hopping across the large stones or the fallen trees that have been placed across the creek. You should be able to keep your feet dry when crossing the creek unless there is an extremely high water flow.

After crossing the creek the second time, the trail enters into a thick and lush forest of mountain laurel and rhododendron. Along this section of the trail, the path becomes increasingly smaller as hikers have apparently abandoned their attempt to find Lee Falls so they turn around and head back to the parking lot. As you get closer to the falls, the trail follows along Tamassee Creek and hugs close to the creek on a steep bank. The amount of erosion in some areas is so great that the trail becomes a half-foot-wide dirt path with a steep drop toward the creek. Keeping your footing can prove difficult along these extremely poorly maintained sections of the trail; exercise extreme caution when hiking along these steep and eroded portions of the trail.

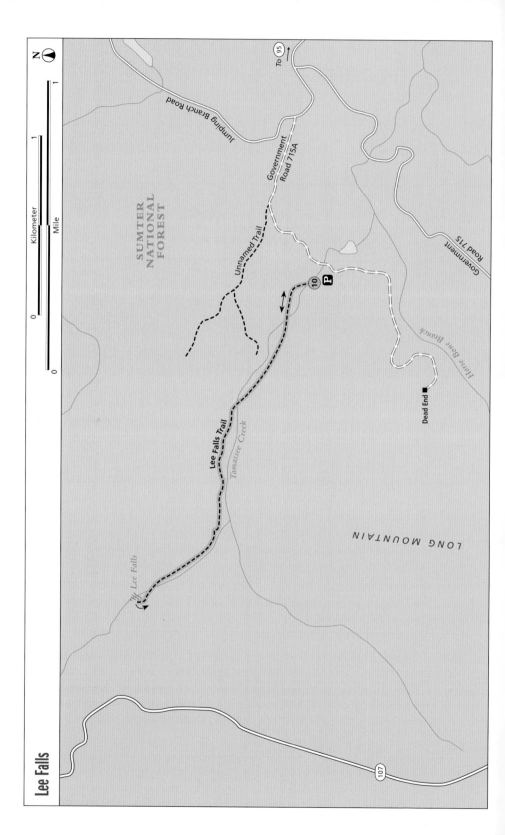

Lee Falls

SUMTER NATIONAL FOREST

LONG MOUNTAIN

Lee Falls

Lee Falls Trail

Tamassee Creek

Unnamed Trail

Jumping Branch Road

Government Road 715A

Government Road 715

Horse Bone Branch

Dead End

To 95

10

P

107

N

Kilometer
0   1

Mile
0   1

Right before you reach the third crossing of the creek, you will come to a large tree where you will find the names of lovers from days gone by inscribed into the bark of the tree. You can only imagine that they were thinking the same thing you may be thinking at this point, "Where did the trail go?" Directly in front of you, a nearly indiscernible path runs practically straight up the mountainside. Save yourself the workout, because this is not the trail. The trail, or the little of it that actually exists, curves around this tree and crosses the creek for the third time.

From here the trail all but disappears. Small footpaths run in almost every direction as most people wander around and look for a clear route to the falls. Surprise! There is no clear route. The best thing to do from here is to follow along the edge of the creek for about 400 feet until you reach a small clearing with a poor view of the cascading falls in front of you. It may be a bit anticlimactic for all the work you had to endure to find the falls, but it was probably an adventure, and you probably had the trail to yourself. From here turn around and retrace your steps, if you can find them, and follow the trail back to the parking lot on FS 715A.

Miles and Directions

0.0 Start from the metal gate at the end of the large dirt parking off FS 715A. A trail leads from the metal gate into a large field. Walk through the field to the forested area on the other side.

0.2 Cross Tamassee Creek. After crossing the creek, walk through two more fields.

0.5 Cross Tamassee Creek. After crossing the creek, walk through one field and then follow the trail as it enters into the forest.

1.3 Do not follow the steep trail up the hill. Utilize the large boulders to cross the creek. The trail will follow along the creek for 400 feet until you are able to get a view of Lee Falls. From here turn around and retrace your steps.

2.6 Arrive back at the parking lot.

Hike Information

Local Information: Mountain Lakes CVB, 105 W. South Broad St., Walhalla, SC 29691; (877) 685-2537; scmountainlakes.com

Local Events/Attractions: Oconee Heritage Center, 123 Browns Square Dr., Walhalla; (864) 638-2224; oconeeheritagecenter.org. Thurs–Fri noon to 6 p.m., Sat 10 a.m. to 3 p.m.

Lodging: Cabins at Oconee State Park, 624 State Park Rd., Mountain Rest; (864) 638-5353. Cabins include fireplace, screened porch, and a grill

Mountain Rest Cabins, 175 Homeland Dr., Mountain Rest; (864) 718-0333; mountainrestcabins.com. Fully furnished cabins

Walhalla Liberty Lodge B&B, 105 Liberty Ln., Walhalla; (864) 638-8239; walhallaliberty lodge.com

Restaurants: Tommy's on Main Italian Restaurant, 124 E. Main St., Walhalla; (864) 638-5005

The Steak House Cafeteria, 316 E. Main St., Walhalla; (864) 638-3311; thesteakhouse cafeteria.com

Dakota Grill, 2911 Highlands Hwy., Walhalla; (864) 718-0553; dakotagrillsc.com

11   Lower Whitewater Falls and Coon Branch Natural Area

This trail is a great half-day hike to the most impressive waterfall in all of South Carolina. At the end of this trail, you reach a large observation deck where you can look across the river gorge at a torrent of water plunging 400 feet toward Lake Jocassee. The route is short and there are only a few moderately steep sections that make hiking this trail more than worth the climb for such a spectacular view.

Start: Bad Creek Access parking lot
Distance: 4.2 miles out and back
Hiking time: About 2 hours
Difficulty: Easy to moderate due to short steep sections on the Lower Whitewater Falls Trail
Trail surface: Gravel path, forested path, gravel road
Best seasons: Spring (Mar–May) for wildflower displays; fall (Sept–Nov) for fall foliage
Other trail users: Hikers only
Canine compatibility: Leashed dogs permitted

Fees and permits: None
Schedule: 6 a.m. to 6 p.m. daily
Maps: TOPO! CD: North Carolina–South Carolina; USGS maps: Reid and Cashiers, North Carolina–South Carolina; USFS maps: Trail Guide, Andrew Pickens Ranger District, available at the National Forest Office in Mountain Rest
Trail contacts: Sumter National Forest, Andrew Pickens Ranger District, 112 Andrew Pickens Circle, Mountain Rest, SC 29664; (864) 638-9568

Finding the trailhead: *From Walhalla:* Drive north on SC 11 (Cherokee Foothills Scenic Highway) for 14 miles and turn left onto SC 130. Drive north on SC 130 for 10.5 miles and turn right (east) at the entrance to Duke Energy's Bad Creek Hydroelectric Station. Pass through the automatic gate. Drive approximately 2 miles to the parking area for the Foothills Trail / Whitewater River. (This is a lighted parking lot with a public telephone and portable toilets.)

From Sapphire, North Carolina: Drive south on NC 281 past the Upper Whitewater Falls overlook area to the state line, where NC 281 become SC 130. Follow SC 130 another mile or so to the Duke Energy Bad Creek Project on the left. You will see an entrance station on the right-hand side of a chain-link gate. Turn right onto Bad Creek Road, drive up to the gate, and if it is closed, wait for it to open. Drive down Bad Creek Road and follow the signs to the hiking trails. The trailhead for the Bad Creek Spur Trail is at the very back of the large gravel parking lot. GPS: N35 00.747' / W82 59.951'

The Hike

If you are only going to hike one trail in this far-north mountain region of South Carolina, this is the one to hike. The trail begins on the Bad Creek Spur Trail, which is an access point to the Bad Creek parking lot and the Foothills Trail. It is also an access point into the Coon Branch Natural Area, a 20-acre area of virgin forest along the Whitewater River that contains a Frasier magnolia with a 6-foot circumference that

A pair of bridges crosses Whitewater River along the Bad
Creek Spur Trail on the route to Lower Whitewater Falls.

stands 86 feet tall. This Frasier magnolia is considered to be the largest in the entire state of South Carolina.

The real highlight along this route, however, is the view of the 400-foot-tall Lower Whitewater Falls. Along the first 0.6 mile of the trail, you follow the Bad Creek Spur Trail. You start out on a gravel path that leads through a young grove of trees. This used to be an open field, but restoration efforts are restoring the field to forested land. After the trail turns sharply to the left, you climb a forested path to a relatively level ridge that offers excellent views of the surrounding Blue Ridge Mountains and of Lake Jocassee and the flatlands to the south. This is a great trail to hike year-round, but in the late fall and early spring, the views on the ridge are the best, before the leaves obscure them slightly.

Near the end of the Bad Creek Spur Trail, you reach a junction with the Coon Branch Trail to the left. If you want to extend your hike to the falls, you can turn left here and follow this out-and-back 0.9-mile trail that follows along Whitewater River back to the small Coon Branch Natural Area. If you choose to hike back to Coon Branch, this will add 1.8 miles to this route, bringing the route to a total of 6.0 miles. Make sure you have enough time and water to add this distance onto your trip. To head directly to the falls, continue straight on the Bad Creek Spur Trail and cross over the pair of bridges that span Whitewater River. The bridges offer nice views of the river. This section of trail, which is close to the river, is the best place to see wildlife. Keep your eyes open for beavers and trout in the river and deer, bears, raccoons, bob-cats, and wild boars that inhabit the forest. The view of the river also gives you long-range view that is perfect for spotting birds. You will often find anglers and birders with their respective poles and binoculars trying to reel in a catch or get a glimpse of the flycatchers, warblers, and other birds that are commonly seen in this forest.

From the pair of bridges, you walk 100 feet to the junction of the Foothills Trail. This is the end of the Bad Creek Spur Trail. The Foothills Trail is to the left and straight ahead. Stay straight on the Foothills Trail and continue toward the Lower Whitewater Falls Trail.

You begin a steep but short ascent and then follow a hilly ridge to the junction with the Lower Whitewater Falls Trail. The Foothills Trail turns to the left and toward a camping area, but stay to the right and follow the blue-blazed Lower Whitewater Falls Trail. You will reach a gravel parking lot and turn left to follow the gravel road for 0.1 mile until you leave the road and enter into the forest again. During the next section of the trail, you descend steeply before climbing over one last steep hill and then descending steeply to an observation deck with spectacular views of the distant Lower Whitewater Falls. From here you can turn around and retrace your steps.

Just as a note, it is an option to take the gravel road back to the parking lot where you started to make this trail a quasi-loop trail. When you reach the gravel road, just turn left and follow the hilly road back to the parking lot at the Bad Creek Access.

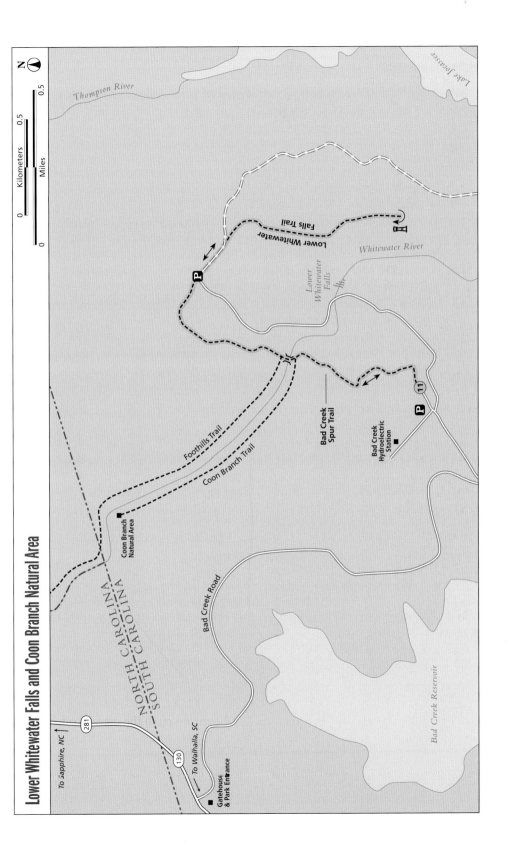

Lower Whitewater Falls and Coon Branch Natural Area

Miles and Directions

0.0 Start from the trailhead to the Bad Creek Spur Trail. Follow the gravel path from the kiosk. This is the white-blazed Bad Creek Spur Trail.

0.6 Just before a pair of bridges, you reach a junction with the Coon Branch Trail to the left. Stay straight on the Bad Creek Spur Trail and cross over the pair of metal railed bridges spanning Whitewater River. After you cross the second bridge, walk 100 feet to the junction with the Foothills Trail. This is the end of the Bad Creek Spur Trail. The Foothills Trail is to the left and straight ahead. Stay straight on the Foothills Trail toward the Lower Whitewater Falls.

1.0 The trail splits. To the left the Foothills Trail continues and leads toward a designated camping area. Stay to the right and start hiking on the blue-blazed Lower Whitewater Falls Trail.

1.2 Reach a gravel parking lot. This is an ATV loading area. Cut across the gravel parking lot and follow the gravel road to the left toward the wooden posts marked with blue blazes.

1.3 Leave the gravel road at the wooden posts marked with blue blazes and veer to the right to enter back into the forest onto a dirt path.

2.1 Reach the observation deck with an impressive view of Lower Whitewater Falls straight ahead. From here you can turn around and retrace your steps back to the Bad Creek Spur Trail access parking lot.

4.2 Arrive back at the parking lot.

Hike Information

Local Information: Mountain Lakes CVB, 105 W. South Broad St., Walhalla, SC 29691; (877) 685-2537; scmountainlakes.com

Local Events/Attractions: Oconee Heritage Center, 123 Browns Square Dr., Walhalla; (864) 638-2224; oconeeheritagecenter.org. Thurs–Fri noon to 6 p.m., Sat 10 a.m. to 3 p.m.

Lodging: Cabins at Oconee State Park, 624 State Park Rd., Mountain Rest; (864) 638-5353. Cabins include fireplace, screened porch, and a grill

Mountain Rest Cabins, 175 Homeland Dr., Mountain Rest; (864) 718-0333; mountainrestcabins.com. Fully furnished cabins

Walhalla Liberty Lodge B&B, 105 Liberty Ln., Walhalla; (864) 638-8239; walhallaliberty lodge.com.

Restaurants: Tommy's on Main Italian Restaurant, 124 E. Main St., Walhalla; (864) 638-5005

The Steak House Cafeteria, 316 E. Main St., Walhalla; (864) 638-3311; thesteakhouse cafeteria.com

Dakota Grill, 2911 Highlands Hwy., Walhalla; (864) 718-0553; dakotagrillsc.com

Organizations: Foothills Trails Conference, PO Box 3041, Greenville, SC 29602; (864) 467-9537; foothillstrail.org

12 Foothills Trail: Jocassee Gorges

Explore the remote backcountry of the Jocassee Gorges on one of the most popular backpacking trips in South Carolina. This three-day trip passes through some of the most scenic land in the entire state, crossing over rugged mountainous terrain and picturesque tributaries of Lake Jocassee, and offers an impressive collection of backcountry campsites along the way. Enjoy the diverse mountain and lakeside terrain of this trail that crosses or hikes along most of the major creeks and waterways in the Jocassee Gorges Wilderness, making this trail an angler's dream come true.

Start: From the Bad Creek Spur Trailhead located in the Duke Energy Bad Creek Project
Distance: 26.1-mile shuttle
Hiking time: About 3 days
Difficulty: Moderate to strenuous due to length and elevation changes
Trail surface: Forested trail, dirt road
Best seasons: Spring (Mar–May) for wildflower displays; fall (Sept–Nov) for fall foliage
Other trail users: Hikers only
Canine compatibility: Leashed dogs permitted

Fees and permits: None
Schedule: Open year-round
Maps: TOPO! CD: North Carolina–South Carolina; USGS maps: Tamassee, Satolah, and Cashiers; South Carolina; USFS maps: Andrew Pickens and Sumter National Forest Trail Guides
Trail contacts: Foothills Trail Conference, PO Box 3041, Greenville, SC 29602; (864) 467-9537; foothillstrail.org

Finding the trailhead: For the Bad Creek Access Trailhead, from Laurel Valley take US 178 south for 8.3 miles, then turn right (west) onto SC 11. Follow 11 for 14.6 miles and pass Lake Keowee. Turn right onto SC 130, then drive 10 miles to the gated entrance of the Duke Energy Bad Creek Station. It looks as if you are not allowed to enter, but it is perfectly fine to enter and go to the trailhead parking lot after registering at the gate. Follow the signs that lead to the trailhead at the Lower Whitewater Falls and Foothills Trail. GPS: N35 01.140'/W82 59.781'

To park a car or be picked up at the end of the hike: From Greenville, take SC 183 west for 18.3 miles toward Pickens. Turn left onto Jewell Street and follow for approximately 400 feet. Take the first right onto East Jones Avenue and follow for 0.6 mile. Turn right onto US 178 west and follow for 16.2 miles. The parking lot and trailhead will be on the left side of the road.

The Hike

The area was named Jocassee, which translates to "Place of the Lost One," by the Native American tribes that originally inhabited this area now managed by the South Carolina Department of Natural Resources. The land was owned by Duke Energy and is now protected land open for recreational use. Traveling east to west, start at the Bad Creek Access and take the Bad Creek Spur Trail over the Whitewater River and past the Coon Branch Trail before reaching the intersection with the Foothills Trail. There is no disperse camping permitted along this first section of the trail so be

A view of Jocassee Creek along the Foothills Trail

prepared for a short hike in before being able to set up camp at the designated campsites on the other side of the Whitewater River. You reach a spur trail that descends
to an observation deck overlooking the distant Lower Whitewater Falls. The view of
the falls is spectacular. The side trip is well worth the hike.

The trail ascends gradually and crosses the North Carolina border, passing through
a lush forest of hemlock, mountain laurel, and rhododendron. A well-constructed
bridge crosses the swift-flowing and beautiful Thompson River. On both sides of
the bridge, you will find excellent camping. During weekends and holidays when
the trail is exceptionally busy, these campsites are very sought after, and it is recommended that you arrive earlier in the day and at the beginning of the weekend if you
intend to camp at these exceptional campsites along the river. If these sites are full,

there is another campsite at Bearcamp Creek about 3.5 miles down the trail. The next section of trails follows along several old roadbeds and follows along the ridge before descending to Horsepasture River and crossing the river on the impressive 115-foot wooden bridge. From here the trail ascends up to a ridge with excellent views of the gorge along Horsepasture River and the surrounding mountains. You descend slightly into Bear Gap and reach an excellent camping site along Bear Creek. This is an ideal resting or stopping point as the next 5.3 miles of trail are exceptionally challenging.

From the bridge spanning Bear Creek, you follow a series of undulating ridges over the next 4 miles and then make a long descent to the western shore of Lake Jocassee and the Cane Brake boat landing. The next 2 miles of trail is much easier and offers a welcome break from the intense climbs and ascents that you have endured between the Horsepasture River and the Cane Brake Access. With Lake Jocassee to the south, you follow the trail along the Jocassee River to the north and pass many excellent level camping sites. You reach one of the most impressive river crossings along the whole trail at the 225-foot suspension bridge spanning the Toxaway River. This is the longest bridge on the entire Foothills Trail and was constructed by Duke Energy engineers.

You will pass over a smaller suspension bridge spanning Toxaway Creek. The trail turns sharply to the south and follows along the eastern bank of the Toxaway River. After 0.5 mile of pleasant hiking along the Toxaway River, you arrive at another extremely challenging section of trail. You must climb nearly 300 wooden steps straight up the bluff ahead. However, along the way you are rewarded for your efforts with excellent views of Rock Creek and the Toxaway River below. The trail descends to Rock Creek Campground, ending this incredibly rigged 1.3-mile stretch of trail. After 4 more miles you reach the short spur trail to Laurel Fork Falls. There are also several points directly along the trail where you will be offered glimpses of the 80-foot falls. The trail follows an old roadbed and follows alongside Laurel Fork Creek for the next 4 miles, crossing the creek several times. Cross Laurel Fork Creek, then ascend the south side of Flatrock Mountain before descending steeply to the Laurel Valley parking area and the end of this rugged but wonderful three-day backpacking trip.

Miles and Directions

0.0   Start from the Bad Creek Spur Trailhead located in the Duke Energy Bad Creek Project.

0.3   Reach a trail junction. To the right is the spur trail that leads down to Lower Whitewater Falls. Stay straight on the Foothills Trail toward the Thompson River.

2.3   Cross the bridge that spans the Thompson River.

4.4   Reach the trail junction with the spur trail to Hilliard Falls on the left. Stay to the right and continue on the Foothills Trail toward Bearcamp Creek.

5.2   Arrive at a nice campsite on Bearcamp Creek.

7.6   Cross the Horsepasture River via a 115-foot wooden bridge.

7.8   Arrive at a spur trail on the right that descends to the Horsepasture River.

8.4   Cross the dry ravine via a 50-foot suspension bridge.

Foothills Trail: Jocassee Gorges

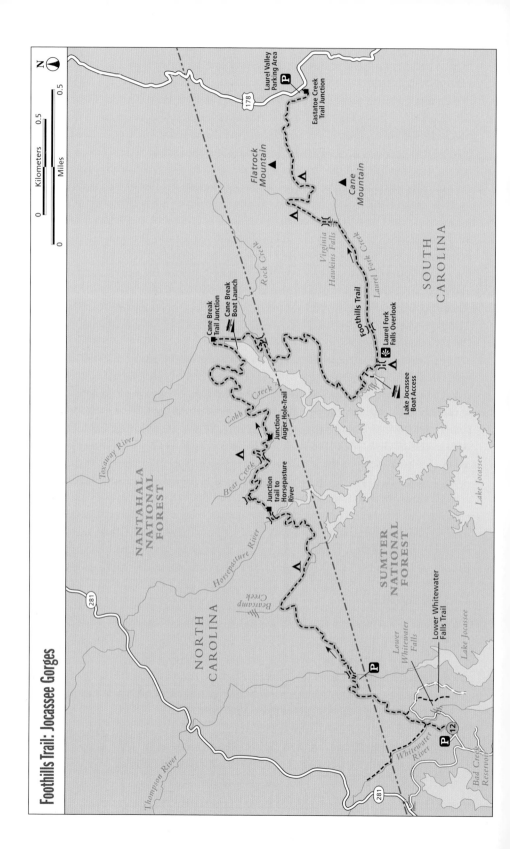

N

Kilometers
0   0.5

Miles
0   0.5

NANTAHALA NATIONAL FOREST

NORTH CAROLINA

SOUTH CAROLINA

SUMTER NATIONAL FOREST

Thompson River

Toxaway River

Rock Creek

Cobb Creek

Bear Creek

Horsepasture River

Bearcamp Creek

Whitewater River

Lake Jocassee

Bad Creek Reservoir

281

178

12

Laurel Valley Parking Area

Eastatoe Creek Trail Junction

Flatrock Mountain

Cane Mountain

Virginia Hawkins Falls

Laurel Fork Creek

Foothills Trail

Laurel Fork Falls Overlook

Lake Jocassee Boat Access

Cane Break Trail Junction

Cane Break Boat Launch

Junction Auger Hole Trail

Junction trail to Horsepasture River

Lower Whitewater Falls

Lower Whitewater Falls Trail

9.6 Descend the wooden steps and walk across Cross Roads Mountain Road.

9.7 Cross the bridge over Bear Creek.

10.5 Reach the junction with the Auger Hole Trail on the left. Stay straight on the Foothills Trail.

11.7 Cross Cobb Creek by hopping over exposed rocks.

13.3 Arrive at the Cane Brake Boat Launch.

13.8 Cross the 65-foot suspension bridge over the Toxaway River.

13.9 Reach a trail junction. The Cane Brake Trail is to the left. Stay straight on the Foothills Trail toward Rock Creek.

15.2 Cross the bridge over Rock Creek

18.8 A spur trail to the right leads down to the Laurel Fork Boat Access. Stay straight on the Foothills Trail toward Laurel Fork Falls.

19.0 A spur trail to the right descends to the Lake Jocassee Boat Access. Stay straight on the Foothills Trail toward Laurel Fork Falls.

19.3 Reach an overlook with an excellent view of Laurel Fork Falls to the right of the trail.

19.4 To the right a spur trail descends down to the top of Laurel Fork Falls. A very nice campsite is near the falls.

19.5 Cross the bridge to a designated campsite.

20.1 Cross a bridge spanning Laurel Fork Creek. Over the next 1.3 miles, the Foothills Trail crosses bridges spanning Laurel Fork Creek five more times.

22.1 Reach a bench that overlooks the Virginia Hawkins Falls.

22.2 Cross the small bridge spanning Laurel Fork Creek. Over the next 0.3 mile, you will cross the creek four more times.

22.7 Arrive at a nice campsite on Laurel Fork Creek.

23.9 Arrive at a large campsite along the creek.

25.8 Reach a T junction at the gravel Horsepasture Road. To the right is the junction with the spur trail to Eastatoe Creek Heritage Preserve. Turn left onto Horsepasture Road, following the Foothills Trail toward the Laurel Valley parking area.

25.9 Arrive at the Laurel Valley parking area. This is a great spot to arrange a shuttle pickup.

26.1 Arrive at US 178 and the end of your hike.

Hike Information

Local Information: Mountain Lakes CVB, 105 W. South Broad St., Walhalla, SC 29691; (877) 685-2537; scmountainlakes.com

Local Events/Attractions: Oconee Heritage Center, 123 Browns Square Dr., Walhalla; (864) 638-2224; oconeeheritagecenter.org. Thurs–Fri noon to 6 p.m., Sat 10 a.m. to 3 p.m.

Lodging: Walhalla Motel, 901 E. Main St., Walhalla; (864) 638-2585; walhallasc.com

Oconee Belle B&B, 302 S. College St., Walhalla; (864) 638-2238

Restaurants: Tommy's on Main Italian Restaurant, 124 E. Main St., Walhalla; (864) 638-5005

The Steak House Cafeteria, 316 E. Main St., Walhalla; (864) 638-3311; thesteakhouse cafeteria.com

Organizations: Foothills Trail Conference, PO Box 3041, Greenville, SC 29602; (864) 467-9537; foothillstrail.org

13 Keowee-Toxaway State Park

If you're thinking of just hiking the beginning of this trail to see the natural bridge, I ask that you reconsider this and hike the entire trail. At almost every bend along this slightly challenging and hilly route, there is a highlight worth noting. After stopping at the natural bridge, where you walk across a large boulder that spans the entire Poe Creek crossing, you venture past the impressive sheer cliffs of Raven Rock, walk out onto rock outcroppings with far-reaching views of Lake Keowee, and then circle around to cross Poe Creek again before returning to the trailhead.

Start: Parking lot behind the visitor center
Distance: 4.1-mile lollipop
Hiking time: About 2 hours
Difficulty: Moderate due to elevation gains
Trail surface: Forested path
Best seasons: Spring (Mar–May) for wildflower displays; fall (Sept–Nov) for fall foliage
Other trail users: Hikers only
Canine compatibility: Leashed dogs permitted. Dogs not allowed in cabins or cabin area.

Fees and permits: None
Schedule: Sun–Thurs 9 a.m. to 6 p.m., Fri 9 a.m. to 8 p.m. (extended to 9 p.m. daily during daylight saving time)
Maps: TOPO! CD: North Carolina–South Carolina; USGS maps: Salem and Sunset, South Carolina
Trail contacts: Keowee-Toxaway State Park, 108 Residence Dr., Sunset, SC 29685; (864) 868-2605; www.southcarolinaparks.com/keoweetoxaway

Finding the trailhead: From I-85 South in Greenville, take exit 40 onto SC 153 toward Easley. Go north on SC 153 for 5 miles. Merge onto Calhoun Memorial Highway / US 123 and drive for 2.5 miles. US 123 becomes SC 93 / Main Street. Continue to drive 3 miles. Go onto SC 8 and continue for 6 miles. Turn left onto SC 183 and then turn right onto US 178 and drive 8.5 miles. Turn left onto SC 11 and drive 8.5 miles. Look for park signs. GPS: N34 55.965' / W82 53.121'

The Hike

This trail underwent major reconstruction in 2012. Ambitious trail crews designed and constructed a new route for the entire trail system in the state park, which has made this trail significantly less challenging because many substantial and steep elevation gains along the route have been eliminated. The new route is much more enjoyable, and it also helps to mitigate erosion in many places. Don't get the wrong idea here though. The trail crew didn't install an escalator, and the trail is still moderately steep in some places along the way. It is enough of a challenge to make this a great route to train for longer-distance and harder backpacking trips or to get a warm-up for a day of tougher trail climbing. The shape of the trail was notably different just a few months before this book was written, so be sure to look over the map before you hit the trail.

Rhododendrons crowd a crossing of Poe Creek
along the Natural Bridge Trail.

The recommended route to hike combines both the Natural Bridge Trail and the Raven Rock Trail. For an easier hike, simply follow the spur trail from the parking lot to the Natural Bridge Trail, follow the Natural Bridge Trail around in a loop, and then return to the parking lot for a 1.5-mile hike. I know this will be tempting, but I really encourage you to hike this entire route. There are so many notable highlights along this route that make this trail very unique and enjoyable.

To follow the recommended route, take the spur trail from the parking lot to the Natural Bridge Trail. At the junction with the Natural Bridge Trail loop, you reach an old roadbed. After 0.4 mile you arrive at a stream crossing. You cross Poe Creek by walking over a large rock slab, and if you aren't paying attention, you might just miss the impressiveness of this natural bridge. The best view of the natural bridge can be seen by following one of the spur trails down to the creek so that you can look back at the bridge from creek level and see the creek flowing under the rock bridge. You climb over a small hill before reaching the junction with the Raven Rock Trail. From here the shape of the Raven Rock Trail is like a balloon, with this first section being the spur that leads to a loop. After 0.1 mile you reach several impressively large boulders on the right side of the trail. From here the trail really starts to climb.

▶ Albert Einstein's son Hans Albert Einstein worked as a research engineer at the nearby Agricultural Experiment Station in Clemson, South Carolina.

After 0.4 mile you reach the junction with the start of the Raven Rock Loop. Turn right and follow the Loop Trail to the north and enjoy the views of the Blue Ridge Mountains to the left side of the trail. You quickly reach the shore of Lake Keowee and a spur trail that descends to designated backcountry campsites that you can reserve online or at the park office if you want to make an overnight backpacking trip of this route. A short climb takes you up to a pair of rock outcroppings with excellent views of the lake and the surrounding mountains. On the hike back you follow the other side of the Raven Rock and Natural Bridge loops so that you can take in a different view on the way back. After a particularly picturesque crossing of Poe Creek, again along the Natural Bridge Trail, you return to the parking lot where you started.

This area is rich in Cherokee and early settler history. The British established an important trading post and Fort Prince George near the park in the mid 1700s. After you're finished hiking the trail, stop by the park's wonderful museum, which offers intriguing exhibits with information on the Cherokee natives that originally inhabited this area and the contribution that early settlers played in the development of the region.

Miles and Directions

0.0 Start from the trailhead marked by a large kiosk in the parking lot behind the visitor center.

0.2 Reach the trail junction with the Natural Bridge Trail, which starts as an old logging road. Turn right at the T junction.

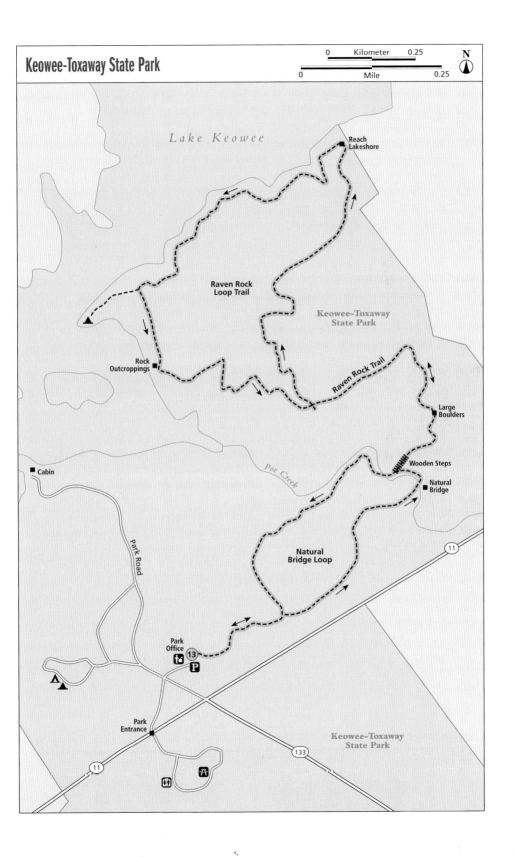

Keowee-Toxaway State Park

Lake Keowee

Reach Lakeshore

Raven Rock Loop Trail

Keowee-Toxaway State Park

Rock Outcroppings

Raven Rock Trail

Large Boulders

Poe Creek

Wooden Steps

Natural Bridge

Cabin

Natural Bridge Loop

Park Road

11

Park Office

13

P

Park Entrance

11

133

Keowee-Toxaway State Park

N

0   Kilometer   0.25

0   Mile   0.25

0.6 Reach a creek crossing and the natural bridge. A very short spur trail leads down to the creek and a better view of the creek flowing under the natural bridge. Once you are back on the Natural Bridge Trail, follow the loop around to the left (west).

0.7 Reach the junction with the Raven Rock Trail. Turn right (north) and ascend the wooden steps.

0.8 There are several notably large boulders on the right side of the trail. These large rocks are impressive. They also mark the point where the trail begins to steeply ascend. Lace up your boots for this climb.

1.2 Turn right onto the gently ascending dirt path at this junction with the start of the Raven Rock loop.

1.8 Arrive at the shore of Lake Keowee. The trail veers to the left.

2.4 A spur trail on the right leads down to campsites on the lakeshore. Stay straight on the Raven Rock loop.

2.5 Arrive at rock outcroppings with excellent views of Lake Keowee.

2.9 At the end of the Raven Rock loop, you reach the junction with the Raven Rock spur. Turn right.

3.4 Once you reach the Natural Bridge Loop, turn right. You can hear Poe Creek rushing in front of you. Follow the wooden steps down to the creek and cross the creek by walking over the large boulders in the stream.

3.8 Reach the junction with the Natural Bridge spur again. Turn right toward the visitor center.

4.1 Arrive at the parking lot and visitor center where you started.

Hike Information

Local Information: Easley Chamber of Commerce, 2001 E. Main St., Easley, SC 29640; (864) 859-2963

Local Events/Attractions: Grand Illumination in downtown Easley. Lighting of the Christmas tree, carolers, and old-fashioned downtown open house takes place in November

South Carolina Botanical Garden, Clemson University, 150 Discovery Ln., Clemson; (864) 656-3405. Open dawn–dusk, free admission

Lodging: Cabins at Keowee-Toxaway State Park, 108 Residence Dr., Sunset; (864) 868-2605

Restaurants: Michael's Pizzeria, 101 NE Main St., Easley; (864) 855-0025; michaelspizzeria.org

Silver Bay Seafood, 7027 Calhoun Memorial Hwy., Easley; (864) 855-9774; www.blueocean-silverbay.com/easley

Bleu VooDoo Grill, 114 E. Main St., Easley; (864) 644-8282

14 Foothills Trail: Sassafras Mountain Segment

This one-day hike begins near the peak of South Carolina's highest summit and ends at Table Rock State Park, one of the most popular state parks in the region. A good pair of hiking poles is highly recommended along this rugged hike, which features long descents for much of the route. Hike over Hickory Nut Mountain and Pinnacle Mountain and across Mill Creek and Carrick Creek as you explore this picturesque mountain landscape steeped in Civil War history.

Start: From the parking area at Sassafras Mountain

Distance: 8.6-mile shuttle

Hiking time: About 5–8 hours

Difficulty: Moderate to strenuous due to elevation gain

Trail surface: Forested trail, dirt roads, gravel paths

Best seasons: Spring (Mar–May) for wildflower displays; fall (Sept–Nov) for fall foliage

Other trail users: Hikers only

Canine compatibility: Leashed dogs permitted. Dogs not permitted in cabin areas.

Fees and permits: Free for kids under age 16; small fee for age 16 and over; senior discount available

Schedule: Sun–Thurs 7 a.m. to 7 p.m., Fri–Sat 7 a.m. to 9 p.m. During daylight saving time, Sun–Thurs 7 a.m. to 9 p.m., Fri–Sat 7 a.m. to 10 p.m.

Maps: TOPO! CD: North Carolina–South Carolina; USGS maps: Table Rock, Estatoe Gap; South Carolina

Trail contacts: Foothills Trail Conference, PO Box 3041, Greenville, SC 29602; (864) 467-9537

Finding the trailhead: From Pickens drive west on US 178 for 15.8 miles. Turn right onto Sassafras Mountain Road / F. Van Clayton Road and follow for 4.8 miles until you arrive at the parking lot and trailhead on Sassafras Mountain. The start of the trail is to the south of the parking lot on the left-hand side. GPS: N35 03.910' / W82 46.631'

The Hike

Begin your long descent from near the peak of Sassafras Mountain at the overlook parking lot. Before you begin your hike, you may want to enjoy the impressive views from the well-constructed overlook that looks toward the southwest. From the parking area you will need to walk down F. Van Clayton Road to the south and then veer to the left to continue on the forested trail that passes through a forest where maples, poplars, pines, and oak trees are most prevalent. Sassafras Mountain is a very popular area for birders, who regularly spot pileated woodpeckers and a variety of beautiful warblers. The trail descends toward Hickorynut Mountain, passing through a section of forest with an understory rich in wildflowers such as pink lady's slippers and trailing arbutus.

In 1.2 miles from the Sassafras Mountain overlook, you reach the remnants of the homestead of John L. Cantrell, who was one of the earliest settlers in this area.

Clouds cast light onto the South Carolina mountains as seen from the Sassafras Mountain Overlook.

The nearby campsite offers an excellent stopping place for those starting late in the day or for anyone looking for a very short hike to a backcountry campsite. From the homestead the trail ascends to near the top of Hickorynut Mountain and then skirts around the western side of the mountain's peak before turning sharply to the left. After briefly following along the Emory Gap Toll Road, you reach an outcropping called the Marion Castles Rock House, where Marion Castles hid to avoid conscription into the Confederate Army.

The trail continues a long descent to a stretch of easy walking, mostly along old roadbeds. It's a good thing you get a break because at the end of this nearly 1.5-mile pleasant section of trail, you have to ascend a series of switchbacks up the side of Pinnacle Mountain. The area is called Drawbar Cliffs, and at the top of the cliffs, you are rewarded with an excellent rock outcropping that offers picturesque views of Lake Keowee and the surrounding mountains. About 60 feet from the outcropping is the border of Table Rock State Park. From the top of the cliffs, the climb is a bit easier, and in 0.5 mile you reach the spur trail that leads to Pinnacle Mountain's peak on the left side of the trail. From here you begin a long and very steep descent toward Table Rock Mountain. In 0.4 mile you reach Bald Rock, a section of the trail that passes through a series of rock outcroppings that offer excellent resting points where you can enjoy spectacular views of the piedmont and Table Rock Mountain. After crossing Mill Creek you pass a 50-foot waterfall 2.4 miles from the end of the trail at the Table Rock Nature Center. After this waterfall the trail crosses several seasonal

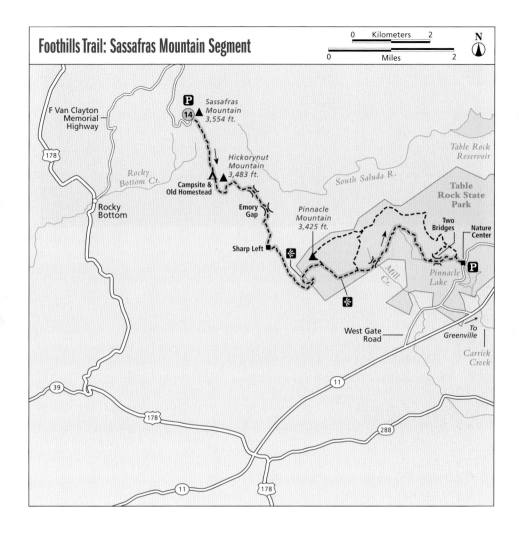

Foothills Trail: Sassafras Mountain Segment

streams via wooden bridges before reaching the junction with the Carrick Nature Trail. Turn left onto the Carrick Nature Trail. You make several creek crossings and then turn sharply right toward the nature center at the trail junction.

In 150 feet you reach a bridge spanning Carrick Creek and then follow the paved path to the nature center and the end of this hike. Here you will find snack machines, water, restrooms, and a very large parking lot where you can leave a vehicle or prearrange a shuttle to pick you up.

Miles and Directions

0.0   Start from the overlook parking lot on F. Van Clayton Road near the peak of Sassafras Mountain. From the parking lot walk south down the road for 0.1 mile and follow the trail to the left, where it descends toward Table Rock State Park.

The Sassafras Mountain Overlook

1.2 Reach an old stone homestead. This is a great place to camp if you arrived late or feel like taking an easy day on the trail.

3.4 The trail turns sharply to the left (east).

4.8 To the left is a large rock outcropping with excellent views of Lake Keowee.

5.2 Arrive a trail junction. To the left is a steep spur trail that leads 0.2 mile to the 3,425-foot peak of Pinnacle Mountain, the second-highest point in South Carolina. Enjoy this side trip or stay straight on the Foothills Trail and continue toward Table Rock State Park.

5.6 Enjoy the rock outcropping with views of the piedmont and Table Rock Mountain to the northeast.

5.9 Stay to the right at the junction with the Mill Creek Pass Trail and cross Mill Creek via the narrow wooden bridge.

7.8 The Carrick Creek Nature Trail turns to the left. Stay to the right and continue on the Foothills Trail toward the Table Rock Nature Center.

8.1 Cross the two bridges over the rocky seasonal streambeds.

8.5 At the T junction turn right toward the nature center on the paved Table Rock Trail.

8.6 Arrive at the nature center and the end of the hike.

Hike Information

Local Information: Pickens Chamber of Commerce, 222 W. Main St., Pickens, SC 29671; (864) 878-3258

Local Events/Attractions: South Carolina Botanical Garden, Clemson University, 150 Discovery Ln., Clemson; (864) 656-3405. Open dawn–dusk, free admission

Pumpkintown Pumpkin Festival, Highway 135 and Oolenoy Church Road, Pumpkintown; (864) 898-0261. This autumn festival takes place annually in October.

Lodging: Cabins at Table Rock State Park, 158 E. Ellison Ln., Pickens; (864) 878-9813. One-, two-, and three-bedroom cabins available

Inn at Table Rock B&B, 117 Hiawatha Trail, Pickens; (864) 878-0078

Restaurants: Michael's, 301 E. Main St., Pickens; (864) 878-6462; michaelsrestaurant.biz. Mon–Fri 8 a.m. to 2:30 p.m., Sun 11 a.m. to 2:30 p.m.

Aunt Sue's Country Corner, 107 Country Creek Dr., Pickens; (864) 878-4366. Tues–Fri 11 a.m. to 6 p.m., Sat–Sun 11 a.m. to 10 p.m.

15 Table Rock State Park

This is one of the best day hikes in the entire mountainous region of South Carolina. It is also one of the most difficult—this isn't a trail for weak knees. You climb nearly 1,800 feet in 3 miles on a trail that is constantly climbing and is often remarkably steep. Masterfully cut stone steps and numerous switchbacks will make the trail easier along this phenomenally maintained and constructed trail. The group of trails around the nature center can be approached many different ways. The recommended route combines the Carrick Nature Trail and the Table Rock Trail for a hike that takes you past several stunning waterfalls, through beautiful hardwood forests, and up to the top of Table Rock Mountain, where you will find several rock outcroppings with far-reaching views of the surrounding mountains and lakes.

Start: From behind the nature center at the trailhead to the Carrick Nature Trail

Distance: 6.8 miles out and back

Hiking time: About 4 hours

Difficulty: Strenuous due to elevation gains and length

Trail surface: Paved path, boardwalk, forested trail

Best seasons: Spring (Mar–May) for wildflower displays; fall (Sept–Nov) for fall foliage

Other trail users: Hikers only

Canine compatibility: Leashed dogs permitted. Dogs are not permitted in cabins or cabin area.

Fees and permits: Free for kids under age 16; small fee for age 16 and over; senior discount available

Schedule: Sun–Thurs 7 a.m. to 7 p.m., Fri-Sat 7 a.m. to 9 p.m. During daylight saving time, Sun–Thurs 7 a.m. to 9 p.m., Fri-Sat 7 a.m. to 10 p.m.

Maps: TOPO! CD: North Carolina–South Carolina; USGS maps: Table Rock, South Carolina

Trail contacts: 158 E. Ellison Ln., Pickens, SC 29671; (864) 878.9813; www.southcarolina parks.com/tablerock

Finding the trailhead: *From I-26:* Take exit 5 onto SC 11 toward Campobello. Travel for approximately 45 miles. Turn left onto East Ellison Lane.

I-85 at the North Carolina line: Travel south to SC 11 exit 92 at Gaffney, proceed on SC 11 for approximately 75 miles, and turn left on East Ellison Lane. GPS: N35 01.926' / W82 42.050'

The Hike

After driving to the nature center, walk up the wooden steps that lead through the breezeway and to the large observation deck with the entrance to the nature center on the right. Walk across the wooden bridge that spans Carrick Creek. The first section of the trail, a spur that leads to the Carrick Creek Loop Trail, is mostly paved with several sections of boardwalk and wooden bridges that cross Carrick Creek and its tributaries. If you have no interest in a very strenuous hike all the way up Table

Enjoy the view of Table Rock Reservoir from an outcropping on the Table Rock Trail.

Rock Mountain, I still suggest that you at the very least hike this spur trail to the Carrick Creek Loop and include the loop trail if you can.

After just 400 feet along the spur trail you reach a beautiful and very picturesque but small waterfall. The large observation deck and multitude of benches off to the right side of the trail and in front of the waterfall is a testament to the type of high traffic that this trail and Table Rock Park receive. Table Rock is one of the most popular state parks in South Carolina, so be prepared for crowds during the earlier sections of this route, especially if you're choosing to hike the trails on a weekend, holiday, or the peak leaf and wildflower seasons. Rest assured though, once you get a few hundred feet onto the Table Rock Trail, the crowds rapidly diminish and then get even smaller the farther you hike, as an increasing number of people abandon their unprepared attempt of the difficult climb to the summit.

Table Rock Mountain holds special meaning for the Cherokee Indians who were the original inhabitants of this region. They believed that the Great Spirit used the remarkably level granite dome of Table Rock as a dining table and used the smaller mountain knows as the Stool as a seat. During the climb up to the summit of Table Rock, take notice of the large boulders that you will find in the forest, boulders that have fallen from higher points on the mountain face. The forest along the hike is dominantly composed of oak and hickory, with sparse pines and hemlocks scattered

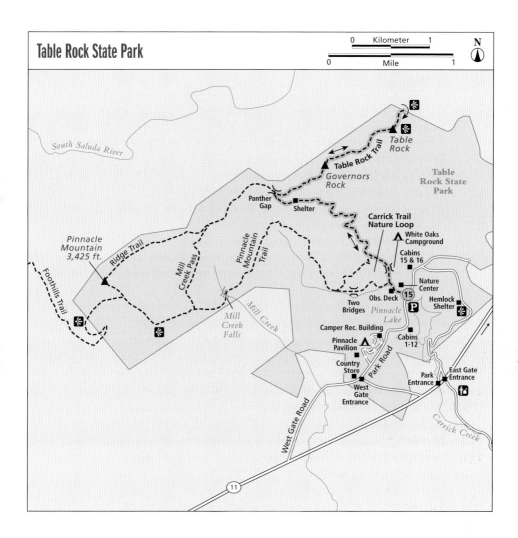

0   Kilometer   1

0   Mile   1

N

South Saluda River

Table Rock

Table Rock Trail

Table Rock State Park

Governors Rock

Panther Gap

Shelter

Carrick Trail Nature Loop

Pinnacle Mountain 3,425 ft.

Ridge Trail

Mill Creek Pass

Pinnacle Mountain Trail

White Oaks Campground

Cabins 15 & 16

Foothills Trail

Nature Center

Mill Creek Falls

Mill Creek

Two Bridges

Obs. Deck 15

Pinnacle Lake

P

Hemlock Shelter

Camper Rec. Building

Cabins 1-12

Pinnacle Pavilion

Park Road

Country Store

Park Entrance

East Gate Entrance

West Gate Entrance

West Gate Road

Carrick Creek

11

throughout the woods. During spring a variety of blooming wildflowers decorate the understory of the forest and the edges of the trail.

The trail gets progressively more challenging the closer you get to the summit of Table Rock. Along the way you pass a shelter built by the Civilian Conservation Corps (CCC) in the 1930s where you can sit and enjoy views of the surrounding mountains. The shelter is a great place to rest because the trail becomes significantly more challenging from this point. The steep climb takes you first up to the summit of Table Rock, where you will find a sign marking the peak, but unfortunately there are no impressive views from the peak. To get the views you really want, you have to continue on the trail, which will take you to several major outcroppings of granite rock and then dead-end at a large, open outcropping that looks out toward Caesars Head and the Table Rock Reservoir. At the last outcropping be sure to look to the left for a breathtaking view of Slicking Rock Falls. From here turn around and retrace your steps back to the nature center and the trailhead parking lot where you started your hike.

Miles and Directions

0.0 Start from the Carrick Creek Nature Trailhead behind the nature center. Follow the wooden bridge over Carrick Creek. A paved trail leads to a small waterfall and observation deck 300 feet from the bridge. After another 300 feet you cross over a bridge that spans Carrick Creek once again.

0.1 Reach the junction with the Carrick Creek Nature Trail and the end of the paved trail. Turn right onto the Carrick Creek Nature Trail toward the Table Rock Trail.

0.2 Cross the bridge spanning Carrick Creek. Notice the beautiful cascades to the left of the bridge.

0.4 Cross another bridge over Carrick Creek. After 500 feet you reach a split in the trail. To the left the Carrick Creek Nature Trail continues to loop around back toward the visitor center. Turn right onto the Table Rock Trail and ascend on the forested path toward the summit of Table Rock.

1.6 A shelter built by the CCC stands on the left side of the trail. Relax at the shelter and enjoy the views, or just continue ascending toward the summit of Table Rock.

1.8 The trail splits. The Ridge Trail is to the left. Stay to the right and continue on the Table Rock Trail.

3.0 Reach the summit of Table Rock Mountain at 3,124 feet. Continue on Table Rock Trail, passing the sign marking the summit and continuing toward overlooks.

3.2 The first overlook is to the right of the trail.

3.4 The trail dead-ends at a large, open, granite overlook with views of Caesars Head and the Table Rock Reservoir straight ahead and Slicking Falls to the left. Enjoy the views, then turn around and head back the way you came.

6.8 Arrive back at the trailhead.

Hike Information

Local Information: Pickens Chamber of Commerce, 222 W. Main St., Pickens, SC 29671; (864) 878-3258

Local Events/Attractions: South Carolina Botanical Garden, Clemson University, 150 Discovery Ln., Clemson; (864) 656-3405. Open dawn–dusk, free admission

Lodging: Cabins at Table Rock State Park, 158 E. Ellison Ln., Pickens; (864) 878-9813. One-, two-, and three-bedroom cabins available

Inn at Table Rock B&B, 117 Hiawatha Trail, Pickens; (864) 878-0078, theinnattablerock.com

Restaurants: Michael's Pizzeria, 101 NE Main St., Easley; (864) 855-0025; michaelspizzeria.org

Silver Bay Seafood, 7027 Calhoun Memorial Hwy., Easley; (864) 855-9774; www.blue ocean-silverbay.com/easley

Bleu VooDoo Grill, 114 E. Main St., Easley; (864) 644-8282

16 Mountain Bridge Wilderness Loop

This extremely popular day hike is filled with breathtaking scenery and memorable challenges that are sure to delight the day hiker searching for a trail packed with excitement and beauty. This lollipop hike combines segments of the Raven Cliff Falls Trail, the Dismal Trail, Naturaland Trust Trail, and the Gum Gap Trail to form an adventurous exploration through the western section of the Mountain Bridge Wilderness. Don't let the relatively short distance fool you. Embark on this route early in the morning and with plenty of water and snacks. Along the route you will enjoy spectacular views of Raven Cliff Falls from three varying positions, a thrilling cable-crossing of Matthews Creek, a stop by the stunning rock formation known as the Cathedral, and a strenuous calf-chiseling climb. Do it! You won't regret it.

Start: From the Raven Cliff Falls parking lot

Distance: 7.6-mile lollipop

Hiking time: About 5–8 hours

Difficulty: Strenuous due to the technical challenges and elevation changes along the Naturaland Trust Trail section

Trail surface: Forested trail, gravel path, old roadbed

Best seasons: Spring (Mar–May) for wildflower displays; fall (Sept–Nov) for fall foliage

Other trail users: Hikers only

Canine compatibility: Leashed dogs permitted

Fees and permits: None

Schedule: Open year-round

Maps: TOPO! CD: North Carolina–South Carolina; USGS maps: Table Rock; South Carolina; USFS maps: Mountain Bridge Wilderness Map available at Caesars Head State Park

Trail contacts: Foothills Trail Conference, PO Box 3041, Greenville, SC 29602; (864) 467-9537

Finding the trailhead: From Greenville, take US 276 West for about 30 miles. The park is located at the top of the mountain right off the highway. The North Carolina border is 3 miles away. Continue 1 mile north past the state park entrance on US 276 to the parking lot for the Raven Cliff Falls Trailhead. GPS: N35 06.956' / W82 38.321'

The Hike

Start your adventure from the parking lot and the trailhead for Raven Cliff Falls. After crossing US 276 the trail gently descends to a junction with the Gum Gap Trail following an old roadbed. During the 1900s honeymooners and visitors to the falls were transported along this road via horse and carriage. At the junction veer to the left and continue on Raven Cliff Falls Trail. After 0.4 mile of gently descending trail, you arrive at another junction. The Dismal Trail is to the left. Stay straight and follow the Raven Cliffs Falls Trail to the excellent overlook with views of the Blue Ridge Escarpment and the waterfall where Matthews Creek plunges more than 400 feet over Raven Cliff. The multiple tiers of cascades above the falls total nearly 1,000 feet, making this one of the highest cascades in the east. The view is exceptionally

impressive during the spring and summer when the rhododendrons and mountain laurels are in bloom. The rare monkshood also grows in the spray area of the falls. This is one of only a few locations where this flower can be found in all of South Carolina.

After enjoying the impressive sight of the falls, return to the junction and turn right (south) on the Dismal Trail. Although the name may seem foreboding, this short and pleasant trail derives its name from the dense, mature hardwood forest that grows in this area between Caesars Head nearly to Table Rock Reservoir. In 0.2 mile you reach a section of large boulders on the right side of the trail. From the top of these boulders, you are able to get a stunning view of Raven Cliff Falls. The trail continues steeply down the hill and traverses a series of steep switchbacks. You hike downhill, staying alongside Matthews Creek for most of the way until you reach the junction with the Naturaland Trust. This is where the trail gets really interesting and also very challenging. If you're not up for an intense hike, now is the time to turn around.

Turn right on the Naturaland Trust Trail heading west toward the top of Raven Cliff Falls. In 0.2 mile you arrive at a crossing with Matthews Creek. Two heavy cables are strung over the creek and attached to trees at either end to allow hikers to safely ford the stream during high water. The cables run parallel to one another with the bottom cable intended to be used for feet and the top cable designed to be used to hold on to with your hands. It is a simple and exciting way to get across the creek. Enjoy and be safe. If the water is low, you can easily get across by hopping across the rocks in the creek bed. The trail follows alongside Matthews Creek and ascends a series of steep switchbacks up Raven Cliff Mountain. After 0.7 mile you reach a 120-foot-tall rock formation called the Cathedral that is unbelievably impressive when you are right underneath it. The trail continues the steep climb, crossing steps, switchbacks, and ladders until you reach the top and cross Raven Cliff Falls via a fun and exciting swinging bridge. From the bridge you get a phenomenal bird's-eye view of the falls as they plunge over Raven Cliff. Look across to the other side and you can see the observation deck where you were earlier along the Raven Cliff Falls Trail. Incredible.

Continue to climb for 0.2 mile more until you reach the junction with the Gum Gap Trail. The hard part is finally over. Turn right and follow an old roadbed gently uphill. In 0.4 mile you reach a side trail on the left. Continue straight on the old roadbed until you reach the junction with the Raven Cliff Falls Trail. Turn left and follow the Raven Cliff Falls Trail back to US 276 and the parking lot where you started this exciting and challenging hike.

◁ *A gravel road leads the way along the Gum Gap section of the Foothills Trail.*

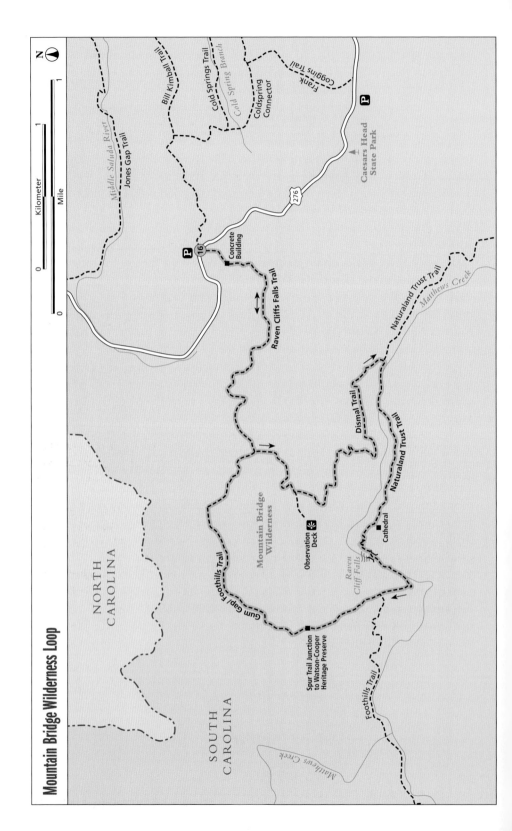

Mountain Bridge Wilderness Loop

Miles and Directions

0.0 Start from the Raven Cliff Falls parking lot. Cross the highway to the trailhead and descend down the gravel path.

0.2 Pass the small concrete building, which is owned by the state park.

1.4 Reach a trail junction. To the right the Gum Gap Trail heads north. Veer left and stay on the Raven Cliff Falls Trail.

1.8 At the Y junction the Raven Cliff Falls Trail continues to the right to an overlook of the falls. This is a great side trip to an observation deck with excellent views of the distant falls. To continue on the loop, veer to the left and join the Dismal Trail heading south.

3.1 Turn right onto the Naturaland Trust Trail.

3.3 Cross Matthews Creek, using the cables during high water.

3.9 Climb the steep steps to the Cathedral, a 120-foot rock wall covered in clinging vegetation.

4.2 Cross the suspension bridge, which offers incredible views from the top of Raven Cliff Falls as Matthews Creek plunges over a cliff.

4.6 Turn right onto the Gum Gap Trail.

5.0 On the left a spur trail leads to the gate of the Watson-Cooper Heritage Preserve. Continue straight on the Gum Gap Trail.

6.2 Turn left onto the Raven Cliff Falls Trail.

7.5 Cross US 276.

7.6 Arrive at the Raven Cliff Falls parking lot where you started.

Hike Information

Local Information: Pickens Chamber of Commerce, 222 W. Main St., Pickens, SC 29671; (864) 878-3258

Local Events/Attractions: Victoria Valley Vineyards, 1360 S. Saluda Rd., Cleveland; (864) 878-5307; victoriavalleyvineyards.com

Caesars Head Hawk Watch, Caesars Head State Park, 8155 Geer Hwy., Cleveland; (864) 836-6115. A rare chance to see thousands of hawks before they migrate to Central and South America. Sep–Nov

Lodging: Solitude Pointe Cabins, 102 Table Rock Rd., Cleveland; (864) 836-4128; www.solitude pointe.com/our-cabins.php

Foxfire Mountain Cabins, (864) 836-6712; foxfiremtncabins.com. Cabins located in Mountain Bridge Wilderness. Office hours 10 a.m. to 6 p.m. daily

Restaurants: Mountain House at Caesars Head, 8101 Geer Hwy., Cleveland; (864) 836-7330

Doris' Family Kitchen, 2800 Geer Hwy., Marietta; (864) 836-4071

Organizations: Foothills Trail Conference, PO Box 3041, Greenville, SC 29602; (864) 467-9537

17 Raven Cliff Falls

This quick and easy day hike traverses gently sloping trails to one of the highest cascades in northwest South Carolina. Follow this extremely well-maintained trail to a masterfully crafted and covered observation deck where you are treated to picturesque and sweeping views of the Blue Ridge Escarpment and Matthews Creek as it plunges more than 400 feet over Raven Cliff in a captivating display of power and beauty.

Start: From the Raven Cliff Falls Trailhead parking lot

Distance: 3.8-mile out and back

Hiking time: About 1–2 hours

Difficulty: Easy due to distance and small amount of elevation

Trail surface: Gravel path, forested trail, old roadbed

Best seasons: Spring (Mar–May) for wildflower displays; fall (Sept–Nov) for fall foliage

Other trail users: Hikers only

Canine compatibility: Leashed dogs permitted

Fees and permits: Small per-person day-use fee

Schedule: Open year-round

Maps: TOPO! CD: North Carolina–South Carolina; USGS maps: Cleveland and Table Rock; South Carolina; USFS maps: Mountain Bridge Wilderness Area maps available at Caesars Head State Park

Trail contacts: Caesars Head State Park, 8155 Geer Hwy., Cleveland, SC 29635; (864) 836-6115; www.southcarolinaparks.com/caesarshead

Finding the trailhead: From Greenville, take US 276 West for about 30 miles. The park is located at the top of the mountain right off the highway. The North Carolina border is 3 miles away. Continue 1 mile north past the state park entrance on US 276 to the parking lot for the Raven Cliff Falls Trailhead. GPS: N35 06.956' / W82 38.321'

The Hike

You have two options on this hike. This section outlines a short hike to the observation deck and back, which is by far the more popular choice for most hikers. For something more challenging, try the Mountain Bridge Wilderness Loop, also outlined in this book. The loop trail will take you on a challenging and scenic journey along a difficult trail that offers three different views of the Raven Cliff Falls, including a crossing on a suspension bridge with a spectacular bird's-eye view from the top of the falls as Matthews Creek plunges over the cliff. No matter what you decide to do with your day, arrive nice and early for this hike, especially on weekends. This is by far the most popular hike in the Mountain Bridge Wilderness. On weekends and holidays expect the parking lot to be full throughout most of the day and the trail to be busy. During the winter the trail is often very sparsely populated and this is an excellent time if you would like to enjoy more views of the surrounding mountains and some solitude for your hike.

The Raven Cliff Falls observation deck

For the short hike to the observation deck and back, start at the trailhead across US 276 and follow the gently sloping trail to the Gum Gap Trail junction. This portion of the trail follows an old buggy road that was originally built for honeymooners and tourists who wanted to ride a horse-drawn carriage down to the falls. As a result the trail is rather wide and level, which makes it easy to follow and enjoy on your way to the observation deck. This place has been a popular hiking and tourist destination for centuries, and you're about to find out firsthand why. At the junction the Gum Gap trail continues to the right. Keep left and follow the Ravens Cliff Falls Trail as it descends toward the overlook.

Along this section of trail, you are likely to see a collection of excellent wildflowers in the summer and spring that include pinxter flower and flame azalea in a variety of colored blossoms. This is also a wonderful location to spot hawks, a diversity of warblers including the black-and-white, worm-eating, and hooded varieties, as well as scarlet tanagers and others. After 0.4 mile you reach another junction, this time with the Dismal Trail. Veer right and continue on the Raven Falls Trail toward the overlook.

Raven Cliff Falls

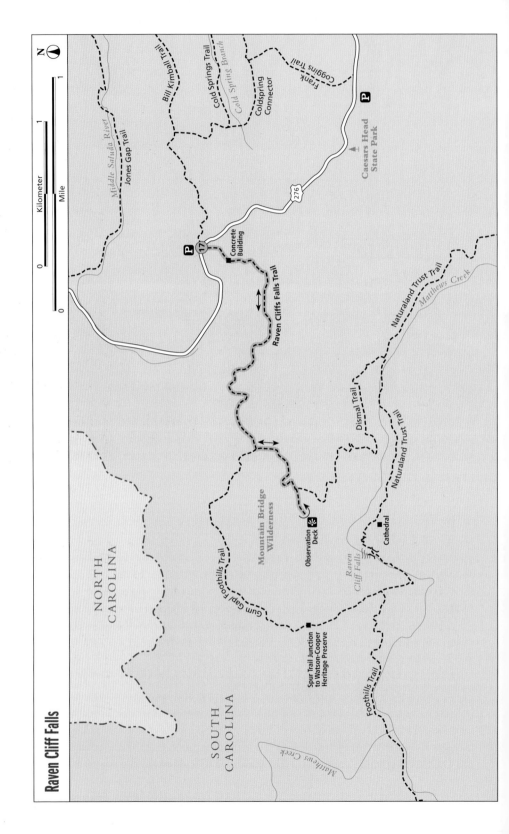

N

Kilometer
0   1

Mile
0   1

NORTH CAROLINA

SOUTH CAROLINA

Jones Gap Trail

Middle Saluda River

Bill Kimball Trail

Cold Springs Trail

Cold Spring Branch

Coldspring Connector

Frank Coggins Trail

276

Caesars Head State Park

P

17

P

Concrete Building

Raven Cliffs Falls Trail

Gum Gap/ Foothills Trail

Mountain Bridge Wilderness

Observation Deck

Raven Cliff Falls

Dismal Trail

Naturaland Trust Trail

Matthews Creek

Naturaland Trust Trail

Cathedral

Spur Trail Junction to Watson-Cooper Heritage Preserve

Foothills Trail

Matthews Creek

Over the next 0.2 mile you descend the steepest section of the trail. However, a short segment of switchbacks makes this descent easier on your knees. After descending a set of stairs, you emerge from the dense forest of rhododendron and mountain laurel to an expansive covered deck, with benches for resting. The deck protrudes from the forested cliff and offers stunning and truly breathtaking views of Matthews Creek as it drops more than 600 feet in a cascading torrent before plummeting an impressive 400 feet over Raven Cliff. It is an awe-inspiring view of the falls and the expansive Blue Ridge Escarpment, filled with azaleas, rhododendrons, and mountain laurels. The covered observation deck is large enough to accommodate a considerable number of people and is an excellent spot to stop for a long break or a snack. Bringing a picnic to enjoy on the benches as you listen and see the falls in the distance is highly recommended. After enjoying the falls you simply turn around and follow the trails back the way you came to return to the parking lot and trailhead where you started this short and spectacularly scenic day hike.

Miles and Directions

0.0 Start from the Raven Cliff Falls parking lot. Cross the highway to the trailhead and descend down the gravel path.

0.2 Pass the small concrete building, which is owned by the state park.

1.4 Reach a trail junction. To the right the Gum Gap Trail heads north. Veer left and stay on the Raven Cliff Falls Trail.

1.8 At the Y junction veer right and follow the Raven Cliff Falls Trail to an overlook of the falls.

1.9 Arrive at the observation deck and pavilion, which offers a wonderful view of Raven Cliff Falls to the southwest. From here turn around and return to the Raven Cliff Falls parking lot.

3.8 Arrive back at the parking lot.

Hike Information

Local Information: Pickens Chamber of Commerce, 222 W. Main St., Pickens, SC 29671; (864) 878-3258

Local Events/Attractions: Victoria Valley Vineyards, 1360 S. Saluda Rd., Cleveland; (864) 878-5307; victoriavalleyvineyards.com

   Caesars Head Hawk Watch, Caesars Head State Park, 8155 Geer Hwy., Cleveland; (864) 836.6115. A rare chance to see thousands of hawks before they migrate to Central and South America. Sept–Nov

Lodging: Solitude Pointe Cabins, 102 Table Rock Rd., Cleveland; (864) 836-4128; www.solitude pointe.com/our-cabins.php

   Pettigru Place B&B, 302 Pettigru St., Greenville; (864) 242-4529

Restaurants: Mountain House at Caesars Head, 8101 Geer Hwy., Cleveland; (864) 836-7330

   Doris' Family Kitchen, 2800 Geer Hwy., Marietta; (864) 836-4071

18 Bill Kimball-Coldspring Branch Loop

This half-day hike combines the difficult and spectacularly scenic Bill Kimball Trail with the easier and relaxing Coldspring Branch Trail. Together they create a wonderful hike recommended for more experienced hikers looking for a workout along with a healthy dose of adventure. Highlights include playful hiking along Coldspring Branch and views of El Lieutenant, a spectacular rock dome reminiscent of El Capitan in Yosemite National Park.

Start: From the trailhead at the Ravens Cliff Falls parking area
Distance: 4.8-mile lollipop
Hiking time: About 3-4 hours
Difficulty: Strenuous due to the steep elevation changes and technical hiking
Trail surface: Forested trail, rock
Best season: Any time when the trail is dry and free of ice so that you can get a grip on the steep trail sections. This trail is not recommended after snow, rain, or times when ice may be present.

Other trail users: Hikers only
Canine compatibility: Leashed dogs permitted
Fees and permits: Small per-person day-use fee
Schedule: Open year-round
Maps: TOPO! CD: North Carolina-South Carolina; USGS maps: Cleveland; South Carolina; USFS maps: Mountain Bridge Wilderness Area maps available at Caesars Head State Park
Trail contacts: Jones Gap State Park, 303 Jones Gap Rd., Marietta, SC 29661; (864) 836-3647; www.southcarolinaparks.com/jonesgap

Finding the trailhead: From Greenville, take US 276 West for about 30 miles, passing through Travelers Rest, Marietta, and Cleveland. Look out for the Caesars Head State Park entrance and continue north on US 276 about 1 more mile past the park entrance to the parking lot for the Coldspring Branch Trail. The trailhead is located in the south end of the parking lot. GPS: N35 06.933' / W82 38.271'

The Hike

To ensure your own safety along this hike, make sure that you are wearing a suitable pair of hiking shoes with a generous amount of grip left on the soles. To ensure the longevity of your knees, I highly recommend a pair of excellent and sturdy hiking poles along this hike. This trail has long sections of extremely steep trail. I do not recommend attempting this rocky, steep, and uneven trail if you are an inexperienced hiker. Start from the parking area for the Raven Falls Trail. You will find the trailhead for the Coldspring Branch Trail at the southern end of the parking lot.

Before this trail was rerouted, hikers would hike along US 276 and then hike onto an old roadbed that led northeast toward El Lieutenant. The trail has been expanded to have its own trailhead at the parking lot, but it makes for some rather unnecessary hiking in my opinion. You start from the parking lot and head down the mountain only to climb back up to the shoulder of the road and join the old roadbed that used

Sections of this trail are so steep that a chain has been installed to help hikers down the trail.

to be the start of the trail. Then again, if you are going to complain about a short climb that may be somewhat unnecessary at the beginning of this hike, you probably don't need to be embarking on a difficult trail like this.

After you rejoin the old roadbed, the trail ascends before following a level ridge and then descends steeply to the junction with the Bill Kimball Trail. The Coldspring Branch Trail continues to the right. Veer left and follow the pink-blazed Bill Kimball Trail. Don't worry about the pink blazing. This trail is hard. You're definitely not going to see any Susan G. Komen fundraising hike events on this difficult trail anytime soon. If it is solitude you want, you will find it on the Bill Kimball Trail. The trail was named after the San Francisco philanthropist who funded the conservation efforts of the Naturaland Trust and made several of the trail projects within the Mountain Bridge Wilderness possible. The California connection goes further as the trail leads to the base of El Lieutenant, which is often compared to El Capitan in Yosemite, the California national park 3.5 hours east of San Francisco. This trail leads to the base of this nearly sheer granite cliff, which is more than 300 feet high.

From the junction with the Coldspring Branch Trail, you ascend for 0.1 mile to the top of a ridge through a forest of mountain laurel and hardwoods. You follow this mostly level ridge for close to 0.5 mile. Along this section you will enjoy excellent views of the surrounding ridges, particularly in winter. You descend briefly and climb back onto the ridge before starting your long and steep descent toward the face of El Lieutenant following a long series of steep switchbacks. Exercise caution along this section of trail as it can be extremely slick after a rainfall and in the morning when a heavy dew has collected along the trail surface. Along some sections of the trail, it is so steep that chains have been placed at chest level so that hikers may hold on to them as they descend the rocky and steep path.

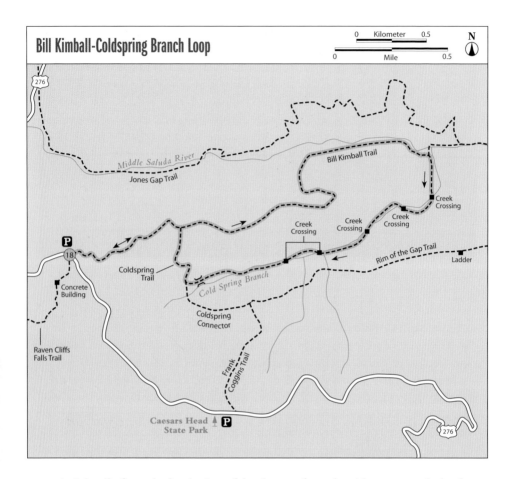

At 0.5 mile from the beginning of the descent from the ridge, you reach the first of four outcroppings of El Lieutenant, which offer views of the surrounding mountains. The next outcropping is definitely more impressive. I suggest pressing on and breaking at the next outcropping, which is just 0.1 mile farther down the trail. This second outcropping is perfect for a long break or lunch and has a more flat surface for sitting and resting and really enjoying the spectacular views. In 0.1 mile you reach the actual base of El Lieutenant and are rewarded with a picturesque view of the north face of the granite cliff. The trail continues to descend, passing another outcropping and then descending more steeply down a series of switchbacks again.

You arrive at a section of trail that is surrounded by downed trees. These trees have been here for decades and are in fact what remains of the American chestnut trees that were killed by the Oriental blight that felled these trees in the 1920s. The chestnut is extremely resistant to decomposition and so they remain a relic and a reminder of what was lost in that tragic blight.

The trail follows along the Middle Saluda River for the next 0.7 mile. Along this section of trail, you traverse through a welcomed level and pleasant section of trail and cross several small streams before arriving at a junction with the Coldspring Branch Trail in an area near a designated campsite.

Over the next 1.3 miles, you will cross two small tributaries and cross Coldspring Branch six times, only adding to the adventurous elements of this hike. At the 3.8-mile mark, you will cross a 15-foot bridge spanning a shallow stream. After 0.1 mile you reach the junction with the Coldspring Connector Trail. Stay to the right and continue your ascent to the ridge and the western junction with the Bill Kimball Trail. After 0.4 mile you arrive at this western junction of the Bill Kimball Trail and have completed your loop. Turn left, staying on the Coldspring Branch Trail, and hike over the ridge back to the Raven Cliff Falls parking area where you started your hike.

Miles and Directions

0.0 Start from the Raven Cliff Falls parking lot just off US 276. A kiosk and signage marks the Coldsprings Branch Trailhead at the south end of the parking lot.

0.6 Reach a trail junction. Veer to the left onto the Bill Kimball Trail, marked with pink blazes.

2.3 Arrive at a T junction. Turn right onto the Coldsprings Branch Trail.

2.5 Cross Coldsprings Branch. The smooth granite that you have to cross can be very slick. Use caution at this creek crossing.

2.8 You will cross Coldsprings Branch two more times.

3.0 Cross Coldsprings Branch for the fourth time.

3.3 Veer to the left before crossing Coldsprings Branch for the fifth time.

3.5 Cross two streams, which are tributaries of Coldsprings Branch.

3.6 Cross Coldsprings Branch for the sixth time. This is the last time you will cross Coldsprings Branch on this hike.

3.8 Cross a seasonal stream via the 15-foot bridge, then follow the trail to the left and uphill at the foot of the bridge.

3.9 Reach a trail junction. The Coldsprings Connector is to the left. Turn right and continue uphill on the orange-blazed Coldsprings Branch Trail.

4.2 Reach a T junction. The Bill Kimball Trail is to the right. Turn left and stay on the Coldsprings Branch Trail, heading toward the Raven Cliff Falls parking lot where you started.

4.8 Arrive at the Raven Cliff Falls parking lot and the end of this hike.

Hike Information

Local Information: Pickens Chamber of Commerce, 222 W. Main St., Pickens, SC 29671; (864) 878-3258

Local Events/Attractions: Victoria Valley Vineyards, 1360 S. Saluda Rd., Cleveland; (864) 878-5307; victoriavalleyvineyards.com

Caesars Head Hawk Watch, Caesars Head State Park, 8155 Geer Hwy., Cleveland; (864) 836-6115. A rare chance to see thousands of hawks before they migrate to Central and South America. Sept–Nov

Lodging: Solitude Pointe Cabins, 102 Table Rock Rd., Cleveland; (864) 836-4128; www.solitude pointe.com/our-cabins.php

Pettigru Place B&B, 302 Pettigru St., Greenville; (864) 242-4529

Restaurants: Mountain House at Caesars Head, 8101 Geer Hwy., Cleveland; (864) 836-7330

Doris' Family Kitchen, 2800 Geer Hwy., Marietta; (864) 836-4071

19 Rainbow Falls

Hike the newest addition to the Mountain Bridge Wilderness Trails. Opened in 2008, this has been a longtime favorite trail for hikers exploring the Cox Camp area, but now that it is officially part of the wilderness area, the popularity of the trail has grown substantially. Explore the mountainous terrain with highlights that include sections of boulder fields, steep rock faces, and impressive overlooks. At the end of the trail, you reach the true star of the show: Rainbow Falls tumbles more than 100 feet against a granite cliff.

Start: From the trailhead for the Jones Gap Trail

Distance: 4.4-mile out and back

Hiking time: About 2–3 hours

Difficulty: Moderate to strenuous due to elevation changes and steep sections of trail

Trail surface: Forested path, old roadbeds

Best seasons: Spring (Mar–May) for wildflower displays; fall (Sept–Nov) for fall foliage

Other trail users: Hikers only

Canine compatibility: Leashed dogs permitted

Fees and permits: Free for kids under age 16; small fee for age 16 and over; senior discount available. Fees higher Oct 1 to Nov 30, including a small fee for children 6–15

Schedule: Daily 9 a.m. to 9 p.m. during daylight saving time; daily 9 a.m. to 6 p.m. remainder of the year. Trails close 1 hour before dark year-round.

Maps: TOPO! CD: North Carolina–South Carolina; USGS maps: Standingstone Mountain; South Carolina; USFS maps: Mountain Bridge Wilderness Area maps available at Caesars Head State Park

Trail contacts: Jones Gap State Park, 303 Jones Gap Rd., Marietta, SC 29661; (864) 836-3647; www.southcarolinaparks.com/jonesgap

Finding the trailhead: From Greenville, take US 276 through Travelers Rest, Marietta, and Cleveland. Approximately 2 miles north of Cleveland, turn right at the park sign onto River Falls Road. Stay on River Falls Road until the name changes to Jones Gap Road. The park is 6 miles off US 276. GPS: N35 07.523' / W82 34.477'

The Hike

To hike back to this spectacular waterfall, you have to start at the trailhead to the Jones Gap Trail and follow the Jones Gap Trail along the Middle Saluda River. This portion of the trail is incredibly scenic and picturesque, especially during the spring and fall. Enjoy the many resting spots along the creek that are perfect for relaxing, fishing, and picnicking. You quickly reach a trail junction with the Rim of the Gap Trail to the left side of the trail. Stay to the right and continue on the Jones Gap Trail. Along this section you pass by several extremely well-maintained backcountry campsites. These are designated sites that must be reserved in advance. One of the best campsites along this section is site number six, which is level and located near the river and

A bridge to Rainbow Falls

provides a very scenic and peaceful camping experience. I highly recommend these backcountry sites.

The trail follows along a wide and rocky path that is very pleasant and mostly level and passes through a forest of hemlock, pine, and oak with a dominant understory of rhododendron. Continue for 0.5 mile until you arrive at the junction with the Rainbow Falls Trail. Join the Rainbow Falls Trail and cross the bridge spanning the Middle Saluda River. At the foot of the bridge, the trail continues west, paralleling the river, and joins the old roadbed of the original Jones Gap Road. In 0.2 mile you cross the Cox Camp Creek. This is the source of Rainbow Falls. Over the next short section of trail, you will cross the creek two more times before beginning a gradual ascent toward the falls. You cross Cox Camp Creek via a 35-foot bridge and then continue the ascent of switchbacks and stone steps, passing a small cascade along the way. Just 1.0 mile from the Middle Saluda River crossing, you reach an overlook that

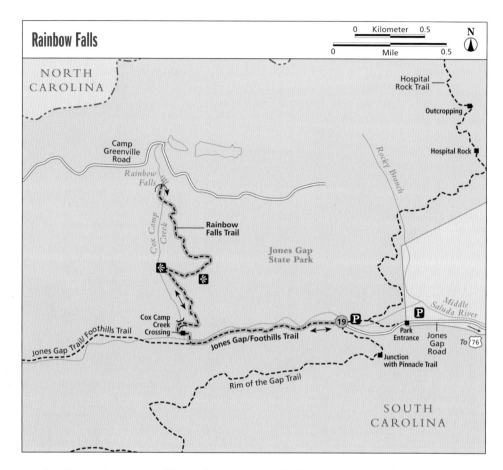

Rainbow Falls

0   Kilometer   0.5

0   Mile   0.5

N

NORTH
CAROLINA

Hospital
Rock Trail

Outcropping

Camp
Greenville
Road

*Rainbow
Falls*

Hospital Rock

Cox Camp Creek

Rainbow
Falls Trail

Jones Gap
State Park

Rocky Branch

*Middle
Saluda River*

Cox Camp
Creek
Crossing

Foothills Trail

Jones Gap Trail

Jones Gap/Foothills Trail

19

Park
Entrance

Jones
Gap
Road

To 76

Junction
with Pinnacle Trail

Rim of the Gap Trail

SOUTH
CAROLINA

offers impressive views of Jones Gap to the south. You continue to climb stone steps before arriving at an artfully crafted stone bridge. You cross this stone bridge and then turn to the left at a sheer rock face. You cross Camp Creek and then climb a last stone staircase before arriving at the base of the beautiful 100-foot waterfall, which is considered to be one of the most beautiful waterfalls in South Carolina. If you are here at the right time of day, the sunlight shining through the spray of the falls will often create a rainbow, a stunningly beautiful sight indeed.

This part of the trail is located on property owned by Camp Greenville YMCA. No camping is permitted in this area, and a spur trail leading to the camp can only be used if you have gained explicit permission from the camp. In recent years the falls have become extremely popular, almost as popular as the nearby Raven Cliff Falls. If you are looking for solitude, I highly recommend that you hike this trail during the winter or early morning on weekdays. Weekends and holidays are going to be extremely busy, and during the summer when Camp Greenville is in full swing, the trail can be exceptionally crowded with campers and visitors. From here turn around and follow the trail back to the parking lot and trailhead for the Jones Gap Trail.

Miles and Directions

0.0 Start from the trailhead near the wide wooden vehicle bridge leading to the Jones Gap State Park office. The trailhead is marked by a kiosk. Follow the Jones Gap Trail alongside the Saluda River.

0.1 Reach the trail junction with the Rim of the Gap Trail to the left. Stay straight on the Jones Gap Trail.

0.6 At this split in the trail, stay to the right and join the Rainbow Falls Trail. The Jones Gap Trail continues to the left toward Caesars Head State Park. In 150 feet you cross a bridge spanning the Middle Saluda River. The trail then takes a sharp turn to the left (west).

0.8 Cross Cox Camp Creek. In 140 feet the trail turns sharply to the right (northeast).

0.9 Cross the 35-foot wooden bridge spanning Cox Camp Creek. In 400 feet the trail veers sharply to the left (north). From here the trail begins an ascent toward the falls.

1.4 The trail rejoins Cox Camp Creek. From the trail you can view some beautiful cascades.

1.6 Reach an overlook on the right side of the trail that offers nice views toward the southeast of the southern edge of Jones Gap.

2.1 Cross Cox Camp Creek using the stepping stones in the creek.

2.2 Arrive at the bottom of Rainbow Falls. After enjoying this impressive waterfall, turn around and hike back to the Jones Gap parking lot where you started.

4.4 Arrive back at the parking lot.

Hike Information

Local Information: Pickens Chamber of Commerce, 222 W. Main St., Pickens, SC 29671; (864) 878-3258

Local Events/Attractions: Victoria Valley Vineyards, 1360 S. Saluda Rd., Cleveland; (864) 878-5307; victoriavalleyvineyards.com

Caesars Head Hawk Watch, Caesars Head State Park, 8155 Geer Hwy., Cleveland; (864) 836-6115. A rare chance to see thousands of hawks before they migrate to Central and South America. Sept–Nov

Lodging: Solitude Pointe Cabins, 102 Table Rock Rd., Cleveland; (864) 836-4128, www.solitudepointe.com/our-cabins.php

Pettigru Place B&B, 302 Pettigru St., Greenville; (864) 242-4529

Restaurants: Mountain House at Caesars Head, 8101 Geer Hwy., Cleveland; (864) 836-7330

Doris' Family Kitchen, 2800 Geer Hwy., Marietta; (864) 836-4071

20 Rim of the Gap Trail

Highlights of this half-day hike include stunning views of Jones Gap, the gorges of the northern rim, the Cleveland Cliff, and Rainbow Falls. This trail can be hiked from east to west for a very strenuous climb or from west to east for a long, steep descent. We decided to feature the challenge of the climb and detail this hike from the east to west route.

Start: From the trailhead near the Jones Gap State Park office
Distance: 5.1-mile shuttle
Hiking time: About 2–4 hours
Difficulty: Strenuous due to elevation changes
Trail surface: Forested path, old roadbeds
Best seasons: Spring (Mar–May) for wildflower displays; fall (Sept–Nov) for fall foliage
Other trail users: Hikers only
Canine compatibility: Leashed dogs permitted
Fees and permits: Free for kids under age 16; small trail-access fee for age 16 and over; senior discount available

Schedule: Daily 9 a.m. to 9 p.m. during daylight saving time; daily 9 a.m. to 6 p.m. remainder of the year. Trails close 1 hour before dark year-round.
Maps: TOPO! CD: North Carolina–South Carolina; USGS maps: Cleveland, Standingstone Mountain, Table Rock; South Carolina; USFS maps: Mountain Bridge Wilderness Area maps available at Caesars Head State Park
Trail contacts: Mountain Bridge Headquarters (Caesars Head State Park), 8155 Geer Hwy., Cleveland, SC 29635; (894) 836-6115

Finding the trailhead: From Greenville, take US 276 West for about 30 miles. The park is located at the top of the mountain right off the highway. The North Carolina border is 3 miles away. GPS: N35 07.533' / W82 34.371'
   To park a car or be picked up at the end of the shuttle: From Jones Gap State Park drive east on CR 97/Jones Gap Road and follow for 5.4 miles. Turn right onto SC 11 and continue for about 4 miles. Turn right onto US 276 and follow for about 7.4 miles until you reach the parking lot and park visitor center on the left side of the road. The Frank Coggins Trail starts across the road from the visitor center.

The Hike

As the name implies, the Rim of the Gap Trail traverses the southern rim of the Jones Gap and offers picturesque and impressive views of the spectacular cliffs along this ancient cleft. However, you will need to climb up to the rim of the gap before you can enjoy these excellent views. This trail is very difficult and I highly recommend hiking this trail as a one-way or shuttle trip. This will require leaving another vehicle at the parking lot and trailhead for the Frank Coggins Trail at Caesars Head State Park or arranging a shuttle from this location back to Jones Gap State Park. It is definitely possible to hike this trail as an out-and-back, but it would be very challenging and would certainly require a very early start.

A mossy boulder sits along the Rim of the Gap Trail.

To reach the start of the Rim of the Gap Trail, you must hike a short section of the Jones Gap Trail, which begins at the main kiosk near the vehicular bridge that crosses the Middle Saluda River in Jones Gap State Park. The beginning of the trail is pleasant and level and follows alongside the Middle Saluda River through a dense understory of rhododendron. After less than 0.1 mile, you reach the intersection with the Rim of the Gap Trail, which immediately begins to climb and turn toward the left, offering a bird's-eye view of the parking lot and trailhead where you started this hike. The first impressive feature you will encounter on this hike is a large rock shelter on the right side of the trail. A faint trail leads to the shelter, evidence of the curiosity that the shelter struck in hikers before you. Continue on the yellow-blazed trail and pass through a section of trail with several rock outcroppings and interesting rock formations along the way. One particular rock formation looks very similar to the moai statues at Easter Island.

The trail continues to climb steeply, and after 0.4 mile you reach a junction with the Pinnacle Pass Trail. Stay to the right and continue on the Rim of the Gap Trail. After 0.6 mile the steepness of the trail eases a bit, and during the next 0.4 mile if you are hiking in the winter, late fall, or early spring, you will have several opportunities to enjoy excellent winter views of Jones Gap to the north, with the Middle Saluda River rushing down below. Sometimes the river can be heard from this section of trail. At 1.3 miles from the junction with the Jones Gap Trail, you will have the opportunity to enjoy a winter view of Rainbow Falls if you look to the north and toward the other side of the rim of Jones Gap. Along this section of trail, you will also encounter a wide variety of spring wildflowers as you travel through a forest of mostly poplar, beech, birch, maple, and basswood trees.

Continue climbing for another 0.5 mile until you reach the junction with the connector trail that leads to the Pinnacle Trail on the left. The trail is only 700 feet long. Taking this trail to the Pinnacle Trail and then turning left on the Pinnacle Trail will take you back to the trailhead where you started to complete an excellent loop trail in the Mountain Bridge Wilderness. However, stay to the right and continue on the yellow-blazed Rim of the Gap Trail.

You will climb for just another 0.7 mile until you reach the junction with the John Sloan Trail straight ahead, which follows an old roadbed. Turn right and stay on the Rim of the Gap Trail, which navigates through dense rhododendron and mountain laurel before descending a section of steps and switchbacks that lead along the edge of the ridge. The next 1.5 miles of trail are spectacular. The trail holds close to the base of the south rim of Jones Gap while the trail passes by several waterfalls that plunge over the edges of cliffs, rock walls, and rocky outcroppings. This is also the portion of the trail that introduces some slightly technical hiking. You will cross ladders, navigate through a tight rock opening called Weight Watchers Rock, pass impressive rock outcroppings with stunning views of the surrounding mountains, cross several streams, and endure a few steep descents. You finally reach the intersection with the Frank Coggins Trail, which you can take to the parking lot and trailhead at Caesars State Park or turn around and head back the way you came and return to the trailhead for the Jones Gap Trail at Jones Gap State Park where you started.

Miles and Directions

0.0 Start from the trailhead near the Jones Gap State Park office. A kiosk near a wooden vehicle bridge marks the start of the Jones Gap Trail, which follows along the Middle Saluda River to the southwest.

0.1 Reach the trail junction with the Rim of the Gap Trail to the left. Turn left onto the yellow-blazed Rim of the Gap Trail.

0.4 The junction with the Pinnacle Trail is on the left. Veer right and stay on the yellow-blazed Rim of the Gap Trail.

1.9 Arrive at a trail junction. The connector trail to the Pinnacle Trail is on the left. Veer right and stay on the yellow-blazed Rim of the Gap Trail.

2.6 Arrive at a trail junction. The John Sloan Trail is straight ahead and follows the wide old roadbed. Turn right and stay on the Rim of the Gap Trail.

Rim of the Gap Trail

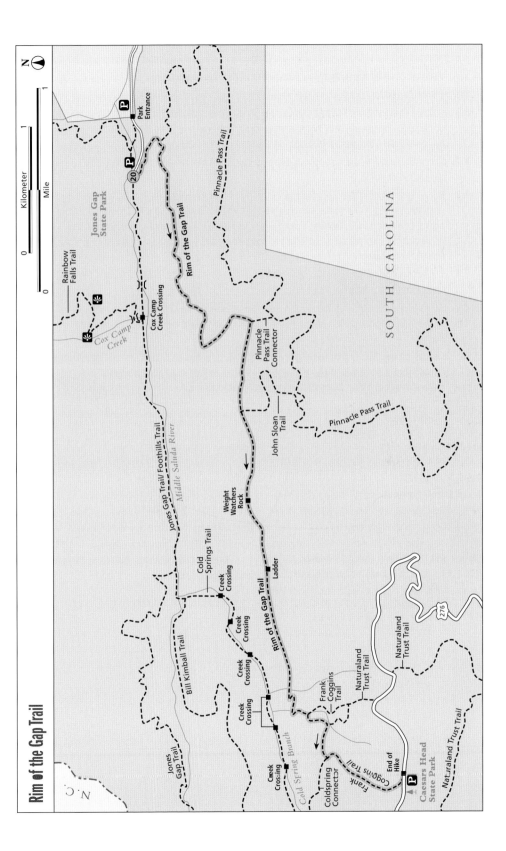

N.C.

Jones Gap State Park

SOUTH CAROLINA

Caesars Head State Park

Park Entrance

Rainbow Falls Trail

Cox Camp Creek

Cox Camp Creek Crossing

Jones Gap Trail/ Foothills Trail

Middle Saluda River

Rim of the Gap Trail

Pinnacle Pass Trail

Pinnacle Pass Trail Connector

John Sloan Trail

Pinnacle Pass Trail

Weight Watchers Rock

Cold Springs Trail

Creek Crossing

Bill Kimball Trail

Creek Crossing

Creek Crossing

Creek Crossing

Ladder

Rim of the Gap Trail

Cold Spring Branch

Jones Gap Trail

Creek Crossing

Coldspring Connector

Frank Coggins Trail

Frank Coggins Trail

Naturaland Trust Trail

Naturaland Trust Trail

Naturaland Trust Trail

End of Hike

276

Kilometer

Mile

N

2.9 The trail passes beneath a large boulder called Weight Watchers Rock. There is also a trail that goes around the rock if your pack won't fit through the opening.

3.3 Climb the ladder up the short rock wall.

3.9 Cross a small stream. The trail climbs steeply and then reaches the bottom of a small, unnamed waterfall. The trail turns sharply to the right (west). Climb down the short ladder and then follow the narrow trail against the sheer wall of granite.

4.1 Cross the short wooden footbridge over a seasonal stream and follow the switchbacks uphill.

4.3 Reach a split in the trail and the end of the Rim of the Gap Trail. The Frank Coggins Trail goes both straight and to the left. Stay straight on the Frank Coggins Trail toward the Coldspring Connector Trail. (*Option:* From here, if you don't have a shuttle, turn around and hike back the way you came to return to the parking lot and trailhead at Jones Gap State Park 4.3 miles away.)

4.4 The return side of the Frank Coggins trail loop is to your left. Stay straight toward the Coldspring Connector Trail.

4.6 Arrive at the junction with the Coldspring Connector Trail. The Coldspring Connector veers to the right. Stay to the left on the Frank Coggins Trail toward the Caesars Head Visitor Center.

5.1 Cross highway 276 and arrive at the parking lot and trailhead at the Caesars Head Visitors Center. This is an excellent place to leave a second vehicle or arrange a shuttle back to the trailhead at Jones Gap State Park where you started your hike.

Hike Information

Local Information: Pickens Chamber of Commerce, 222 W. Main St., Pickens, SC 29671; (864) 878-3258

Local Events/Attractions: Victoria Valley Vineyards, 1360 S. Saluda Rd., Cleveland; (864) 878-5307; victoriavalleyvineyards.com

Caesars Head Hawk Watch, Caesars Head State Park, 8155 Geer Hwy., Cleveland; (864) 836-6115. A rare chance to see thousands of hawks before they migrate to Central and South America. Sept–Nov

Lodging: Solitude Pointe Cabins, 102 Table Rock Rd., Cleveland; (864) 836-4128; www.solitude pointe.com/our-cabins.php

Pettigru Place B&B, 302 Pettigru St., Greenville; (864) 242-4529

Restaurants: Mountain House at Caesars Head, 8101 Geer Hwy., Cleveland; (864) 836-7330

Doris' Family Kitchen, 2800 Geer Hwy., Marietta; (864) 836-4071

21 Falls Creek and Hospital Rock Trails

Discover the gorgeous 100-foot-high Falls Creek Falls along this rugged day hike that combines the Falls Creek Trail and the Hospital Rock Trail in the Mountain Bridge Wilderness. Encounter sweeping views at the numerous rock outcroppings as you traverse through a variety of mountain terrains and lush forest. Along the way you pass Hospital Rock, an old hideout for Civil War deserters.

Start: From the Hospital Rock Trailhead in Jones Gap State Park
Distance: 6.2-mile shuttle
Hiking time: About 3-6 hours
Difficulty: Strenuous due to intense elevation change along the route
Trail surface: Forested path, old roadbed, gravel path
Best seasons: Spring (Mar-May) for wildflower displays; fall (Sept-Nov) for fall foliage
Other trail users: Hikers only
Canine compatibility: Leashed dogs permitted
Fees and permits: Free for kids under age 16; small fee for age 16 and over; senior discount available. Fees higher Oct 1 to Nov 30, including a small fee for children 6-15

Schedule: Daily 9 a.m. to 9 p.m. during daylight saving time; daily 9 a.m. to 6 p.m. remainder of the year. Trails close one 1 hour before dark year-round
Maps: TOPO! CD: North Carolina-South Carolina; USGS maps: Standingstone Mountain, Cleveland; South Carolina; USFS maps: Mountain Bridge Wilderness Area maps available at Caesars Head State Park
Trail contacts: Jones Gap State Park, 303 Jones Gap Rd., Marietta, SC 29661; (864) 836-3647; www.southcarolinaparks.com/jonesgap

Finding the trailhead: From Greenville drive northwest on US 276 to the junction of US 276 and SC 11. Continue approximately 1.5 miles and turn right onto River Falls Road (Greenville County S-23-97), which changes to Jones Gap Road, and continue to Jones Gap State Park. From the parking lot, walk toward the park buildings on a short trail that crosses the Middle Saluda River. At the fishpond of the former Cleveland Fish Hatchery, bear right and angle for the orange-blazed trailhead and registration box straight ahead. The Hospital Rock Trail ends at Falls Creek Waterfall and the only access from the east is via the Falls Creek Trail. GPS: N35 07.607'/W82 34.194'

To park a car or be picked up at the end of the shuttle: From the trailhead at Jones Gap State Park, head east on CR 97/Jones Gap Road and follow for 1.6 miles. Turn left onto Duckworth Road and follow for 0.5 mile. Take the second right onto Falls Creek Road and follow for 0.4 mile. The trailhead and small parking lot for the Falls Creek Trail will be on the left side of the road.

The Hike

You can start this hike either from the parking lot and trailhead for Falls Creek Trail at the end of Falls Creek Road or from the Hospital Rock Trailhead in Jones Gap State Park. Either way, I highly recommend that you approach this trail as a one-way hike

and leave a vehicle at the opposite end of the trail or arrange a shuttle to get you back to where you started. This trail can definitely be hiked in one day as an out-and-back 12.4-mile hike, but it would be extremely strenuous and would require an early start for most hikers.

If you are mostly interested in seeing the falls, then simply start from the Falls Creek Falls Trailhead and turn around after enjoying the falls. For the route described here, start from the Hospital Rock Trailhead in Jones Gap State Park. At the beginning of the trail, you hike past many backcountry campsites to the left and right of the trail. These campsites are highly recommended, as are the sites to the west along the Middle Saluda River and the Jones Gap Trail. The campsites are only a short walk from the backcountry-camping parking lot. They are very reasonably priced and a simple way to get out of those crowded front-country campsites that are often loud, crowded, and feel more akin to a parking lot for RVs than an outdoor wilderness experience. These campsites, however, must be reserved in advanced.

From the very start this trail begins a long, hard climb up to the ridge. This is one of the hardest trails in the Mountain Bridge Wilderness, but the views from the numerous outcroppings and at the top of the ridge are worth the hike. Along the steep climb to Hospital Rock, you traverse through a hardwood forest of chestnut, oak, and Frasier magnolia and dense sections of rhododendron and mountain laurel. In spring the wildflower displays are wonderful and include violets, hydrangea, asters, and galax. The dense forest makes this stretch of trail less than ideal for birding. You will have much better luck around the peak of Sassafras Mountain for this activity. However, along this route you may be able to spot quick glimpses of pileated woodpeckers, chickadees, and red-shouldered hawks soaring above the canopy.

If you are hiking during hunting season, I highly recommend that you wear bright-orange-colored clothing and hat. Hunting season is generally between October 1 and January 1. This section of the trail does pass through a wildlife management area where hunting is permitted, so be advised and be safe! Getting shot by a trigger-happy hunter is the quickest way to spoil your hiking and picnic plans.

After 1.1 miles you reach Hospital Rock, a cavern and house-size rock that was used by Civil War deserters as a hideout. It is an inviting campsite given the fact that the cavern is high enough to stand under. However, the state park service has found some ridiculous reason to ban people from camping under this rock, which is easily the most logical and superior camping site in the entire Mountain Bridge Wilderness. After exploring Hospital Rock, enjoying the wonderful views, and deeply contemplating the validity of bureaucracy in the American wilderness, continue to climb the steep and rocky trail toward the top of the ridge. Along this section of trail there are several excellent rock outcroppings with superb views of the surrounding mountains that also make excellent and much-welcomed resting spots along this difficult section.

◀ *Falls Creek Falls*

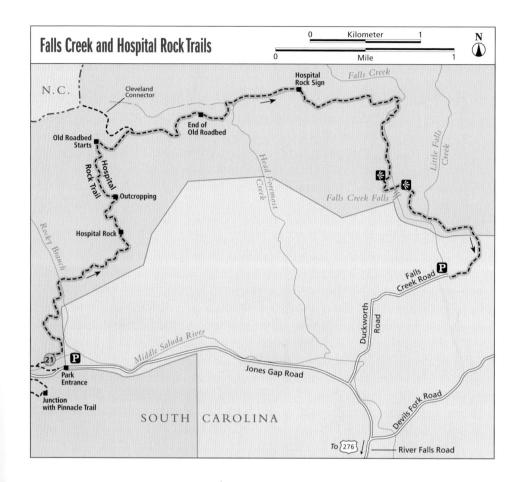

Falls Creek and Hospital Rock Trails

The trail levels off briefly atop the ridge before plunging down steep switchbacks and long descents toward Falls Creek Falls. You encounter more excellent rock outcroppings and cross several streams and tributaries of the Headforemost Creek before arriving at Falls Creek Falls and the end of the Hospital Rock Trail. You arrive at the base of the falls and are treated with an excellent view of the 100-foot waterfall cascading and plunging toward you. At the base of the falls are large rocks that make excellent resting and picnic spots. You cross Falls Creek by hopping across the exposed stones and join the Falls Creek Falls Trail, which leads up beside the falls on a steep forested trail that offers excellent varying perspectives of the falls. The trail turns to the right and you leave the falls behind.

You pass an excellent outcropping before beginning a steep climb down to the parking lot and trailhead at the end of the Falls Creek Falls Trail, which mostly follows an old and wide roadbed for much of the way. This section takes you through sections of impressive boulder fields and past another rock shelter to the left of the trail right before you reach the parking lot and the end of this dynamic hike.

Miles and Directions

0.0 Start from the trailhead for the Hospital Rock Trail in Jones Gap State Park. At the beginning of the trail, you pass campsites to the left and right of the trail.

0.5 Cross the small stream and climb up a steep hill. The trail passes under power lines, and the swath offers excellent views of the surrounding ridges.

1.1 A spur trail on the left leads to Hospital Rock, a massive rock that is quite fun to explore. Spend some time exploring this impressive feature and then rejoin the Hospital Rock Trail.

1.5 A large rock outcropping on the left side of the trail offers excellent views.

2.0 The trail reaches an intersection with an old roadbed. Turn right onto the old road.

2.2 Arrive at a trail junction. The Cleveland Connector Trail is to the left. Veer to the right and stay on the Hospital Rock Trail.

2.8 Leave the old roadbed and veer to the left onto the narrow trail.

3.1 Cross the small stream.

3.5 A sign marks the Hospital Rock Trail.

4.7 Reach a large rock overlook with some decent views of the surrounding ridges.

4.9 Reach the bottom of Falls Creek Falls. Enjoy the waterfall and then cross the creek at the base of the falls. On the other side of the creek is the Falls Creek Trail.

5.0 Arrive at a small rock outcropping with nice views of the surrounding mountains.

5.4 Cross the small stream and continue on the Falls Creek Trail. During the next 0.2 mile, the trail passes through an impressive boulder field.

6.2 Arrive at the end of the Falls Creek Trail marked by a kiosk on Falls Creek Road. This is a choice location to arrange a shuttle back to Jones Gap State Park.

Hike Information

Local Information: Pickens Chamber of Commerce, 222 W. Main St., Pickens, SC 29671; (864) 878-3258

Local Events/Attractions: Victoria Valley Vineyards, 1360 S. Saluda Rd., Cleveland; (864) 878-5307; victoriavalleyvineyards.com

Lodging: Solitude Pointe Cabins, 102 Table Rock Rd., Cleveland; (864) 836-4128, www.solitude pointe.com/our-cabins.php

Pettigru Place B&B, 302 Pettigru St., Greenville; (864) 242-4529

Restaurants: Mountain House at Caesars Head, 8101 Geer Hwy., Cleveland; (864) 836-7330

Doris' Family Kitchen, 2800 Geer Hwy., Marietta; (864) 836-4071

22 Palmetto Trail: Poinsett Reservoir Passage

Enjoy views of the Blue Ridge Mountain foothills on this long day hike that explores the northern perimeter of the Poinsett Watershed. A long and gradual ascent takes you to Brushy Ridge and Rocky Spur Mountain, where you are offered winter views of the surrounding mountains and piedmont. The additions of switchbacks and stone steps make navigating this trail easy and enjoyable.

Start: From the trailhead at the Orchard Lake Campground
Distance: 13.2-mile out and back
Hiking time: About 5-7 hours
Difficulty: Moderate due to elevation changes
Trail surface: Forested trail, paved road, gravel path, old roadbed
Best seasons: Spring (Mar–May) for wildflower displays; fall (Sept–Nov) for fall foliage
Other trail users: Hikers only
Canine compatibility: Leashed dogs permitted

Fees and permits: None
Schedule: Open year-round. Check palmetto conservation.org for updates and trail closings.
Maps: TOPO! CD: North Carolina-South Carolina; USGS maps: Saluda, Landrum; South Carolina; USFS maps: Palmetto Trail maps available online at palmettotrail.org
Trail contacts: Palmetto Conservation, 722 King St., Columbia, SC 29205; (803) 771-0870; palmettoconservation.org

Finding the trailhead: From Greenville drive north on US 25. After you cross SC 11, turn right onto Old Highway 25 (Greenville County Road S23969). Drive for approximately 7 miles and turn right onto Saluda Road, which changes to Mountain Page after you cross into North Carolina. Drive approximately 3.5 miles and make a sharp right turn onto Mine Mountain Road. The campground is approximately 2.0 miles farther. GPS: N35 11.882' / W82 21.059'

The Hike

It's a long, slow, and gradual climb of nearly 6.0 miles to the top of Rocky Spur Mountain so be sure to have your boots laced up for this hike and bring plenty of snacks and water with you before embarking on this long day hike. This trail does connect with the Blue Wall Passage of the Palmetto Trail, and combined they can make an ambitious day hike or a comfortable overnight backpacking adventure. Unfortunately, there is no vehicle access to the trailhead where the Blue Wall Passage and the Poinsett Passage meet, so plan accordingly for an out-and-back trip that is more than 12 miles long if you intend to hike the entire length of the Poinsett Passage. For something slightly less challenging, I recommend hiking the Poinsett Passage for the first 4.5 miles until you reach the start of Hogback Mountain Road. The rest of the trail follows along this doubletrack gravel road and does not offer much for spectacular scenery, challenge, or interesting highlights. If you turn around at Hogback Mountain Road, the out-and-back total for the trail is 9 miles, which makes a very comfortable and enjoyable day hike that can be accomplished in 3 to 5 hours depending on your conditioning and hiking speed. And don't feel like you're missing much if you turn around at Hogback Mountain Road. The most impressive sections of trail and scenery are encountered before this junction. Therefore, I highly recommend this route.

The Poinsett Passage traverses mostly through the Poinsett Watershed, a 19,000-acre tract of land that is a part of the Greenville Watershed, which feeds the Poinsett Reservoir and Greenville Water System. This area provides water to the city of Greenville, and the watershed is recognized by water professionals as producing some of the cleanest water in the nation. So please don't go mucking it up and disregarding Leave No Trace principles. Let's keep this water clean and healthy for our neighbors to the south of the trail. The close proximity to Greenville makes this trail and area a popular destination for cubicle dwellers living in the city who are desperate for an escape to the outdoors. For dramatic overlooks and spectacular views of the mountains, hikers will want to head farther to the west and explore the extensive network of trails in the Mountain Bridge Wilderness Area.

A hiking stick has been abandoned at the trailhead to the Poinsett Reservoir Passage.

While you do have the opportunity to catch glimpses of the surrounding mountains along this route, the views are mostly obscured by forest that continues unobstructed for the most part throughout the entire length of the trail. However, this is a good choice if you are content with a nice climb through a forest and don't mind if you see a few houses and paved roads along the way. While the trail is far from a wilderness experience, it is a very nice option for a challenging walk in the woods and offers great opportunities to see a variety of wildlife and plants along the way.

Start on this hike from the Orchard Lake Campground trailhead. There is a small gravel parking lot that has been constructed specifically for Palmetto Trail hikers. From the parking lot follow the gravel road to a kiosk that marks the start of the trailhead. The first section of the trail is quite uneventful and somewhat difficult to follow.

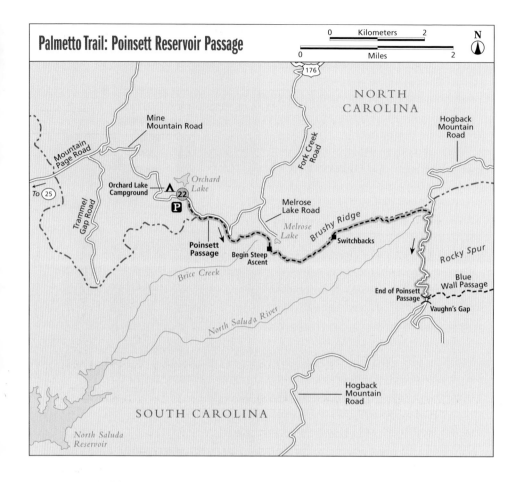

Palmetto Trail: Poinsett Reservoir Passage

Counterintuitively, you leave the trailhead and follow a gravel road to a small bridge over a seasonal stream and then climb the road embankment to follow the paved road to Fork Creek Road to where the trail rejoins a forested trail. The trail follows along the paved road, and after 1.1 mile you leave the road and continue a gradual ascent toward Brushy Ridge. The trail is heavily forested along this section, which closely parallels the South Carolina–North Carolina border. At 1.8 mile from the start of the trail, you begin the very steep ascent. Several sections of newly constructed switchbacks and a series of rock steps help you manage the climb. During the winter you will have decent views of the surrounding mountains.

At the 2.8-mile mark you reach the top of Brushy Ridge and then quickly climb in and out of a steep gap before continuing along the undulating ridge that follows along Brushy Ridge and over Rocky Spur Mountain. You reach the junction with the gravel Hogback Mountain Road at the 4.5-mile mark. This is a great turnaround point. The trail follows the gravel road for the rest of the way to Vaughn's Gap, where you reach the trailhead for the Blue Wall Passage. From here simply turn around and follow the trail back the way you came in to return to the trailhead and parking lot at Orchard Lake Campground.

Miles and Directions

0.0 Start from the trailhead at the Orchard Lake Campground. The trail follows a gravel road to the right of the trailhead kiosk. Cross the short, wooden footbridge over a small stream and then ascend to Fork Creek Road. Turn left onto Fork Creek Road and follow the road for 150 feet before turning off the road to the right and taking the narrow trail back into the forest. The trail follows beside Fork Creek Road for about the next 1.1 miles, keeping the road to the left.

1.2 Leave Fork Creek Road behind and continue on the trail.

1.9 The trail begins to climb steeply toward Brushy Ridge. During the climb you encounter several sections of switchbacks.

3.1 Climb the steep set of switchbacks along Brushy Ridge.

4.7 Reach the start of Hogback Mountain Road. The trail turns sharply to the right (south) and follows the gravel road for the next 2 miles. This is a good spot to turn around and head back to the Orchard Campground Trailhead, unless you want to continue on the Blue Wall Passage Trail. Otherwise there is not much reason to hike the last 2 miles of the trail.

6.6 You reach the end of the Poinsett Passage Trail and the start of the Blue Wall Passage at Vaughn's Gap. The end of the trail is marked with a kiosk and trailhead for the Blue Wall Passage segment of the Palmetto Trail. From here, turn around and follow the gravel Hogback Mountain Road back toward Brushy Ridge.

8.5 Arrive at the end of Hogback Mountain Road and continue to follow the Poinsett Passage Trail toward Brushy Ridge.

10.1 Reach the start of the switchbacks and descend Brushy Ridge.

11.3 Reach the end of the switchbacks and continue on the Poinsett Passage Trail.

12.0 The trail begins to run alongside Fork Creek Trail to the right for about the next 1.1 miles. Turn left onto Fork Creek Road. In about 150 feet turn right and descend from the road to the stream crossing via the wooden bridge. From here follow the gravel road back toward the trailhead.

13.2 Arrive at the trailhead and kiosk where you started your hike.

Hike Information

Local Information: Greenville Chamber of Commerce, 24 Cleveland St., Greenville, SC 29601; (864) 242-1050

Local Events/Attractions: Greenville Zoo, 150 Cleveland Park Dr., Greenville; (864) 467-4300

Falls Park, West Camperdown Way, Greenville. Open 7 a.m. to 9 p.m. daily; free admission

Lodging: Red Horse Inn, 45 Winstons Chase Ct., Landrum; (864) 895-4968; theredhorse inn.com

Saluda Mountain Lodge, 1783 Holbert Cove Rd., Saluda; (828) 749-4951; saludamountain lodge.com

Restaurants: Drake House Restaurant, 511 N. Howard Ave. (US 176 North), Landrum; (864) 457-2533; www.drakehouselandrumsc.com. Open daily 11 a.m. to 2:30 p.m.

Hare & Hound Pub, 101 E. Rutherford St., Landrum; (864) 457-3232. Open daily 11 a.m. to 10 p.m.

23 Blue Wall Preserve

This easy day hike takes you through most of the Nature Conservancy's Blue Wall Preserve. Along the route you will pass by two small ponds called "twin ponds" and explore the surrounding hardwood, pine, and shrubland forest. A looping spur trail leads to a beautiful waterfall that drops 20 feet into a small pool.

Start: From the upper parking lot at the end of Doug Hill Road

Distance: 3.4-mile lollipop

Hiking time: About 2 hours

Difficulty: Easy due to length and light elevation gains

Trail surface: Gravel road, dirt path, forested trail

Best seasons: Early spring and late fall for cooler temperatures and wildflowers. Good in winter for cool temperatures and bird watching.

Other trail users: Hikers only

Canine compatibility: Leashed dogs permitted

Fees and permits: None

Schedule: Open during daylight hours year-round

Maps: TOPO! CD: North Carolina–South Carolina; USGS maps: Tigerville-Saluda, South Carolina

Trail contacts: The Nature Conservancy, 27 Cleveland St., Greenville, SC 29601; (864) 233-4988

Finding the trailhead: From I-26 to exit 1 (SC 14), turn west toward Landrum and travel 2.6 miles. Turn right on Mountain View Road and continue through the stop sign onto Blue Mill Road. At the fire station turn right on Oak Grove Road and drive 0.9 mile to Lake Road. Turn right on Lake Road and drive 1.2 miles to the stop sign. Turn left onto Lakeshore Drive, go around Lake Lanier, and turn left onto Doug Hill Road. Turn left again onto Pennel Road. Park vehicles in the upper parking lot and walk down the road to the information kiosk at the Palmetto Trailhead. GPS: N35 10.968' / W82 15.166'

The Hike

A bridge that crosses Vaughn Creek has been deemed impassable by vehicles. Therefore, you must park your vehicle at the upper parking lot and hike the extra 0.4 mile to the lower parking lot and the actual trailhead to the network of trails within the Blue Wall Preserve. The hike along the descending gravel road is pleasant and still passes through a dense forest, so you'll still feel as if you are on a hike through the woods, even while hiking along the road to the trailhead. The entrance to the preserve and the trailhead is marked by a large kiosk and sign. The Blue Wall Preserve is managed by the South Carolina chapter of the Nature Conservancy. You can access the preserve from the east at the trailhead on Doug Hill Road or from the west at the trailhead at the intersection of the Poinsett Reservoir Passage and the Blue Wall Preserve Passage at Vaughn's Gap.

Acquired in 1997 by the Nature Conservancy, the preserve is comprised of a patchwork of 20,000 acres that provides an important habitat for wildlife and flora of

Twin Pond along the Blue Wall Passage Trail in the Blue Wall Preserve

the southern Appalachian Blue Ridge Escarpment. The preserve is a favorite among bird enthusiasts. Bring your binoculars and look for the 114 bird species that have been spotted in the preserve, which has been deemed an Important Bird Area by the Audubon Society. Some of the birds that you may encounter include the Canada goose, blue-headed vireo, ruby-throated hummingbird, broad-winged hawk, mourning dove, brown thrasher, wood thrush, Carolina wren, downy woodpecker, Carolina chickadee, chimney swift, and the pileated woodpecker, just to name a few. You may also notice some impactive management of the preserve as the Nature Conservancy continues to work toward eradicating destructive invasive plant species such as kudzu, multiflora rose, English ivy, and princess tree.

The trail reaches the first of the twin ponds and an optional spur trail to the left leads to a very nice stream. Staying straight along the northern edge of the pond, the trail reaches a junction with a loop trail that circles around the second pond and makes a stop at a lovely 20-foot waterfall along the way. This trail occasionally veers away from the edge of the pond and traverses through a mix of hardwood and pine forest and several low-lying bogs and scrubland areas. The trail returns to the pond and follows along the southern edge of the pond before reaching an intersection with

Blue Wall Preserve

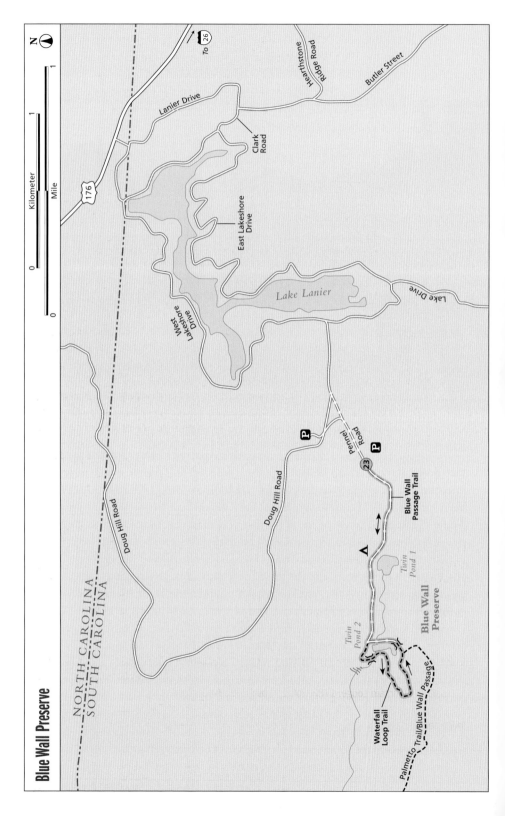

the Blue Wall Passage Trail. If you want to make this hike longer, you can turn right here and follow the Blue Wall Passage Trail 2 miles to the Vaughn's Gap Trailhead.

To stay on the recommended route, turn left and follow the Blue Wall Passage Trail along the eastern edge of the pond and return to the junction with the start of the loop trail. Turn right and retrace your steps back to the trailhead, then ascend the gravel road back to the upper parking lot.

Miles and Directions

0.0 Start from the upper parking lot at the end of Doug Hill Road. Walk down the gravel Poinsett Road toward the lower parking lot and the entrance to the preserve.

0.4 The lower parking lot and the trailhead to the preserve is marked by a kiosk and a large sign for the preserve.

0.9 An interpretive plaque sits at the northeastern edge of the first of the twin ponds. A spur trail to the left leads to a stream. Stay straight on the dirt path heading toward the second of the twin ponds.

1.3 Arrive at a trail junction. Stay to the right and start the beginning of the loop trail that leads to the falls.

1.4 Cross the wooden bridge that spans the rocky stream. In 75 feet you'll reach a spur trail that leads to a small waterfall 30 feet away. Once you arrive at the falls, turn around and retrace your steps back to the main loop trail. Turn right on the loop trail and continue along the loop trail back toward the pond.

2.0 Reach the trail junction with the Palmetto Trail. The Blue Wall Passage Trail continues to the right and leads to Vaughn's Gap. Turn left, continue to loop around the eastern side of the pond, and head back to the junction with the beginning of the loop trail. In 250 feet you'll cross a small bridge over a stream that is an outlet of the pond.

2.2 Arrive back at the junction with the beginning of the loop trail. Turn right and follow the Blue Wall Passage Trail back to the parking lot where you started.

3.4 Arrive back at the upper parking lot where you started.

Hike Information

Local Information: Greenville Chamber of Commerce, 24 Cleveland St., Greenville, SC 29601; (864) 242-1050

Local Events/Attractions: Greenville Zoo, 150 Cleveland Park Dr., Greenville; (864) 467-4300

Falls Park, West Camperdown Way, Greenville. Open 7 a.m. to 9 p.m. daily; free admission

Lodging: Red Horse Inn, 45 Winstons Chase Ct., Landrum; (864) 895-4968; theredhorseinn.com

Saluda Mountain Lodge, 1783 Holbert Cove Rd., Saluda; (828) 749-4951; saludamountainlodge.com

Restaurants: Drake House Restaurant, 511 N. Howard Ave. (US 176 North), Landrum; (864) 457-2533; www.drakehouselandrumsc .com. Daily 11 a.m. to 2:30 p.m.

Hare & Hound Pub, 101 E. Rutherford St., Landrum; (864) 457-3232. Daily 11 a.m. to 10 p.m.

Organizations: The Nature Conservancy, 27 Cleveland St., Greenville, SC 29601; (864) 233-4988

24 Paris Mountain State Park

This hike combines six trails within Paris Mountain State Park to create a challenging 5.4-mile loop. One of the most popular routes in the park, this trail begins with a descent to Buckhorn Creek. A steep climb takes you to Reservoir 3, where the trail follows across the top of the concrete dam. A spur trail leads to the site of the original fire tower. Enjoy walking mountain ridges with partially obstructed views of the surrounding mountains. The old-growth trees in this forest are remarkable. The trail is challenging, with lots of ups and downs, but the experience is well worth the work.

Start: Buckhorn Gate parking lot
Distance: 5.4-mile loop
Hiking time: About 3 hours
Difficulty: Strenuous due to distance and elevation changes
Trail surface: Dirt trail
Best seasons: Mar–May before the hot temperatures of the summer arrive, and Sept–Nov to enjoy the cool weather of the fall and the turning of the leaves
Other trail users: Mountain bikers share all of the trails with hikers on this loop except the southern section of the Brissy Ridge Trail. The trails are closed to mountain bikers on Sat. The trail is also very popular with runners.
Canine compatibility: Leashed dogs permitted
Land status: State park

Fees and permits: Free for kids under age 16; small fee for age 16 and over; senior discount available
Schedule: Daily 8 a.m. to 9 p.m. during daylight saving time, daily 8 a.m. to 6 p.m. remainder of the year
Maps: TOPO! CD: North Carolina–South Carolina; USGS maps: Paris Mountain and Greenville, South Carolina
Trail contacts: Paris Mountain State Park, 2401 State Park Rd., Greenville, SC 29609; (864) 244-5565; www.southcarolinaparks .com/parismountain
Other: There is a large campground near the state park entrance with 39 sites, 13 with tent pads. Each site has water and electric hookup and access to bathrooms with hot showers.

Finding the trailhead: From I-385 take exit 40 onto North Pleasantburg Road (SC 291) for approximately 4 miles. Turn right onto Piney Mountain Road. Go to the first light and turn right onto State Park Road. Follow for 2 miles and then turn left into the park entrance. Pay the entrance fee at the entrance station and continue straight through the state park until you reach the Buckhorn Gate parking lot on the left. GPS: N34 56.445'/W82 23.506'

The Hike

Named after Richard Paris, the first white European to settle in the Greenville area, preservation of the mountain began as early as 1890. Paris Mountain State Park was formally established in 1923 during the Great Depression. Most of the artfully constructed stone and wood structures within the park were built by Civilian Conservation Corps (CCC) members. The park is 5 miles north of Greenville, and the mountain rises from the piedmont some 15 to 20 miles south from where

Paddlers explore Lake Placid, Paris Mountain's swimming lake in the south end of the park.

the mountains actually begin. Paris Mountain is considered a monadnock, a single mountain that stands alone. Monadnocks are created when a massive rock resists the weathering and erosion of the surrounding mountains. When you first enter the park, one of the most stunning features you will notice is the large number of towering old-growth trees found in the forest. The steep slopes of the mountain made the trees inaccessible to lumber operations before its preservation.

The trailhead begins at the Buckhorn Gate parking lot, where many trails and roads intersect, making it very easy to get confused. The kiosk for the trailhead is at the junction of the yellow-blazed northbound section of the Brissy Ridge Trail and the white-blazed westbound Sulphur Springs Trail. However, for this hike you will follow the eastbound section of the yellow-blazed Brissy Ridge Trail and hike a loop in a counterclockwise direction. The trail begins on the east side of the parking lot at a brown sign labeled Brissy Ridge Trail.

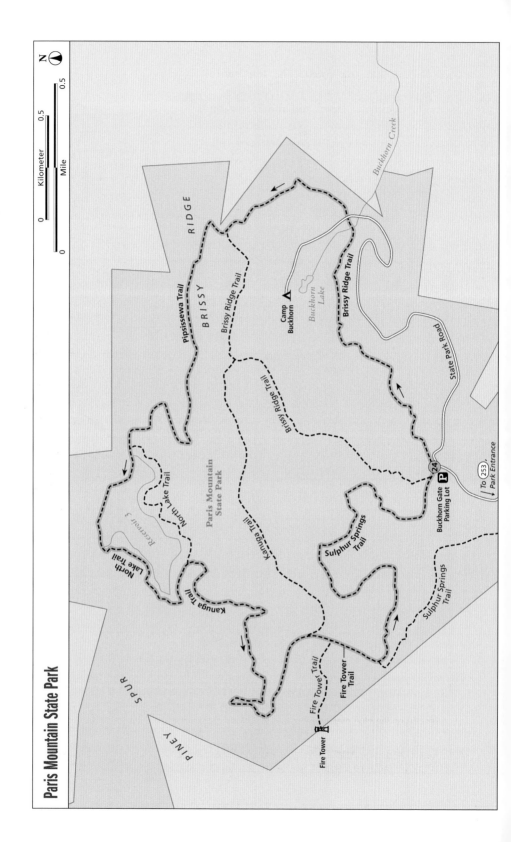

Paris Mountain State Park

The rocky, rooted, thin trail descends steeply through a pine and oak forest. The trail twice crosses Buckhorn Creek, where you will find a thick mix of mountain laurel and rhododendron crowding the creek banks. The park is dominated by Virginia pine, but you can also find honeysuckle and arbutus, also known as strawberry tree for its red edible fruits. Along the trail you may encounter deer, skunks, squirrels, and a variety of birds. Occasionally a black bear is seen in the park, but these sightings are rare. And fortunately, most of the snakes within the park are nonvenomous. But keep an eye out for venomous copperheads, which are sometimes seen along the trail.

▶ **Many of the pine trees in Paris Mountain State Park have fallen due to a massive pine beetle infestation that occurred during the early 2000s.**

After 0.8 mile you cross the park's main road and begin a very steep 0.4-mile ascent up to a T junction with the Pipsissewa Trail. Turn right (northeast) and continue the climb up to a ridge and then follow the rocky, dirt path that descends to Reservoir 3, a man-made lake that once served as a source of drinking water for the city of Greenville. This route passes by four of the five backcountry campsites that are found along the lakeshore, making this an excellent trek for backpackers looking for a short weekend trip or an extended backcountry fishing trip. The reservoir is stocked with bass, brim, and catfish. A South Carolina fishing license is required.

Follow the Pipsissewa Trail for 1.0 mile until you reach the junction with the North Lake Trail, which is blazed with blue markings. Turn right (west) onto the North Lake Trail. Enjoy the level 0.7-mile hike along this well-marked trail that borders the reservoir before you reach the junction with the Kanuga Trail. Turn right (southwest) and begin the steepest climb of the loop, which reaches an optional spur trail leading to the remains of an old fire tower near a cleared mountaintop. Unfortunately, you can no longer climb the tower. Follow the blue-marked Fire Tower Trail for 0.2 mile. The Fire Tower Trail seamlessly becomes the white-blazed Sulphur Springs Trail, which goes over a few small hills before descending steeply, widening over 1.1 miles, and returning to the Buckhorn Gate parking lot where you began your hike.

Miles and Directions

0.0   Start from the Buckhorn Gate parking lot. The trailhead is on the east side of the parking lot and marked with a wooden sign that says "Brissy Ridge Trail."

0.8   Cross paved State Park Road and continue on yellow-blazed Brissy Ridge Trail.

1.3   Reach T junction with the green-blazed Pipsissewa Trail. Turn right (northeast).

2.3   Reach the junction with the purple-blazed North Lake Trail. Turn right (west).

3.0   Reach junction with the red-blazed Kanuga Trail. Turn right (southwest).

4.1   Reach junction with Fire Tower Spur Trail. Stay right (southwest). After 300 feet stay left (south) on the blue-marked Fire Tower Trail. The trail becomes the white-blazed eastbound Sulphur Springs Trail that leads back to the Buckhorn Gate parking lot where you started.

5.4   Reach the Buckhorn Gate parking lot where you began the hike. (***Option:*** Extend this hike by 0.5 mile by taking the blue-blazed, westbound Fire Tower Trail to the site of the old fire tower.)

Hike Information

Local Information: Upcountry South Carolina Visitor Center; 500 E. North St., Greenville, SC 29602; (864) 233-2690; www.upcountrysc.com

Greenville Visitor Center, 206 S. Main St., City Hall Lobby, Greenville, SC 29601; (864) 233-0461; www.greenvillecvb.com

Local Events/Attractions: Music in the Woods, Paris Mountain State Park, 2401 State Park Rd., Greenville; (864) 244-5565; www.pmspf.org/new/pages/music.htm. A family-friendly acoustic music festival at the park's amphitheater, held Saturday nights in the summer

Lodging: The Magnolia Inn, 426 S. Main St., Travelers Rest; (864) 884-1808; www.magnolia inntr.com. Historic home converted into an inn, on 2 acres located 1 mile west of Paris Mountain State Park

Rustic Cabins at Paris Mountain State Park, 2401 State Park Rd., Greenville; (864) 244-5565. Ten cabins are located in the park, each equipped with two sets of bunk beds. No air-conditioning. Heat is available in winter. Hot showers on-site

Restaurants: Sassafras Southern Bistro, 2 W. Coffee St., Greenville; (864) 235-5670; sassafrasbistro.com. Downtown Greenville's award-winning fine-dining Southern comfort food menu. Try the shrimp and grits with beignets for dessert.

Bucky's Bar-B-Q, 1326 N. Pleasantburg Dr., Greenville; (864) 244-5114; buckysbbq.com. Tasty Southern barbecue platters at a low price. Great for families or anyone on a budget

Organizations: Upstate Forever, 507 Pettigru St., Greenville, SC 29601; (864) 250-0500; upstateforever.org. This organization promotes sensible growth and protects special places in the upstate region of South Carolina.

Honorable Mentions

A Opossum Creek Trail

If you find yourself on the far western edge of Oconee County, you can enjoy this wonderful 4.5-mile loop hike that leads to a tall waterfall along Opossum Creek. The trail is located near the town of Long Creek, just a few miles from the Georgia border. Since the hiking trail does not connect to the nearby Chattooga River Trail system, this hike is often less crowded than the other trails in this mountainous region of South Carolina, which is extremely popular with hikers. So if you're searching for a little solitude in this region, this hike may be a good choice.

Starting from the parking lot and trailhead along Turkey Ridge Road, the well-maintained trail gradually descends to the edge of the Chattooga River and enters into the Chattooga Wild and Scenic River area. Along this section of the river, the descent is rather steep. However, switchbacks and masterful trail planning have made the descent as easy as possible given the steep terrain.

Along the descent to the Chattooga River, the trail ventures through the Camp Branch Valley, crossing several tributaries and following along an old roadbed for much of the way. After 1.8 miles from the trailhead, you will be able to hear the rapids and splashing of the Chattooga River, and 2.0 miles from the trailhead, you will reach the Chattooga River at a point where the river makes a big bend toward the west. Right on the edge of the river, you arrive at a beautiful sandy beach that is the perfect spot for a rest or lunch. Directly in front of the sandy beach is an excellent swimming hole. I highly recommend taking a dip in the river, especially on a hot summer day.

After enjoying the river, turn left and continue on the Opossum Creek Trail, which continues to follow alongside Opossum Creek. After crossing Camp Branch Creek, the trail becomes considerably more rocky. At points you will find yourself hiking over boulders before reaching the base of Opossum Creek Falls. From the base of the falls, you have several excellent boulders for sitting, resting, and taking in the excellent view of the beautiful multitiered waterfall.

B Sulphur Springs Loop

This moderately difficult 4.0-mile loop hike is an excellent choice for hikers looking to further explore Paris Mountain State Park. The park is one of the most popular parks for hiking in all of South Carolina, and I highly recommend that you take the time and make a trek on one or more of the extremely well-maintained and excellent trails in the large trail system found within this park. This is also an excellent area to train for long-distance backpacking trips that may take you through more challenging terrain. The hilly ascents and descents found on this trail are a great place to get in shape and become prepared for the more challenging hikes in the far western

Appalachian Mountains and beyond. Some of the highlights along this hike include a stop at Mountain Lake, a trek past cascades on Paris Mountain, and some fairly nice views from the peak of the mountain.

Starting from the trailhead at Sulphur Springs Picnic Area, you will find two artfully constructed stone picnic pavilions that are a wonderful place to enjoy lunch or a snack before or after your hike. Then again, the peak of Paris Mountain is definitely another great choice for a picnic as well. The trail starts by following Sulphur Springs through a lush forest filled with rhododendron and pine and hickory trees. You cross two bridges spanning Sulphur Springs before reaching a beautiful gazebo. If you are looking for a very short and picturesque trek during a visit to Paris State Park, you may want to consider a there-and-back journey to this gazebo along Sulphur Springs Creek. To continue on the Sulphur Springs Loop, you simply follow the trail uphill and quickly arrive at the Mountain Lake dam. You will follow the stone steps that lead around the dam and follow the trail as it traverses along the lake's edge.

After 0.7 mile from the trailhead, you leave the lakeshore and ascend toward the peak of Paris Mountain, following alongside the creek once again. After 1.0 mile you pass through a section of trail with several cascades rolling over rock slab. At 1.5 mile you reach the junction with the spur trail that leads to the old fire tower. You are no longer able to climb the fire tower so I recommend that you continue straight on the Sulphur Springs Trail and continue climbing until you reach the foundation of the old tower foundation as well as the foundation and chimney of the old fire-tower keeper's home. The only thing remaining now of the old house is a few brick chimneys and the foundation. You may be tempted to stop and enjoy the limited views of the surrounding mountains and rolling hills, but keep going. The views are much better when you reach the high point of the trail, very near the actual peak of the mountain, just down the trail. From the high point of the trail, the path dips down then climbs again to a small knob with a nice overlook before steeply descending back to the Sulphur Springs picnic area and the trailhead where you began your hike.

POISON IVY AND POISON SUMAC

These skin irritants can be found throughout South Caroline and come in the form of a bush or a vine, having leaflets in groups of three, five, seven, or nine. Learn how to spot the plants. The oil they secrete can cause an allergic reaction in the form of blisters, usually about twelve hours after exposure. The itchy rash can last from ten days to several weeks. The best defense against these irritants is to wear clothing that covers the arms, legs, and torso. There are also nonprescription lotions you can apply to exposed skin that guard against the effects of poison ivy and poison sumac and can be washed off with soap and water.

If you think you were in contact with the plants, after hiking (or even on the trail during longer hikes), wash with soap and water. Taking a hot shower with soap after you return home will also help to remove any lingering oil from your skin.

Should you contract a rash from any of these plants, use an antihistamine to reduce the itching and apply a topical lotion to dry up the area. If the rash spreads, consult your doctor.

Midlands

The sixteen hikes featured in this section explore a diversity of terrains that range from the hilly trails in Sumter National Forest in the western part of the state and the flat and easy treks through Congaree National Park in the central part of the state, to the paths that take you through the Sandhills belt near Cheraw and South Carolina's northwestern border. Stretching across the central part of the state, the Midlands region is part of what is known as the Piedmont geologic province. While South Carolinians generally refer to this area as part of the Upcountry, the Midlands trails in this book are categorized as the trails you find in the less mountainous terrain of South Carolina between the mountains and the coast. The northern portion of the Midlands features trails that traverse a rolling and hilly landscape. In this region you will find remnants of the ancient mountain ranges in the form of monadnocks, isolated hills and mountains made of rock that remained after the surrounding land was eroded away. Parson's Mountain, located near the western border of the state between Greenville and Columbia, is an excellent example of a monadnock. More-challenging hikes in this area can be found throughout the region. For example, at Poinsett State Park and Kings Mountain, you will find steep hills and challenging ravines even though the parks are a great distance away from each other.

Across the center of the state, you will find the Sandhills region. Twenty million years ago, during the Miocene epoch, this was the coastline. The "sandhills" of this region are actually ancient sand dunes that were built to astounding heights due to the length of time that this location served as coastline. The best example of the Sandhills region can be found by exploring the Carolina Sandhills National Wildlife Refuge, which aims to protect some of the remaining longleaf pine ecosystem of this fascinating landscape.

◀ *Fall boldly displays its colors in the forest around Lick Fork Lake (hike 26).*

25 Parson's Mountain

An easy day hike in the Parson's Mountain Recreation Area takes you around Parson's Mountain Lake. Highlights include the lake and a crossing atop the dam at the southeastern side of the lake. You can extend the length of the trail and get a more challenging hike by walking the optional spur trail that takes you past abandoned gold mines and to the base of the fire lookout tower at the summit of Parson's Mountain.

Start: The trailhead to the right side of the first parking lot on Parson's Mountain Lake
Distance: 1.7-mile loop
Hiking time: About 1 hour
Difficulty: Easy due to length and small elevation gains
Trail surface: Forested trail, dirt path, paved road
Best seasons: Early spring and late fall for cooler temperatures and wildflowers. Good in winter for cool temperatures and bird watching.
Other trail users: Hikers only
Canine compatibility: Leashed dogs permitted

Fees and permits: Small daily fee per OHV operator; annual pass available. Also good for Cedar Springs, Enoree, and Wambaw cycle trails. There is a significant fine for illegal trespass.
Maps: TOPO! CD: North Carolina-South Carolina; USGS maps: Verdery, South Carolina; USFS maps: Parson's Mountain Recreation Area Map, Long Cane Ranger Station
Trail contacts: Sumter National Forest, Long Cane Ranger District, 810 Buncombe St., Edgefield, SC 29824; (803) 637-5396

Finding the trailhead: From Abbeville drive southwest on SC 72 for approximately 1.4 miles, then turn left onto SC 28. Drive 2.2 miles on SC 28 and turn left onto Parson's Mountain Road. Follow Parson's Mountain Road for 1.5 miles, then turn right onto Campground Road. Follow Campground Road for 1.2 miles until you reach the trailhead and parking lot on the right. GPS: N34 05.853' / W82 21.458'

The Hike

You don't have to climb to the top of Parson's Mountain to enjoy the park. A quick hike around Parson's Mountain Lake gives you the opportunity to circle around the beautiful lake and explore some of the surrounding forests. Along the hike you will traverse through bottom and upland hardwood forest and pass through pine and scrub oak sections of woods. In spring and summer you are likely to see wildflowers like sparkleberry, wild ginger, and redbud growing in the forest, along the trailside, and around the lakeshore. Geologists consider the mountain a monadnock, which is a high point of rock that has resisted the erosion that has washed away the surrounding landscape.

Beautiful fall foliage along the Parson's Mountain Trail.

Parson's Mountain Lake at sunset

From the first parking lot on the lake, follow the concrete steps down to the paved path. There are restrooms just to the right. Follow the paved path to the lakeshore. This lake has a no-motor rule so the only background noise you will hear will likely be from other campers and hikers in the area and the occasional four-wheeler on one of the four-wheeler trails in the park. During hunting season the surrounding national forest is a popular hunting ground, so you may want to exercise caution and wear bright clothing. From the lakeshore follow the paved path to the right, then follow the path along the lakeshore to a small wooden sign that marks the start of the Parson's Mountain Lake Trail. After 0.1 mile you cross over an earthen bank that was created when the man-made lake was constructed. This portion of the trail can be severely overgrown during the summer. Tall grasses and dense shrubs grow very well on the lakeshore here, and the trail can be obscured by the thick vegetation. Luckily there isn't much of anywhere else you can go without ending up in the water, which is located on both sides of the bank. Watch out for snakes if the trail is severely overgrown, as they like to hang around the edges of the lake. Cross the earthen bank and then cross the short wooden bridge that spans a tributary that flows into the lake. To your left is a great view of the surrounding lake and forest.

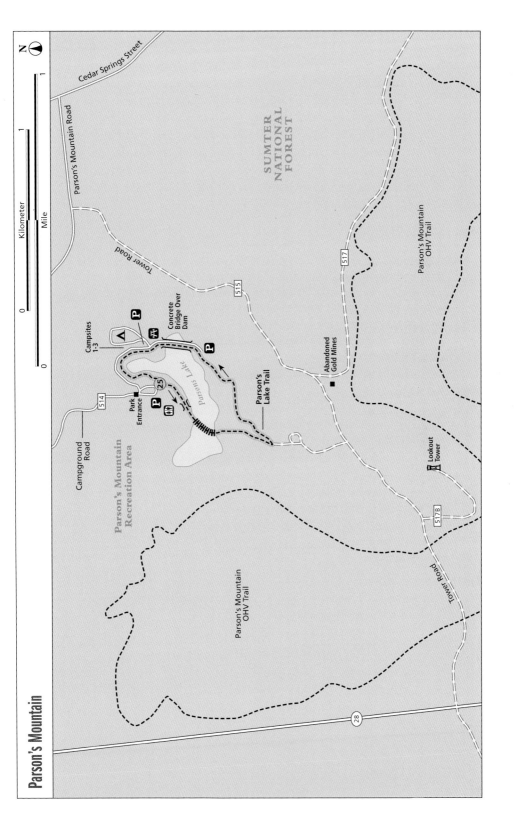

Parson's Mountain

N

Kilometer
0 · · · 1

Mile
0 · · · 1

Cedar Springs Street

Parson's Mountain Road

Tower Road

Campground Road

514

Park
Entrance

Parson's Mountain
Recreation Area

Campsites
1-3

P

P

25

Parsons Lake

Concrete
Bridge Over
Dam

515

Parson's
Lake Trail

SUMTER
NATIONAL
FOREST

517

Abandoned
Gold Mines

Parson's Mountain
OHV Trail

Parson's Mountain
OHV Trail

Lookout
Tower

517B

Tower Road

28

The trail enters into a bottomland hardwood forest and ascends an old road-bed to a junction with a spur trail. If you turn right here, the spur trail will gently ascend to the top of Parson's Mountain and past several abandoned gold mines that are really no more than just holes in the ground. The view from the top of Parson's Mountain is quite nice, and on a clear day you can see for miles. Staying to the left, the Parson's Mountain Lake Trail continues around the southern edge of the lake. You reach a parking lot and trailhead for the Parson's Mountain Trail and then follow the paved road across the dam on the eastern edge of the lake, before veering to the right and returning to a forested trail that returns to the parking lot and trailhead where you started.

Miles and Directions

0.0 Start from the first parking lot on Parson's Mountain Lake. Follow the paved path down the steps, past the restrooms on the right, and to the edge of the lake. Follow the path to the right. After 100 feet you reach the trailhead marked by a small wooden sign. Follow the dirt path that follows alongside the lake and enters into the forest.

0.1 Cross the wooden bridge that spans a tributary of the lake that flows into a smaller arm of the lake to the right of the trail. The trail can be overgrown in the summer. Watch for snakes along this portion of the trail.

0.2 Cross a boardwalk spanning a seasonal stream.

0.5 Reach a trail junction with the Fire Tower Trail. Stay to the left on the Lake Trail.

1.0 Arrive at a parking lot and alternate trailhead for the hiking trails. Cross the parking lot and follow the paved road across the short dam at the southeast edge of Parson's Mountain Lake.

1.2 Pass the lakeshore picnic area on the right side of the paved road.

1.4 Campsites 1 through 3 are on the right and left sides of the paved road. About 150 feet from the campsites, you'll reach a junction on the right side of the road with an unpaved trail. Follow the forested trail toward the lakeshore.

1.7 Arrive at the parking lot and trailhead where you started.

Hike Information

Lodging: Parson's Mountain Recreation Area, 454 Parson's Mountain Rd., Abbeville. Open 6 a.m. to 10 p.m. for campers and recreation use, trails close at sunset; closed Nov 16 to Apr 30. www.fs.usda.gov/scnfs

26 Lick Fork Lake

This easy hike circles around Lick Fork Lake and explores the surrounding pine and hardwood forest. Along the route you will cross Lick Fork Creek twice, including one crossing where you hop across the large rocks of the streambed. The no-gas-motor rule on the lake gives hikers the opportunity to hear the sounds of birds and other wildlife in the forest as they circumnavigate the lakeshore.

Start: Paved parking lot at the end of CR 392
Distance: 1.7-mile loop
Hiking time: About 1 hour
Difficulty: Easy due to length and small elevation changes
Trail surface: Forested path
Best seasons: Early spring and late fall for cooler temperatures and wildflowers
Other trail users: Hikers only
Canine compatibility: Leashed dogs permitted

Fees and permits: Small fee per car per day; annual pass available
Schedule: Dawn-dusk daily; closed Dec 15 through Apr 1
Maps: TOPO! CD: North Carolina-South Carolina; USGS maps: Colliers, South Carolina; USFS maps: Lick Fork Lake Recreation Area, Long Cane Ranger Stations
Trail contacts: Sumter National Forest, Long Cane Ranger District, 810 Buncombe St., Edgefield, SC 29324; (803) 637-5396

Finding the trailhead: From exit 1 on I-20 at North Augusta, go north on SC 230 through Colliers. Approximately 3 miles past Colliers, turn right onto Edgefield County S-19-263, Lick Fork Road. Follow Lick Fork Road for 2 miles; turn right onto CR 392 at the entrance to the Lick Fork Lake Recreation Area. Follow CR 392 for 0.2 mile and park in the north parking area. Walk through the picnic area to the lake and look to the right for the trailhead sign to the Lick Fork Lake Trail. GPS: N33 43.767'/W82 02.475'

The Hike

The Lick Fork Lake Recreation Area may only be 12 acres, but sometimes good things come in small packages. One of the best features of the park is Lick Fork Lake. The Lick Fork Hiking Trail circles around this lake and occasionally veers away from the lakeshore and gives you the opportunity to experience the hardwood and pine forest of the park. There is one other trail in the park, the Horn Creek Trail, which intersects twice with the Lick Fork Hiking Trail. The longer Horn Creek Trail gives you the opportunity to further explore the forest of the park and is more popular with mountain bikers than the Lick Fork Lake Hiking Trail.

The Lick Fork Lake Hiking Trail begins at the first parking lot after the park entrance. There is not a particularly distinct trailhead at this parking lot for the trail. Simply follow the paved path past the picnic area and down to the edge of the lake. A roped-off swimming area and small beach on the lakeshore are a welcome site on a hot South Carolina summer day and the swimming area is a great spot to jump in

A pier extends into Lick Fork Lake.

the lake and cool off before and after your hike on the nature trail. At the lakeshore veer left and cross the long wooden bridge that spans an arm of the lake. The trail stays alongside the lakeshore, but there are several different paths along this section of the trail that you can take to get to a pier and observation deck that extends into the lake and offers excellent views of the lake and the surrounding forest. Notice that there are no motorboats on this lake. The no-gas-motors rule on the lake keeps the lake peaceful and quiet, making this the perfect location for a quiet hike around the lake. Adding to the wilderness experience is the fact that the park is rarely very crowded, with exception maybe to the beach area. You are likely to be the only one on the trail and can often find some nice solitude on this trail.

Along the hike during the spring and fall, a variety of wildflowers, ferns, and wild blackberries line the trail and fill the understory of the forest, which is mostly comprised of pine, oak, red maple, and dogwood trees. Wildlife that you may

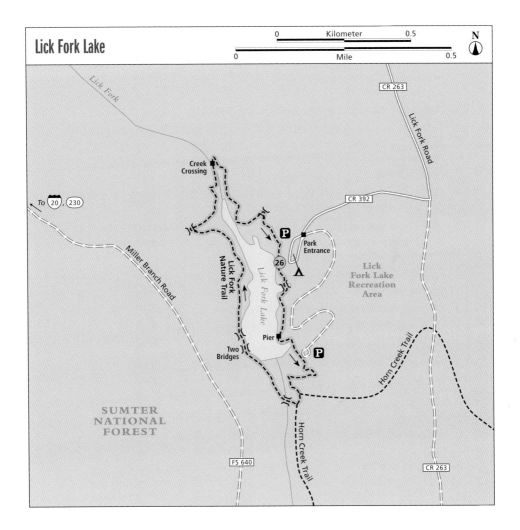

encounter includes deer, squirrels, turtles, frogs, and a variety of birds such as pine warblers, nuthatches, and red-cockaded woodpeckers. After crossing through the parking lot for the Horn Creek Trail, the Lick Fork Lake Hiking Trail circles around the southern end of Lick Fork Lake and follows along the western side of the lake. Small wooden bridges provide crossings for streams that are dry most of the year. At the northern end of the lake, you must rock-hop across the large rocks in Lick Fork Lake. These rocks are often slippery and slick, so make sure that you have good footwear with excellent grip for this creek crossing. From here the trail veers sharply to the right and gently ascends back to the parking lot and the swimming area where you started.

Miles and Directions

0.0 Start from the paved parking lot at the end of CR 392. Follow the paved path past the picnic area. The paved path ends at the lake and the trail splits. Turn left and follow the dirt trail along the lakeshore.

0.1 Cross a long wooden bridge that spans an arm of the lake.

0.2 A pier with an observation and fishing deck, as well as excellent views, extends out into the lake. The trail becomes paved and in 400 feet you arrive at the parking lot and trailhead for the Horn Creek Trail. Walk through the parking lot. A kiosk marks the start of the Horn Creek Trail.

0.3 The trail splits at a trail junction 150 feet from the kiosk. The Horn Creek Trail is to the left. Stay to the right on the Lick Fork Lake Hiking Trail.

0.5 Cross the wooden bridge spanning a seasonal stream. The trail begins to follow alongside the creek on your right. One hundred feet from the bridge, the trail splits. The Horn Creek Trail is to the left. Stay to the right on the Lick Fork Lake Hiking Trail.

0.7 Cross the wooden bridge spanning a seasonal stream. Then cross another bridge over a seasonal stream in just 150 feet.

1.1 Cross the wooden bridge spanning a seasonal stream.

1.3 Large rocks in the streambed allow you to easily cross the creek.

1.6 Cross the wooden bridge spanning a seasonal stream.

1.7 Arrive at the parking lot and picnic area where you started.

Hike Information

Local Information: Edgefield County Chamber of Commerce, 416 Calhoun St., Johnston, SC 29832; (803) 275-0010

Local Events/Attractions: Jane Bess Pottery, 206 Lynch St., Edgefield; (803) 637-2434

Magnolia Dale, 320 Norris St., Edgefield; (803) 637-2233. This historic home built in 1830 is now home to the Edgefield County Historical Society. Open by appointment only

Lodging: Camping at Lick Fork Lake Recreation Area, 256 Lick Fork Lake Rd., Edgefield. Small parking and nightly camping fees required. First-come, first-served

Edgefield Inn, 702 Augusta Rd., Edgefield; (803) 637-2001

Restaurants: Old Edgefield Grill, 202 Penn St., Edgefield; (803) 637-3222. Open Tues–Sat 11 a.m. to 2 p.m. and Wed–Sun 5 to 9 p.m.

10 Governors Café, 303 Main St., Edgefield; (803) 637-9050; tengovernorscafe.com

Organizations: Sumter National Forest, Long Cane Ranger District, 810 Buncombe St., Edgefield, SC 29324; (803) 637-5396

27 Palmetto Trail: Blackstock Battlefield Passage

Follow this interpretive trail along the Tyger River and through the site of the Battle of Blackstock, an important battle of the Revolutionary War that was fought on William Blackstock's farm. The trail begins with a short descent through a young forest of oak and pine to the banks of the Tyger River. You follow along the riverbank, hiking over gentle hills before ascending to an open field where the Blackstock farm once stood and the site where the battle occurred. A paved path encircles a picturesque monument placed on a high hill overlooking the open battlefield.

Start: Dirt parking lot on the right side of Battlefield Road
Distance: 1.3-mile loop
Hiking time: About 1 hour
Difficulty: Easy due to length and minimal elevation gain
Trail surface: Forested trail, old roadbed, dirt path, gravel road
Best seasons: Spring and fall for cooler temperatures and wildflowers

Other trail users: Hikers only
Canine compatibility: Leashed dogs permitted
Fees and permits: None
Schedule: Open year-round
Maps: TOPO! CD: North Carolina- South Carolina; USGS maps: Spartanburg and Greer/Wellford, South Carolina
Trail contacts: Palmetto Conservation Foundation, 722 King St., Columbia, SC 29205; (803) 771-0870; palmettoconservation.org

Finding the trailhead: From exit 44 on I-26: drive through Cross Anchor on SC 49 and enter Union County. Turn left onto Blackstock Road (Union County S-44-51), drive 1.6 miles, and turn right onto Monument Road. At the fork bear left onto Battlefield Road (maps may differ; follow street signs). The dirt parking lot is approximately 1 mile farther on the left. A kiosk marks the trailhead.

From Spartanburg: Drive south on SC 56 and cross over the Tyger River. Turn left onto Blackstock Road (Spartanburg County S-42-115). Drive 1.4 miles and turn left onto Monument Road. At the fork bear left onto Battlefield Road. The parking area is approximately 1 mile farther on the left. GPS: N34 05.124'/W80 54.442'

The Hike

Whether you are interested in the historical significance of this area or just want to take a nice walk in the woods, this is a wonderful, easy day hike that in a very short distance explores a significant diversity of landscapes. Starting with a short walk through a young forest of oak and pine, this well-maintained path built with the help of AmeriCorps volunteers quickly arrives at the bank of the Tyger River. The relatively tucked-away location of this hike is an advantage if you want to view birds or other wildlife along the trail, or if you simply want a little solitude. From the steep banks along the river, you will have the benefit of a bird's-eye view of the swiftly moving river, which is often teeming with wildlife, especially in the early morning

The Battlefield Monument pays tribute to the Battle of Blackstock, a significant conflict of the Revolutionary War and a victory for the Patriot forces.

hours. Keep an eye out for the white-tailed deer, turkeys, and great blue herons that are commonly seen around the river.

The forested trail follows alongside the Tyger River, and along this section you will traverse over several small hills. During the warmer months of the year, and especially after heavy spring rains, you are likely to see canoes and flat-bottom boats drifting down the river. Paddlers pass this area along the 24-mile Tyger River Canoe Trail. The river is mostly flat water; however, there is some notable whitewater in the upper sections of the river. If the water is at normal levels, after following along the river for 0.2 mile, you reach a small beach of sand and pebbles on the edge of the river. This is a great place to take a break, have a picnic, or just relax and listen to the sound of the river rushing through the forest. From this beach the trail gently descends to the edge of a large, open field. This is the original site of William Blackstock's farm and the site of the Blackstock Battlefield.

The Battle of Blackstock was fought on November 20, 1780, and was a significant victory for the Patriot Militia. The battle followed the major British defeat at Kings Mountain less than a month earlier and strengthened the momentum of the American forces. The Patriots also made significant advances that contributed to the British defeat at Cowpens. At the time of the battle, this large field had several log-built outbuildings. These buildings were not chinked between the logs. These spaces between the logs allowed the Patriot forces to stay protected inside the buildings and shoot through the spaces of the logs instead of engaging in the open-field warfare preferred by the British. This battlefield was the site where the Patriot General Thomas Sumter faced the previously undefeated British General Lieutenant Colonel Banastre Tarleton. When the battle was over, ninety-three of the British forces had been killed, and it is believed that seventy-five to one hundred men were wounded compared to the three American deaths and four American wounded, making the battle a decisive Patriot victory. Historian Henry Lumpkin wrote that the road to the ford was completely blocked with the bodies of dead soldiers, the wounded, and their horses.

The trail follows along the edge of the forest and cuts through the edge of the field. During the summer this section of the trail is often overgrown and can become obscured and difficult to follow. If you stay close to the edge of the forest, keeping the forest to your right, you'll have an easy time staying on the trail. Follow the gently ascending path through the field. As you reach the top of the hill, you will see the Battlefield Monument in the distance to your left. The monument sits atop a hill and is surrounded by a cluster of trees. Near the top of the hill, you reach a split in the trail marked by a split-rail fence on both sides of the trail where the Battlefield Trail enters back into the forest. Stay to the left and follow the gravel road to the Battlefield Monument on top of the hill, where you'll have a remarkable view of the surrounding battlefield. From here retrace your steps along the gravel road and back to the split-rail fence. Follow the Battlefield Trail back into the forest and descend to the parking lot and trailhead where you started.

Miles and Directions

0.0 Start from the dirt parking lot on the right side of Battlefield Road.

0.3 Reach the bank of the Tyger River. Follow the trail to the right alongside the river.

0.5 Enjoy the small, sandy beach on the left side of the trail on the edge of the river. The trail leaves the riverside and ascends along an old roadbed.

0.9 The trail enters into the large field and the site of the battle. The trail is often overgrown in the summer. Stay along the edge of the forest, keeping the forest to your right. To your right you can see the Battlefield Monument on the hill in the shade of the surrounding cluster of trees.

1.0 The dirt path splits. To the right a split-rail fence on both sides of the trail marks the junction where the Battlefield Trail reenters the forest. Stay to the left and follow the spur trail that leads to the gravel road that encircles the Battlefield Monument 250 feet away. Once you reach the Battlefield Monument, turn around and walk the 250 feet back to the split-rail fence and follow the Battlefield Trail into the forest.

1.3 Reach the parking lot and trailhead where you started.

Palmetto Trail: Blackstock Battlefield Passage

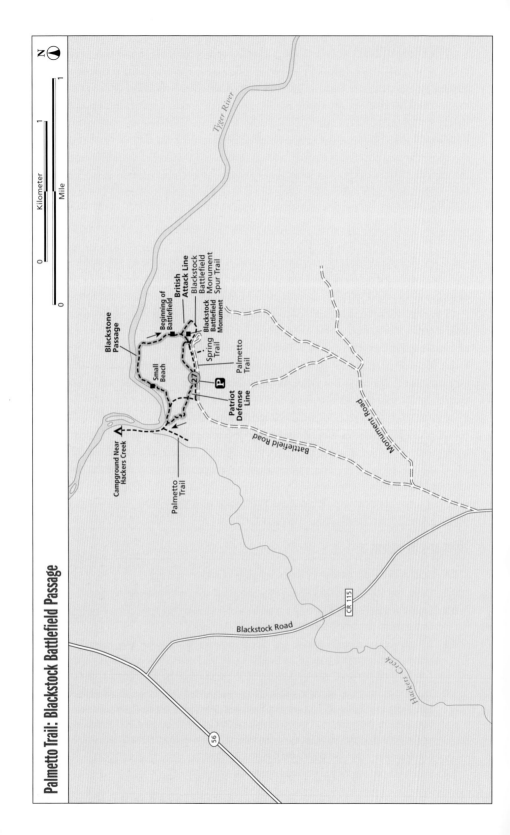

Hike Information

Local Information: Spartanburg Convention and Visitors Bureau, 105 N. Pine St., Spartanburg, SC 29302; www.visitspartanburg.com

Local Events/Attractions: BMW Zentrum Museum, 1400 Highway 101 S., Greer; www.bmwusfactory.com. Open daily. Group factory tours may resume in 2014

Lodging: Inn on Main B&B, 319 E. Main St., Spartanburg; (864) 585-5001; innonmainofspartanburg.com

Camping at Croft State Park, 450 Croft State Park Rd., Spartanburg; (864) 585-1283.

Restaurants: Lime Leaf Thai, 101 E. Main St., Spartanburg; (864) 542-2171; www.limeleaf101.com. Open daily at 11:30 a.m.

The Beacon Drive-In, 255 John B. White Sr. Blvd., Spartanburg; (864) 585-9387; beacondrivein.com. Open Mon–Sat at 9 a.m., Sun at 11 a.m.

Organizations: Palmetto Conservation Foundation, 722 King St., Columbia, SC 29205; (803) 771-0870; palmettoconservation.org

28 Buncombe Trail

This hike northwest of Columbia explores a short section of the Buncombe Trail through the Sumter National Forest. The hike traverses a mostly pine forest that is pleasantly hilly. Highlights include several stream crossings and opportunities for wildlife viewing. The forest has had ongoing logging activity in recent years, but the logging is suspended on weekends. Saturday and Sunday are exceptionally good days to explore this trail.

Start: From the Blue Trailhead
Distance: 8.0-mile out and back
Hiking time: About 3–6 hours
Difficulty: Easy to moderate due to length
Trail surface: Forested path, dirt road
Best season: Year-round
Other trail users: Equestrians and mountain bikes
Canine compatibility: Leashed dogs permitted
Fees and permits: Small per-vehicle fee

Schedule: Open year-round sunrise–sunset
Maps: TOPO! CD: North Carolina–South Carolina; USGS maps: Newberry NW; South Carolina; USFS maps: Buncombe Trail Map available at Enoree/Tyger Ranger District Stations within the Sumter National Forest
Trail contacts: Sumter National Forest, Enoree/Tyger Ranger District, 20 Work Center Rd., Whitmire, SC 29178; (803) 276-4810

Finding the trailhead: From I-26 take exit 60 (SC 66) and drive east for 3.5 miles. Turn right onto FR 358 and drive 0.3 mile. You will first pass the Buncombe Trailhead parking area on the left and Brickhouse Campground will be past it on the right. GPS: N34 27.055' / W81 42.253'

The Hike

You have a large number of opportunities to extend the length of this hike and create several different loops if you prefer a more challenging hike. The area is often referred to as the Buncombe Trail, but this is actually quite misleading. The forest surrounding the Brickhouse Campground contains a large network of trails and spur trails that are integrated into a much larger network of gravel and dirt roads. When you consider creating routes that include both trails and roads, the options become nearly limitless for loops and routes to explore this area. Primitive and disperse camping is also permitted along the trail unless it is otherwise posted, which makes this area a good option for backpacking if you don't have time to drive to the much more scenic and challenging trails in the more northwestern part of the state. The route that I recommend starts from the Brickhouse Campground and combines three trails to form a trip that gives you a great introduction to this region of the Sumter National Forest. No matter how far you choose to hike along the Buncombe Trail, the trail traverses over exceptionally hilly terrain that will pose only a small degree of challenge for well-conditioned hikers and crosses over seasonal streams and creeks that give hikers

A pine grove canopy along the Buncombe Trail

exploring the heavily forested region the sense that they are traversing though a more deep wilderness at times.

To hike the route I suggest in this book, you start from the trailhead for the Blue Trail. The kiosk is slightly misleading and confusing. While most kiosks are right next to the start of the trail, this kiosk is standing alone in a large grassy field without much direction to guide you toward the start of the trail. Regardless, the Blue Trail begins to the east of the kiosk. Follow the Blue Trail into the forest and cross several gravel roads to a junction with the Green Trail. Turn right and follow the Green Trail to the Red Trail. Turn right and follow the Red Trail to the junction with the Purple and Blue Trails. At this point most casual day hikers have experienced the beauty of the pine forests and would be ready to turn around or start heading back toward the parking lot. You have several options here. If you want the shortest way back to the trailhead, simply turn around and hike the way you came, taking the Red Trail to the Green Trail and then following the Green Trail to the west back to the Blue Trail, which leads to the parking lot. However, if you would like a slightly longer hike, turn right and follow the Blue Trail to the northwest on a winding trail that will take you back to the parking lot after passing through the campground.

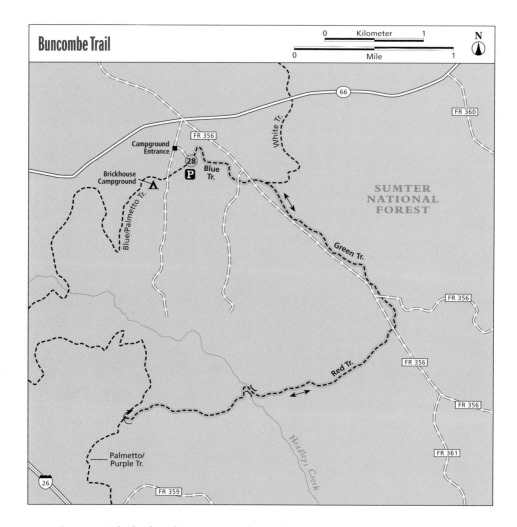

0   Kilometer   1

N

0   Mile   1

66

FR 360

FR 356

White Tr.

Campground
Entrance

28

Brickhouse
Campground

Blue
Tr.

P

SUMTER
NATIONAL
FOREST

Blue/Palmetto Tr.

Green Tr.

FR 356

Red Tr.

FR 356

FR 356

Palmetto/
Purple Tr.

Headley's Creek

FR 361

26

FR 359

An overnight backpacking trip can be easily created at this junction by keeping left on the Purple Trail and traversing the southernmost section of trail that leads to the Grey Trail, which will connect you back to the Green Trail before joining the Blue Trail and returning to the parking lot. For an even longer two- to three-day backpacking trip, you can combine the hike I describe in this book with the Purple and White Trails to form a 27-mile-long hike that forms a large loop back to the Blue Trail, which will take you back to the parking lot where you started. It is certainly not a destination hike, and if you are looking for spectacular scenery, I would suggest the trails to the west in the Mountain Bridge Wilderness. However, the trails to the west are much more challenging and this is an excellent choice for a quick backpacking trip if you live close to this area or if you are just getting into backpacking and want to test out your gear. It's also good if you want to ease into more challenging hikes with something a little easier and forgiving on the less-conditioned hiker.

Miles and Directions

0.0 Start from the trailhead for the trail complex marked with a large kiosk. This hike begins on the Blue Trail, which begins at the back of the large field to the east of the kiosk. Follow the Blue Trail into the forest.

0.6 You reach a junction with a gravel road, the first of many along this trail. Cross the gravel road and continue on the Blue Trail.

0.7 Cross another gravel road.

0.9 Arrive at a T junction. The White Trail is to the left. Turn right and follow the Green Trail.

1.8 Cross the gravel road.

2.0 Reach a split in the trail. The Grey Trail is to the left. Veer right and follow the Red Trail.

3.1 Cross the creek via the wooden footbridge.

4.0 Arrive at a T junction. From here you have several options. You can take a right and follow the 4.5-mile Blue Trail to the right and return to the Brickhouse Campground and trailhead parking area. If you are backpacking, you can turn left and follow the 9-mile Purple Trail. However, I recommend simply turning around and taking the shorter route back the way you came to return to the trailhead where you started to complete this 8-mile hike.

8.0 Arrive back at the trailhead.

Hike Information

Local Information: Newberry County Chamber of Commerce, 1109 Main St., Newberry, SC 29108; (803) 276-4274; newberrycounty.org

Local Events/Attractions: Newberry Opera House, 1201 McKibben St., Newberry; (803) 276-6264; newberryoperahouse.com

Carter and Holmes Orchids, 629 Mendenhall Rd., Newberry; (803) 276-0579. Open Mon–Sat 9 a.m. to 5 p.m.

Newberry Oktoberfest, historic downtown Newberry. Takes place the first weekend in Oct; free admission

Lodging: Brickhouse Campground in Sumter National Forest; (803) 276-4810. First-come, first-served

Hampton Inn Newberry Opera House, 1201 Nance St., Newberry; (803) 276-6666

Restaurants: Steven W's Downtown Bistro, 1100 Main St., Newberry; (803) 276-7700, stevenws .com. Open Tues–Sun 5:30 to 10 p.m.

Ronnie's, 2067 Wilson Rd., Newberry; (803) 276-3016; ronniesbuffet.com. Open daily 7 to 10 a.m. and 11 a.m. to 8:30 p.m.

29 Palmetto Trail: Peak to Prosperity Passage

This trail follows an old railroad bed that spans Crims Creek from Alston to Pomaria over ten restored railroad trestles. The picturesque and well-maintained trail would be an easy hike if it were not for the length. However, the nearly 13-mile trail can easily be hiked in a single day by a reasonably fit hiker. Highlights include the 1,100-foot bridge that spans the Broad River and the great burgers at Wilson's Grocery at the end of the trail in Pomaria.

Start: From the trailhead and gravel parking lot in Alston

Distance: 12.8-mile out and back

Hiking time: About 6 hours

Difficulty: Moderate due to length

Trail surface: Gravel path, boardwalk, restored train trestles

Best seasons: Early spring and late fall for wildflowers and cooler temperatures. Good in the winter for cooler temperatures and bird watching

Other trail users: Bikers, runners

Canine compatibility: Leashed dogs permitted

Fees and permits: None

Schedule: Open year-round

Maps: TOPO! CD: North Carolina-South Carolina; USGS map: South Carolina

Trail contacts: Palmetto Conservation Foundation, 722 King St., Columbia, SC 29205; (803) 771-0870; palmettoconservation.org

Finding the trailhead: From I-26 exit 85, take SC 202 east to US 176, turn left, and drive into Pomaria, turning right on Angella Street, beside Wilson's Grocery. Parking is available behind the kiosk. GPS: N34 14.619' / W81 19.090'

The Hike

We have all heard of a one-stoplight town. Well, Alston is a no-stoplight town with the distinguishing feature being a wooden sign that reads ALSTON posted on a power pole just before you reach the gravel parking lot for the trailhead. Don't try to ask directions on your way to the Peak to Prosperity Trail. Case in point, at the other end of the trail in Pomaria, I asked a young woman working behind the counter of Wilson's Grocery if it would be faster to walk along the highway back to Alston. She said, "Alston! Where's that?" Alston is less than 7 miles from Pomaria—and the woman said she had lived in Pomaria her whole life.

Nonetheless, Alston is the starting point for the beautiful Peak to Prosperity Trail and serves as an apt introduction to the small rural towns scattered throughout South Carolina. You can access this trail from the east-end trailhead in Alston, or from the west-end trailhead in Pomaria. I recommend starting from the east end in Alston so that if you want a very short hike, you can hike a very short distance across the impressive bridge that spans the Broad River. There is also a well-maintained campground at the Alston trailhead that can be accessed by a short spur trail to the right of

Looking through the restored 1,100-foot-long bridge over the Broad River

the trailhead. A canoe launch is located just up the gravel road from the trailhead and is clearly marked with a sign at the gravel parking lot.

While crossing the artfully restored bridge, you have excellent and picturesque views of the Broad River. The trail is open to both bikers and hikers, so watch out for bikers. The bridge crossing is the busiest section of the trail and a spot that is especially popular with photographers, bird enthusiasts, and wildlife watchers, who comb the banks and waters of the river with their binoculars and cameras in hopes of catching a glimpse of the diverse birds and wildlife seen along the bridge. You may see bald eagles soaring overhead along the river. The bridge is 1,100 feet long and the decking and handrails were made possible by a grant from the South Carolina Department of Parks, Recreation, and Tourism.

After crossing the bridge, the trail quickly passes under SC 213. The trail is easy to follow, and several whimsical sculptures are placed alongside the trail as you pass under the highway overpass. The trail from this point becomes a nearly perfectly straight, old railroad bed that stretches out in front of you for miles. The railroad ballast, or medium-size gravel that is laid down as a base material for the railroad bed, acts as a trail surface for most of the trail. The ballast is hard on the feet so it is important that you wear a good pair of hiking boots when hiking this trail.

Along the trail you will cross over fourteen wooden trestles crossing Crims Creek. The decking and reconstruction of these trestles was completed in 2009 by two

Palmetto Trail: Peak to Prosperity Passage

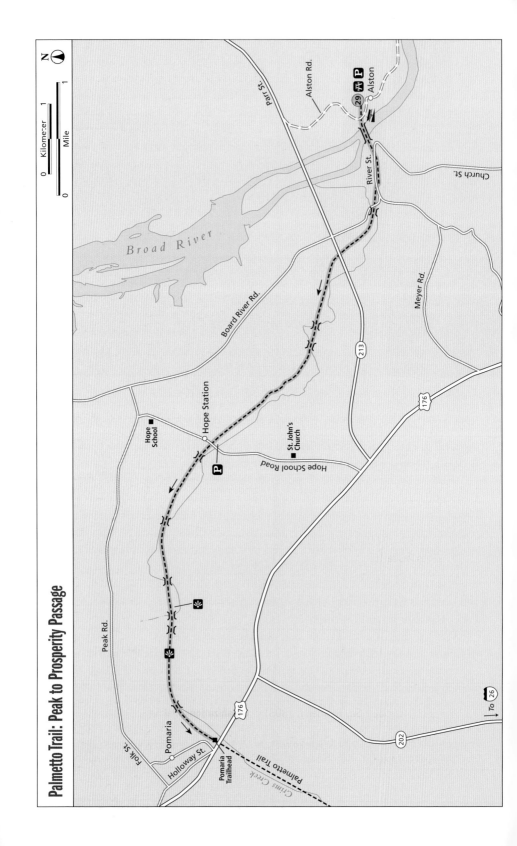

devoted volunteers, Charles Webber and Furman Miller. After 3.5 miles from the trailhead, you cross Hope School Road and the trail continues on the other side of the road. In 0.4 mile from the Hope School Road crossing, you reach a junction in the trail. A dirt road veers off to the right, and misleading signage makes you think you should turn right and follow this dirt road to nowhere. Do not turn right. Stay straight on the old railroad bed. The trail is easy to follow from here, and an observation deck on the left side of the trail offers excellent views of a small pond before you arrive at the western end of the trail at the town of Pomaria. You will see Wilson's Grocery straight ahead. This a great place to get a cold Gatorade, some snacks, or one of the fresh-cooked burgers that the store is known for. From here, simply turn around and retrace your steps back to the trailhead at Alston where you started.

Miles and Directions

0.0 Start from the gravel parking lot in Alston.

0.1 Cross the 1,100-foot bridge over Broad River.

0.9 Cross over Trestle 2. In 200 feet the trail crosses under SC 213.

2.1 Cross Trestle 3.

2.3 Cross Trestle 4.

3.5 Cross Hope School Road.

3.6 Cross Trestle 5.

3.9 Arrive at a trail junction. A dirt road that seems to be the trail veers off to the right. Do not turn right onto this dirt road. Stay straight on the old railroad bed with ballast.

4.3 Cross Trestle 6.

4.8 Cross Trestle 7.

5.1 Cross Trestle 8. In 100 feet a spur trail to the left leads down to several campsites on Crims Creek.

5.2 Cross Trestle 9.

5.4 An observation deck on the left side of the trail overlooks a small pond.

5.9 Cross Trestle 10.

6.4 Arrive at the Pomaria Trailhead. Wilson's Grocery is straight ahead.

12.8 Turn around and retrace your steps back to the Alston trailhead.

Hike Information

Local Information: Newberry Chamber of Commerce, 1109 Main St., Newberry, SC 29108; (803) 276-4274; newberrychamber.org

Local Events/Attractions: Newberry Opera House, 1201 McKibben St., Newberry; (803) 276-5179; newberryoperahouse.com

Lodging: Bernibrooks Inn, 200 W. Pinckney St., Abbeville; (864) 366-8310

Restaurants: Wilson's Grocery, 5941 Highway 176, Pomaria; (803) 276-9685

The Palms Grill and Bar, 612 Wilson Rd., Newberry; (803) 276-4688

Organizations: Palmetto Conservation Foundation, 722 King St., Columbia, SC 29205; (803) 771-0870; palmettoconservation.org

30 Harbison State Forest: Stewardship Trail

A popular trail with hikers and mountain bikers, this hike moves up and over constant hills for a moderately challenging hike through a pine and oak forest in one of the most popular parks in the Columbia area. A short spur trail along the route takes you to a rock outcrop with an excellent view of the Broad River.

Start: At the Stewardship Trail parking lot and trailhead

Distance: 3.3-mile loop

Hiking time: About 2 hours

Difficulty: Easy to moderate due to elevation gains

Trail surface: Forested path

Best seasons: Early spring and late fall for cooler temperatures and wildflowers

Other trail users: Mountain bikers, runners

Canine compatibility: Leashed dogs permitted

Fees and permits: Permits not required for hikers; daily permit (small fee) required for bikers, with annual pass available; daily parking permit required (small fee)

Schedule: Dawn–dusk daily year-round

Maps: TOPO! CD: North Carolina–South Carolina; USGS maps: Columbia Northeast, South Carolina; USFS maps: Harbison State Forest brochure

Trail contacts: Harbison State Forest, 5500 Broad River Rd., Columbia, SC 29221; (803) 896-8890

Finding the trailhead: From Columbia take I-26 to exit 101 and go southeast on US 176 (Broad River Road) 2.8 miles. The forest is on the left side of the road. GPS: N34 06.056' / W81 07.556'

The Hike

Only 9 miles from downtown Columbia, you find this 2,137-acre green space. There are more than 18 miles of trails in the park, and all of the trails are open to mountain bikers, runners, and hikers, so exercise extreme caution when hiking on these trails. It is not uncommon to see inconsiderate mountain bikers riding at extremely fast speeds around blind turns, even though these mountain bikers know that hikers and runners are sharing the trail. More than once while hiking these trails I have had to dodge bikers who are riding at dangerous speeds. There are many trails that are more popular than the stewardship trail for bikers, making this trail a good choice for hiking, yet many bikers ride through the trails in a random route and so it is difficult to gauge when the best time to enjoy the trails in this park would be. Having said that, this is hands down one of the best collections of trails within the Columbia city limits, so don't let the fact that bikers are on the trail deter you from enjoying these great hiking paths.

A wooden bridge crosses a seasonal stream along the Stewardship Trail.

The land that these trails explore was once exhausted cotton fields and farming fields. Today, the fields have been transformed through sound forest-management practices into a healthy forest that is predominately longleaf and loblolly pine with an assortment of hickory, oak, and red maple. In the spring and fall, you are likely to see wildflowers such as butterfly peas, elephant's feet, and flame azaleas growing along the trailside. Common wildlife seen in the forest include white-tailed deer, eastern box turtles, and wild turkeys. The park is a great place to spot birds, and you are likely to see woodpeckers and eastern wood peewees.

Note that in the wintertime the eastern section of the Stewardship Trail is located in the Broad River floodplain and the low-lying portions of the trail can become rather muddy at high water, especially the spur trail that leads down to the River Rest overlook. While you are in the park, consider launching a canoe or kayak from the boat put-in that is just south of the River Rest overlook. You will need to fill out a float plan at the park's Environmental Center before you launch your boat. However, there is no extra fee to launch boats from the canoe put-in.

The Stewardship Trail is a loop trail in the northeast section of the forest and one of the easier trails to hike in the park. Be sure to note that the ubiquitous gates throughout the park are closed at 5 p.m. The park is open from dawn to dusk, but the gates that allow vehicle access back to the Stewardship Trailhead close at 5 p.m. The parking lot at the entrance to the park remains accessible until dusk, so if you are going to be hiking the Stewardship Trail past 5 p.m., you need to park your car at the front parking lot and walk along the gravel road back to the trailhead.

A gravel parking lot and kiosk marks the beginning of the trail. After only 1 mile you reach a spur trail that leads down to the River Rest overlook. It is optional to hike down to the benches and rock outcropping that overlooks the river, and I highly recommend it. The rock outcropping is an especially nice spot to sit and enjoy views of the river, and if you are looking for a very short trail to hike in the Columbia area, you can always simply turn around at this point and head back to the parking lot for a 2-mile out-and-back hike. The rest of the hike follows over undulating hills through a mostly pine forest, and the hike really gets your heart racing with all the ups and downs. You intersect other trails in the area, but the trail is very well marked and maintained and it is very easy to follow the loop trail back around to the parking lot.

Miles and Directions

0.0 Start from the gravel parking lot and Stewardship Trail parking lot.

0.1 The trail junction with the Midland Mountains Trail is to the right. Stay straight on the Stewardship Trail. After 300 feet you cross a small bridge over a seasonal stream, and then you cross another similar bridge after another 250 feet.

0.7 Cross the gravel road that leads to the canoe put-in and continue on the Stewardship Trail on the other side of the road.

0.9 Take the spur trail to the right toward the River Rest overlook, a rock outcropping along the Broad River and several benches with excellent views of the river.

Harbison State Forest: Stewardship Trail

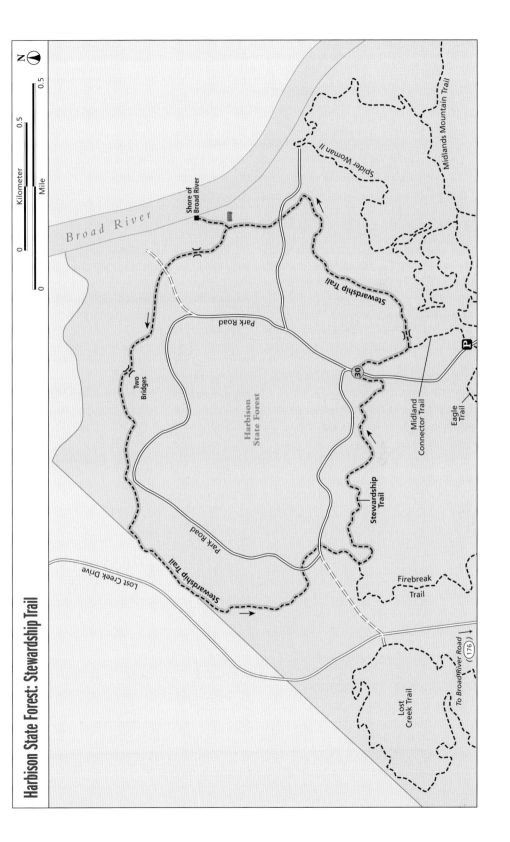

1.0 Reach River Rest. Turn around and retrace your steps the 0.1 mile back to the Stewardship Trail.

1.2 Cross a small wooden bridge spanning a seasonal stream.

1.3 Cross the dirt service road and continue on the Stewardship Trail on the other side of the road.

1.5 Cross the two wooden bridges spanning seasonal streams.

2.5 Cross the gravel road and continue on the Stewardship Trail on the other side of the road.

2.7 The Firebreak Trail connector is to the right. Stay straight on the Stewardship Trail.

3.3 Reach the gravel parking lot and trailhead where you started.

Hike Information

Local Information: Greater Irmo Chamber of Commerce, 1248 Lake Murray Blvd., Irmo, SC 29063; (803) 749-9355; greaterirmochamber .com

Local Events/Attractions: Lake Murray, South Carolina. Call (803) 781-5940 for information on 78-square-mile Lake Murray, or visit lake murrayfun.com

University of South Carolina, 945 Bull St., Columbia; (803) 777-0169; www.sc.edu

Lodging: Dreher Island State Park (camping), 3677 State Park Rd., Prosperity; (803) 364-0756

Sesquicentennial State Park (camping), 9564 Two Notch Rd., Columbia; (803) 788-2705

Restaurants: Lizard's Thicket, 7569 St. Andrews Rd., Irmo; (803) 732-1225; lizardsthicket.com. Open daily from 7 a.m.

Catch 22, 1085-D Lake Murray Blvd., Irmo; (803) 749-4700; catch22irmo.com. Open Tues–Sat 4 to 11 p.m.

Organizations: South Carolina Forestry Commission, PO Box 21707, Columbia, SC 29212; (803) 896-8800; www.state.sc.us/forest

31 Sesquicentennial State Park Sandhills Trail

Located in northwest Columbia, this wonderful, easy day hike circles the 30-acre lake in Sesquicentennial State Park. The trail, which opened in December 2012, features a paved section that is wheelchair accessible. A perfect choice for a lunch-break day hike, a short weekend stroll, or a quick escape from the city, this hike crosses several streams and ventures through forest and wetlands rich in bird-watching and other wildlife-viewing opportunities.

Start: From Sandhills Trailhead, the parking lot near the park office
Distance: 2.1-mile loop
Hiking time: About 1 hour
Difficulty: Easy
Trail surface: Paved path, forested trail, gravel path, boardwalk
Best season: Year-round
Other trail users: Hikers only
Canine compatibility: Leashed dogs permitted
Fees and permits: Small fee for adults; senior discount available

Schedule: Daily 8 a.m. to 6 p.m.
Maps: TOPO! CD: North Carolina–South Carolina; USGS maps: Fort Jackson North and Killian; South Carolina; USFS maps: Sesquicentennial State Park map available online at southcarolinaparks.com and at the state park office
Trail contacts: Sesquicentennial State Park, 9564 Two Notch Rd., Columbia, SC 29223; (803) 788-2706

Finding the trailhead: From Spartanburg head east on I-26 for 86 miles to I-20 East via exit 107B. Continue on I-20 for 10 miles to exit 74 (Two Notch Road). Turn left and continue 3.2 miles to Sesquicentennial State Park on the right. GPS: N34 05.124'/W80 54.442'

The Hike

Following a renovation project costing more than $160,000 that was funded mostly by donations from the Richlands County Commission, the Sandhills Trail was completely resurfaced and greatly improved in December 2012. If you haven't ventured northwest of Columbia in a while and hiked this pleasant day hike, you should definitely take the time to revisit this extremely well-maintained hiking trail that is a perfect choice for runners, hikers, children, and those who enjoy hiking with dogs. New boardwalks and bridges were added to the trail as well as a paved portion of the trail that leads from the trail's beginning at the state park office to the southern edge of the lake. Much of the trail has also been improved with sections of gravel path that makes it very easy to hike around the lake.

For much of the hike you will explore a quintessential sandhill ecosystem of pine and oak mixed with sections of wetland that can be crossed via boardwalks that were built as part of the renovation project. Along the way you may encounter wildlife

Canadian geese land on Sesquicentennial Lake.

such as deer, fox, squirrels, river otter, owls, and a variety of bird species including a diversity of ducks. Many of the buildings were constructed by the Civilian Conservation Corps (CCC) as part of the FDR New Deal program that brought work to the struggling economy during the Great Depression era. You can still see the evidence of the fine craftsmanship and artful stonework around the park at the many buildings throughout the grounds. The park has an excellent campground if you would like to extend your stay. The campsites are suitable for RVs and tent camping and have full hookups, power, and water at each site and on-site restrooms with hot showers.

Start the hike from the kiosk next to the park office. Follow the paved and level path toward the lake, passing several picnic pavilions and a playground to the left. At the T junction you can go either way around the lake. The trail is very easy to follow, and anytime there is a junction, it is very well marked. If you head to the right and walk toward the south end of the lake, you walk under a collection of large, arching oak trees of impressive beauty and have far-reaching views of the 30-acre lake to the left. Along this section there are several benches for resting and enjoying the serene landscape. You cross over several streams on well-constructed bridges before reaching a short section of wetland that is easily navigated via the wooden boardwalks that

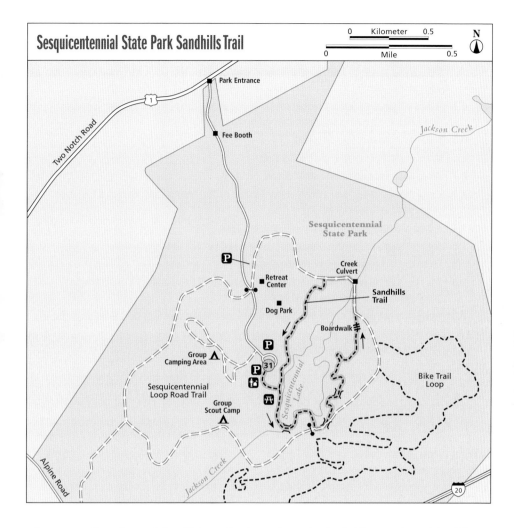

Sesquicentennial State Park Sandhills Trail

keep your feet nice and dry. This wetland marsh marks the halfway point of the hike. You cross several small streams and briefly join a dirt road before returning to a paved path again and returning to the parking lot and trailhead where you started your hike.

There are more than 12 miles of trails in Sesquicentennial State Park. The 0.4-mile Jackson Creek Nature Trail is one of the most popular trails in the park. This trail explores a wooded hillside and a small wetland area and journeys past a very small waterfall, all within a short distance along a very easy trail. Also in this book is the Loop Road Trail, which I highly recommend. Sesquicentennial is an excellent example of how valuable it is to integrate green spaces into metropolitan areas, and I encourage anyone living in the Columbia area to make a trip to this wonderful park and hike some of these excellent and well-maintained trails that are easily accessible for anyone living in the region.

Miles and Directions

0.0 Start from the visitor center parking lot. A kiosk to the left of the visitor center marks the start of the Sandhills Trail. Follow the paved path past the restrooms and picnic area to the edge of the lake.

0.1 Reach a T junction. You can go either way to complete a loop around the lake. Turn right and follow the paved path toward the south end of the lake.

0.3 Cross a bridge over the lake outlet.

0.5 Cross a short bridge over a seasonal stream.

0.7 Cross another bridge over a small stream.

1.1 Cross the boardwalk over a short boggy section. In 300 feet the trail reaches a T junction with a service road. Turn left.

1.4 A creek flows under the trail through a large culvert.

1.5 The trail splits. The service road continues straight. Turn left onto the trail.

1.6 Cross the bridge over a small seasonal stream.

1.8 The trail splits again. A spur trail leads to the right uphill to a parking lot. Stay straight. In 250 feet the path becomes paved again.

2.0 Arrive at a trail junction and complete the loop around the lake. Turn right to return to the visitor center.

2.1 Reach the visitor center where you started.

Hike Information

Local Information: Columbia CVB, 1101 Lincoln St., Columbia, SC 29201; (800) 264-4884; www.columbiacvb.com

Local Events/Attractions: World Beer Festival, Columbia Convention Center, 1101 Lincoln St., Columbia; www.allaboutbeer.com. This festival occurs annually in January.

SC Oyster Festival, 1616 Blanding St., Columbia; (803) 252-2128. Admission fee is charged; advance purchase is discounted. Takes place annually in November

Lodging: Camping at Sesquicentennial State Park, 9564 Two Notch Rd., Columbia; (803) 788-2706. Both primitive group sites and sites with electric and water hookups are available.

Chestnut Cottage Bed and Breakfast, 1718 Hampton St., Columbia; (803) 256-1718; www.chestnutcottage.com

Restaurants: Lizard's Thicket, 7620 Two Notch Rd., Columbia; (803) 788-3088; lizards thicket.com

Alodia's, 2736 N. Lake Dr., Columbia; (803) 781-9814; alodias.com. Open Tues–Sat 11 a.m. to 10 p.m., Sun 11 a.m. to 2 p.m. and 5 to 9:30 p.m.

32 Sesquicentennial State Park Loop Road Trail

This short day hike in northwest Columbia deeply explores the oak and pine forest found throughout Sesquicentennial State Park. Along this level and easy route, you mostly follow park roads that are closed to unofficial traffic, giving you a better opportunity to spot more of the wildlife found in this dynamic Sandhills ecosystem.

Start: From the trailhead to the Mountain Bike Trail
Distance: 3.4-mile loop
Hiking time: About 1-2 hours
Difficulty: Easy
Trail surface: Dirt road, forested path
Best season: Year-round
Other trail users: Mountain bikers
Canine compatibility: Leashed dogs permitted
Fees and permits: Small fee for adults; senior discount available

Schedule: Daily 8 a.m. to 6 p.m.
Maps: TOPO! CD: North Carolina–South Carolina; USGS maps: Fort Jackson North and Killian; South Carolina; USFS maps: Sesquicentennial State Park map available online at southcarolinaparks.com and at the state park office
Trail contacts: Sesquicentennial State Park, 9564 Two Notch Rd., Columbia, SC 29223; (803) 788-2706

Finding the trailhead: From Spartanburg head east on I-26 for 86 miles to I-20 East via exit 107B. Continue on I-20 for 10 miles to exit 74 (Two Notch Road). Turn left and continue 3.2 miles to Sesquicentennial State Park on the right. GPS: N34 05.523'/W80 54.487'

The Hike

Keep your eyes open along this hike and you just may spot wildlife such as deer, fox, squirrels, owls, and a variety of other bird species as you explore this impressive stretch of mature pine and oak forest. The trail is mostly level with a few sections of small rolling hills that make this an excellent trail for hikers and runners looking for an easy trail in the Columbia area that is long enough to give them a little challenge. The trail is one of the less popular trails in the park, which makes this an excellent choice for those looking to walk dogs and find a little solitude in a usually busy park nestled in a crowded metropolitan area of South Carolina.

You will start your hike near the retreat center. The parking lot is easy to miss and the trailhead is marked as the start of the Mountain Bike Trail. After entering the park from the entrance gate, look for the sand-and-grass parking lot on the left side of the road. As the name suggests, the first section of the trail is very popular with mountain bikers so be cautious and give mountain bikers the right-of-way when hiking on the trail. After the first mile you are much less likely to encounter mountain bikers because most of them tend to bike on the outer loop while hikers tend to prefer the inner loop that leads back around to the park road.

The beginning section of the trail can be confusing as you cross the network of Mountain Bike Trail and access roads that crisscross the Loop Road Trail. Adding to the confusion is the fact that there is never a mention of the Loop Road Trail on any of the trail markers along the way. However, if you simply follow the directions below, you will be able to navigate this trail just fine. There are plenty of opportunities to create a variety of loops, longer routes, and shortcuts along the way. This route is the official Loop Road Trail and definitely the route that I would suggest taking. However, this is intended only as an introduction to this network of trails and I strongly encourage you to explore this part of the park, especially if you live in the Columbia region. This park is a gem for city dwellers looking to get out in nature during a short lunch break and also makes for a great weekend escape.

The trail curves around to the north and along the Sandhills Trail, offering occasional views of the 30-acre Sesquicentennial Lake in the distance. At the 1.8-mile mark you reach a junction with another dirt road. To the right is a sign for the Group Scout Camp, a large clearing at a group camp that is often used by Boy Scouts and other outdoor associations for larger gatherings. There are several picnic tables here at the group camp and this makes for an excellent stopping point to rest or enjoy lunch or just a snack. At the junction of the roads at the Scout Camp, you stay straight and continue to follow the dirt road. In 0.6 mile you reach another split in the trail. A dirt road splits to the left. Stay straight again to get back to the main park road. In just 0.9 mile you are back at the main park road. Cross the paved park road and return to the retreat center where you started and arrive at the end of this easy hike through some of the best forest in Sesquicentennial Park.

Miles and Directions

0.0   Start from the trailhead to the Mountain Bike Trail. The kiosk and start of the trail is in the dirt parking lot on the left side of the main park road near the Retreat Center.

0.5   Reach a split in the trail. The yellow-blazed Lake Trail is to the right. Stay straight on the blue-blazed Loop Trail.

0.6   Walk straight through the junction with the other end of the Sandhills Trail.

0.7   Reach a split in the trail. The Mountain Bike Trail is to the left. Stay straight on the Loop Road Trail.

0.8   Reach a split in the trail. The Mountain Bike Trail splits again to the left. Stay straight on the Loop Road Trail.

1.3   Pass the white metal gate that blocks the road to vehicular traffic and continue straight, following the dirt road alongside the wooden fence.

1.8   Reach a junction. A road veers to the right and leads to the Group Scout Camp. Stay straight.

2.4   Arrive at a split in the trail. A dirt road splits to the left. Stay straight.

3.3   Reach another metal gate. Cross the paved park road. The parking lot is on the other side of the road and the kiosk where you started is to the left.

3.4   Arrive at the kiosk where you started.

The trail follows a sandy-white road for most of the route.

Sesquicentennial State Park Loop Road Trail

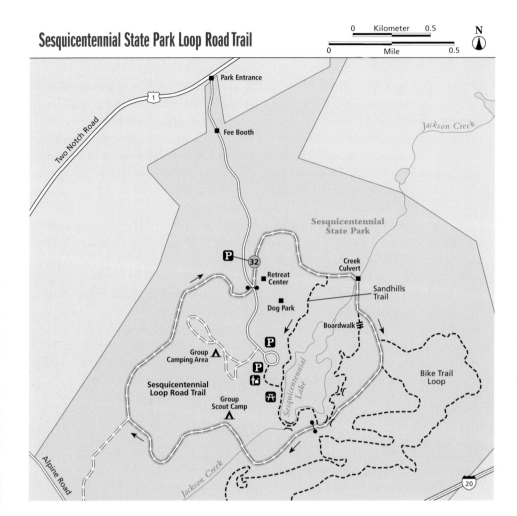

Hike Information

Local Information: Columbia CVB, 1101 Lincoln St., Columbia, SC 29201; (800) 264-4884; www.columbiacvb.com

Local Events/Attractions: Lexington County Peach Festival, Gilbert; (803) 892-5207; lexingtoncountypeachfestival.com. This festival is held annually in the summer.

SC Oyster Festival, 1616 Blanding St., Columbia; (803) 252-2128. Admission fee is charged; advance purchase is discounted. Takes place annually in November

Lodging: Camping at Sesquicentennial State Park, 9564 Two Notch Rd., Columbia; (803)

788-2706. Both electric and water sites and primitive group sites are available.

Chestnut Cottage Bed and Breakfast, 1718 Hampton St., Columbia; (803) 256-1718; chestnutcottage.com

Restaurants: Little Pigs BBQ, 4927 Alpine Rd., Columbia; (803) 788-8238; www.littlepigs.biz. Open Wed 11 a.m. to 2 p.m., Thurs 11 a.m. to 8:30 p.m., Fri–Sat 11 a.m. to 9 p.m., Sun 11 a.m. to 3 p.m.

Solstice Kitchen, 841-4 Sparkleberry Ln., Columbia; (803) 788-6966; solsticekitchen.com. Open Tues–Fri 11:30 a.m. to 2 p.m., Mon–Sat 5:30 to 9:30 p.m.

33 Kings Mountain National Park Battlefield Trail

This paved trail is an excellent choice for anyone interested in history and the Revolutionary War. This easy day hike explores the battleground of one of the most important conflicts of the war, the Battle of Kings Mountain, fought on October 7, 1780. The well-maintained path traverses the route that the over-the-mountain men traveled during the famous battle. As you wind your way around the base of the mountain, you pass many informative interpretive plaques and memorials dedicated to the soldiers who fought here. A short climb to the top of the mountain brings you to two impressive obelisks that commemorate the site where the battle was won by the Revolutionary fighters, considered to be the site of the turning point in the Revolutionary War.

Start: From the trailhead directly behind the visitor center
Distance: 1.6-mile loop
Hiking time: About 1 hour
Difficulty: Easy
Trail surface: Paved
Best season: Year-round
Other trail users: Hikers only
Canine compatibility: Leashed dogs permitted
Fees and permits: None

Schedule: Daily 9 a.m. to 5 p.m.
Maps: TOPO! CD: North Carolina–South Carolina; USGS maps: Grover, Kings Mountain; South Carolina; USFS maps: Kings Mountain State Park Trail Map available online at www.nps.gov/kimo, at the parks visitor center, and at kiosks at the trailhead
Trail contacts: Kings Mountain National Military Park, 2625 Park Rd., Blacksburg, SC 29702; (864) 936-7921

Finding the trailhead: From Greenville travel on I-85 North to NC exit 2. Merge onto Banks Road and take the first right onto Battleground Drive / NC 216. Follow Battleground Drive for 3.2 miles to the park visitor center. GPS: N35 08.484' / W81 22.631'

The Hike

Before you start this wonderful hike, I highly recommend that you stop in at the visitor center and enjoy the short and fascinating film in the theater. This will give you an extensive overview of the historical significance of this area and the walk that you are about to embark upon. This film helps to bring the trail to life, so to speak, as you climb up toward the top of Kings Mountain. If you choose not to watch the film, you can still get plenty of information from the interpretive stations along the paved path. I really enjoy the way that this particular trail was planned out. If you start from the visitor center and walk counterclockwise, the interpretive plaques that you encounter along the way tell the story of the Battle of Kings Mountain in chronological order. You literally follow the route that the fighters took as they battled their way toward victory at the top of Kings Mountain. It is an exciting and very educational hike; a walk that retraces our country's path to independence and democracy.

This memorial commemorates soldiers killed at the Battle of Kings Mountain.

However, this is also simply an enjoyable walk in the woods. Even if you have absolutely zero interest in American history, you will probably enjoy the walk through the mixed hardwood forest that leads past several artfully constructed obelisks. The path is exceptionally maintained and easy to follow, which makes it a favorite of families with young children.

After watching the movie at the visitor center, follow the paved path behind the visitor center to a T junction. Turn right and follow the paved path to two memorials marking the gravesite of Major William Chronicle, Capt. John Mattocks, William Rabb, John Boyd, and Col. Patrick Ferguson. The original gravestone is to the left and barely legible. A replica has been constructed to the right that is very easy to read. From here the trail briefly follows alongside a small stream, which you will cross several times on this hike. The trail crosses the stream via concrete bridges. As the trail winds through the hardwood forest, you pass many benches at regular intervals where you can stop and take a rest or just relax and reflect on the battle that was fought here. After 0.7 mile you reach a trail junction. The short trail to the right leads to a stone memorial that commemorates the speech then–president Herbert Hoover gave on this site in 1930, the 150th anniversary of the battle. Return to the main trail and follow it as it circles around to the left (west) and climbs steeply uphill to the top of the hill, where you are rewarded with views of distant ridges through the trees.

In 0.2 mile you arrive at the first stone monument, the 23-foot-tall Kings Mountain Centennial Monument, which memorializes the soldiers who fought in the

Kings Mountain National Park Battlefield Trail

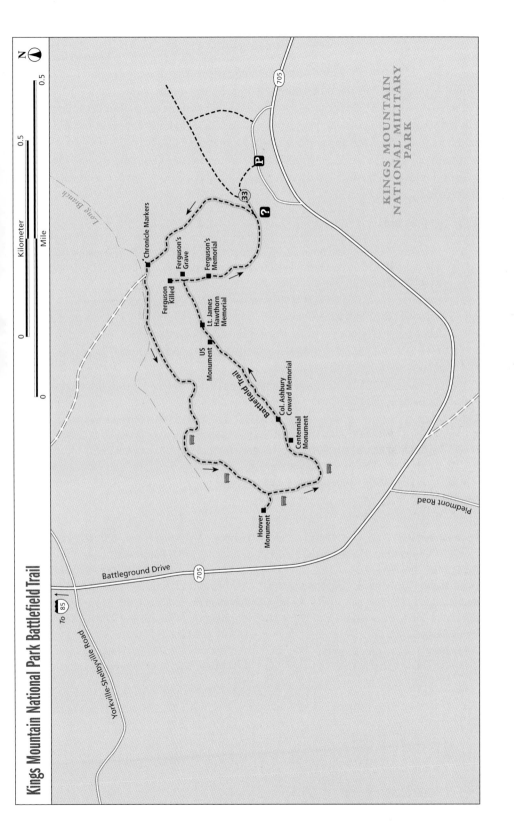

historical battle. Carved in the side of the monument are the words of Thomas Jefferson: "Here the tide of the battle turned in favor of the American Colonists." The trail climbs gently uphill to the more impressive of the two monuments, the US Monument, an 83-foot-tall obelisk that stands in the middle of the path. After 0.1 mile you reach a plaque that marks the exact spot where British colonel Ferguson fell. A spur trail here leads to a stone marker that marks his gravesite. The trail curves to the right and leads downhill to a stone memorial that commemorates Colonel Ferguson. From here you follow the paved path up the steep hill and back to the visitor center where you started your hike.

Miles and Directions

0.0 Start from the paved path behind the visitor center and walk to the right to follow the trail in a counterclockwise direction. After 400 feet you reach a junction with a spur trail back toward the parking lot. Stay to the left.

0.2 Reach the gravesite on the right of Major William Chronicle, Capt. John Mattocks, William Rabb, John Boyd, and Colonel Ferguson.

0.7 Reach the junction with the spur trail that leads to the Hoover Monument.

0.9 Arrive at the 23-foot-tall Kings Mountain Centennial Monument, which memorializes the soldiers who fought in the historic battle.

1.1 The 83-foot-tall US Memorial stands in the middle of the path. The obelisk commemorates the Battle of Kings Mountain.

1.2 Reach a spur trail that leads to the plaque indicating where Colonel Ferguson was killed. Continue on the path down the hill for 250 feet to the memorial commemorating Colonel Ferguson, which was erected as a kind gesture by the United States for the British. The trail climbs steeply from here to the visitor center.

1.6 Arrive at the visitor center and the end of your hike.

Hike Information

Local Information: Greenville Chamber of Commerce, 24 Cleveland St., Greenville, SC 29601; (864) 242-1050

Local Events/Attractions: Cowpens National Battlefield, 4001 Chesnee Hwy., Gaffney; (864) 461-2828. Open daily 9 a.m. to 5 p.m. Free admission

Greenville Zoo, 150 Cleveland Park Dr., Greenville; (864) 467-4300

Lodging: White House Inn, 607 W. Pine St., Blacksburg; (864) 839-0005

Camping at King Mountain State Park, 1277 Park Rd., Blacksburg; (803) 222-3209

Restaurants: Foothills Café, 3155 Peachtree Rd., Chesnee; (864) 592-1652. Open Tues–Sun 11 a.m. to 9 p.m.

Carolina Café, 211 Old Metal Rd., Gaffney; (864) 406-0333. Open Tues–Sun 5 to 9 p.m.

34 Landsford Canal State Historic Site

Along the well-maintained and beautiful Canal Trail, you can explore the site of the old canal system that made the Catawba River commercially navigable from 1820 to 1835. This is a great trail for kids, dogs, and anyone interested in history or taking an easy walk along the rocky and wide Catawba River. Several observation decks and many benches along the trail offer splendid views of the river. A highlight of the trail is an observation deck that overlooks a remarkable display of spider lilies that cover the surface of the Catawba River. Hike the trail between May and July for the best chance to see the lilies in bloom, covering the river in a breathtaking blanket of white flowers.

Start: The trailhead and parking lot at the end of the park road accessed from Entrance Area 1 off US 21 (Landsford Road)
Distance: 3.1-mile out and back
Hiking time: About 2 hours
Difficulty: Easy due to length, well-maintained trail, and level walking
Trail surface: Paved path, dirt trail, boardwalk
Best season: May–June to see blooming spider lilies and fledgling eagle activity around the eagle's nest
Other trail users: Hikers only

Canine compatibility: Leashed dogs permitted
Fees and permits: Free for kids under age 16; small fee for age 16 and over; senior discount available
Schedule: Daily 9 a.m. to 6 p.m.
Maps: TOPO! CD: North Carolina–South Carolina; USGS maps: Catawba, South Carolina
Trail contacts: Landsford Canal State Park, 2051 Park Dr., Catawba, SC 29704; (803) 789-5800; www.southcarolinaparks.com/landsfordcanal

Finding the trailhead: From Rock Hill take I-77 southbound to exit 77 to Highways 5 and 21. Turn left (south), travel 16 miles to the Landsford Canal State Park sign, and turn left. The park entrance is on the left. Follow the park road to where it dead-ends at a parking lot and trailhead. Follow the paved path as it curves to the right, passing the playground, picnic pavilions, and the log cabin. The Canal Trail starts at the end of the paved path, just past the log cabin. GPS: N34 47.471'/W80 52.899'

The Hike

It's easy to spend a lot of time along this trail, so be sure to plan accordingly. Just in the first few hundred feet, there is a playground and several very nice picnic pavilions, so if you are bringing kids along, you may be at the park for several hours before you even step foot on the trail. You see the beautiful Catawba River flowing in front of the trailhead. Once the trail reaches the river, the Eagle Point Trail veers off to the right. This trail leads to a viewing area for the eagle's nest. Plan to visit the park in early June for the best chance to see a baby eagle's first flight. Looking out across the Catawba River, you will notice the rocky shoals sticking out of the water, and where they are

A historic cabin is located near the trailhead of the Canal Trail.

not visible, you may notice rapids in the river. This section along the Catawba made commercial transportation along this river impossible in the early 1800s. In search of a navigable path between Charleston and the Mississippi River, an extensive network of canals and locks was constructed alongside the river as a bypass around these shoals and rapids.

This route combines two trails in the park, the Nature Trail and the Canal Trail, to explore the riverbanks of the Catawba as well as the canals, the three locks, and other historical structures along this stretch of the river. Along the mostly level route, you will pass an ample number of interpretive signs explaining in detail the history of the complex canal system that you see along the trail and the relics of structures you will encounter along the way. Most of the original stonework of the three locks is still intact, making these canals one of the best examples of canals and locks in the entire state.

Late spring is the best time to visit the park, not only because of the eagle activity at the nest, but also because of the abundance of wildflowers along the trails. There is an enormous variety of wildflowers found in the park including the crane-fly orchid, Solomon's seal, and my favorite, the yellow passionflower. The highlight of all the flowers in the park is the spider lily, which grows around the Catawba Rapids. A mile into the hike, you will reach an observation deck and have the chance to see an impressive number of spider lilies blanketing the surface of the river. Also keep your eyes peeled for birds found in the park, which in addition to the bald eagles include osprey, woodpeckers, warblers, and the yellow-billed cuckoo.

The two trails intersect at many points along the route. Start on the Nature Trail, which follows alongside the Catawba River, and follow it to the spider lily observation deck. From here, take the Canal Trail south to the Upper Locks and the masterfully constructed stone arch. There is also a parking lot down here at Entrance 2. Some hikers prefer to leave a second car at the end of the trail instead of hiking back along the Canal Trail. You can also add a half mile to your hike if you want to hike the extra distance to the lower locks just south of the Entrance 2 trailhead. I recommend turning around at the upper locks and hiking back to the junction with observation deck spur trail, then following the Canal Trail on the way back to the parking lot, passing the guard locks along the way. The trail is very well maintained and the signage is clear and easy to follow.

Miles and Directions

0.0 Start from the trailhead and parking lot at the end of the park road from Entrance 1. Follow the paved path past the playground and picnic pavilions. The trail curves to the right and follows alongside the Catawba River on the left. After passing the log cabin on the right, you arrive at the trailhead for the Canal Trail.

0.1 At the trailhead for the Canal Trail, the paved trail ends. Follow the dirt path alongside the river for 300 feet until you reach a split in the trail. The Canal Trail is to the right. Stay to the left and follow the Nature Trail, which follows alongside the river and crosses a wooden bridge.

0.4 A bench on the riverbank overlooks the Catawba River.

0.6 To the left of the trail is a bench that offers wonderful views of the river. Continue 250 feet to a T junction where the Canal Trail rejoins with the Nature Trail. Turn left and continue to follow along the river.

0.7 Cross the wooden bridge spanning a seasonal creek that feeds into the Catawba River. Fifty feet from the bridge, you'll reach a split in the trail. The Canal Trail is to the right. Stay left on the Nature Trail.

0.9 Arrive at a split in the trail. The Canal Trail is to the right. Stay left on the spur trail that leads toward an observation deck 150 feet away. The observation deck looks over the Catawba River at a point where a large number of spider lilies grow on the river's surface. After you enjoy the view, turn around and retrace your steps back to the junction with the Nature Trail and the Canal Trail. Turn left onto the Canal Trail. After 100 feet, cross the wooden bridge, which has no handrails, that spans a seasonal stream. Notice the stone arches on both sides of the bridge.

1.2 Arrive at the Mill Complex.

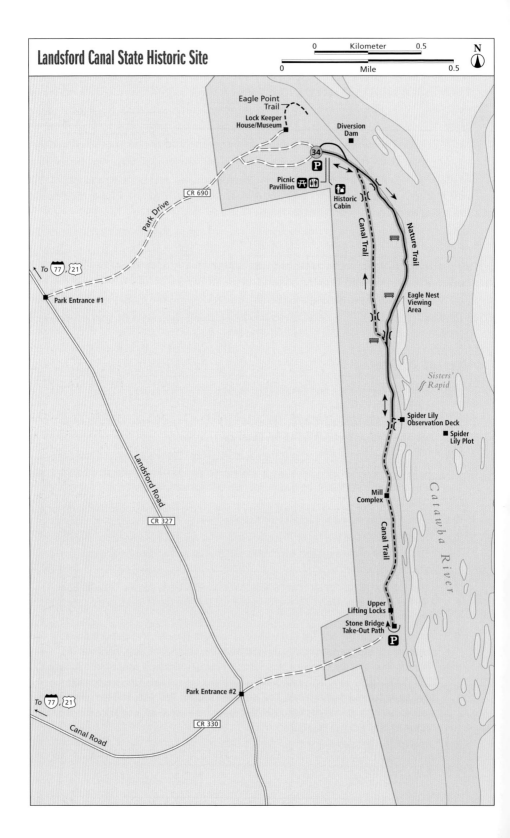

Landsford Canal State Historic Site

0   Kilometer   0.5

0   Mile   0.5

N

Eagle Point Trail

Lock Keeper House/Museum

Diversion Dam

34

Park Drive

CR 690

Picnic Pavillion

Historic Cabin

Canal Trail

Nature Trail

To 77, 21

Park Entrance #1

Eagle Nest Viewing Area

Sisters' ff Rapid

Spider Lily Observation Deck

Spider Lily Plot

Landsford Road

CR 327

Mill Complex

Canal Trail

Catawba River

Upper Lifting Locks

Stone Bridge Take-Out Path

Park Entrance #2

To 77, 21

Canal Road

CR 330

1.5 The upper locks run right beside the trail. Continue south on the Canal Trail for 150 feet until you reach the trailhead at Entrance 2. At the end of the upper locks is an interesting and arching stone bridge. A spur trail on the other side of the stone bridge leads to a boat put-in on the river. From here, you can opt to add a half mile to your hike if you stay straight on the Canal Trail, which ends at the lower locks, or simply turn around and retrace your steps back to the junction with the spur trail to the spider lily observation deck.

2.2 At the junction with the spur trail to the observation deck, turn left onto the combined Nature Trail / Canal Trail.

2.4 Arrive at a split in the trail. The Nature Trail goes straight. Turn left onto the Canal Trail. Fifty feet from the junction, a bench overlooks the forest and a seasonal stream. Continue for 350 feet and cross the 12-foot wooden bridge, with handrails, crossing a stream.

2.8 Cross another wooden bridge that spans a seasonal stream. After 250 more feet you reach the guard locks.

2.9 At the trail junction turn left onto the Canal Trail. Follow the forested path along the Catawba River. After 300 feet the trail becomes paved. Follow the paved path back to the parking lot and trailhead where you started.

3.1 Arrive back at the trailhead where you began.

Hike Information

Local Information: Chester County Chamber of Commerce, 109 Gadsden St., Chester, SC 29706; (803) 581-4142

Local Events/Attractions: Canaan Zipline Canopy Tours, 3111 Sand Island Rd., Rock Hill; (803) 327-6932; canaanzipline.com

Catawba Cultural Center, 1536 Tom Steven Rd., Rock Hill; (803) 328-2427

Lodging: Harmony House B&B, 3485 Harmony Rd., Catawba; (803) 403-1912; harmonyhouse bb.wordpress.com.

Camping at Andrew Jackson State Park, 196 Andrew Jackson Park Rd., Lancaster; (803) 285-3344

Restaurants: Gus' Family Pizza Restaurant, 605 S. Main St., Lancaster; (803) 285-1552; pizzabygus.com. Open Mon–Sat 11 a.m. to 10 p.m. Closed Sun.

Jomars Family Restaurant, 278 Lancaster Bypass E., Lancaster; (803) 286-6482; jomars familyrestaurant.com. Open daily 7 a.m. to 9 p.m.

35 Carolina Sandhills National Wildlife Refuge: Tate's Trail

This route is a favorite among birders and other wildlife enthusiasts. Tate's Trail travels alongside two bodies of water where you are likely to see waterfowl and other wildlife. You pass Martin's Lake and Pool D before taking a spur trail that loops around Lake 12. The terrain is hilly but not difficult.

Start: Gravel parking lot near observation tower
Distance: 6-mile lollipop
Hiking time: About 3 hours
Difficulty: Easy to moderate due to length and moderate elevation gains
Trail surface: Forested path
Best seasons: Early spring and late fall for cooler temperatures and wildflowers; winter for waterfowl
Other trail users: Hikers only

Canine compatibility: Dogs not permitted
Fees and permits: Free admission; permits required for off-road ATV use and hunting
Schedule: Open year-round from 1 hour before sunrise to 1 hour after sunset
Maps: TOPO! CD: North Carolina–South Carolina; USGS maps: Middendorf and Angelus, South Carolina
Trail contacts: Carolina Sandhills NWR, 23734 Highway 1, McBee, SC 29101; (843) 335-8401

Finding the trailhead: From Columbia follow I-20 to US 521 (exit 98). Turn left (north), drive into Camden, and turn right onto US 1. Follow US 1 for 29 miles, pass through McBee, and turn left (north) onto SC 145. Drive approximately 5 miles and turn left (west) onto Wildlife Drive and the entrance to the wildlife refuge. Turn right onto Wildlife Drive and follow the signs to the trailhead and observation tower. GPS: N34 33.293' / W80 13.285'

The Hike

There are a few other shorter hiking trails in this 46,000-acre park, but Tate's Trail is the longest and best way to see the park on foot and on an official hiking trail. Most visitors see the park by driving or biking the 9-mile-long Wildlife Drive, which traverses through a great deal of the park. And there are also more than 100 miles of dirt and gravel roads that crisscross through the park that are also open for mountain biking and hiking. Located in the upper Sandhills belt of South Carolina, this region was once the coastline of South Carolina. In more recent history the region became eroded and exhausted as the result of poor farming practices. It has since been restored by impressive forest management and restoration techniques and today serves as important habitat for wildlife and waterfowl.

A testament to the success of the restoration efforts are the significant variety of birds, wildlife, and flora that can be seen throughout the park. The highlight of the park is the abundance of waterfowl, which is best seen during the winter months when migrating birds are most active in this region. You are likely to see wood ducks and Canada geese as well as the endangered red-cockaded woodpecker. Note that the

A view of Lake 12 along Tate's Trail

trees that are used by the woodpeckers for nests are marked with white rings around the tree trunks.

This is a wonderful park in which to spot wildflowers. You can find yellow jessamine, woolly mullein, lizard's tail, mountain laurel, and St. John's wort growing in this area. Tate's Trail starts in the gravel parking lot just off Wildlife Drive. Turkey and deer are commonly seen in this park, and there are scheduled hunts that take place in the refuge, so take extra precaution during the hunting season. Information about scheduled hunts will be posted throughout the park when they are occurring.

Tate's Trail starts from a gravel parking lot at the southern end of Martin's Lake. After 0.6 mile a short but steep spur trail leads down to the shore of Martin's Lake. This is an excellent place to view waterfowl and other wildlife. I recommend making your approach to the lake softly to try to avoid spooking the many birds that are often wading on the lake. During some parts of the year, the park sets up a photography blind at this spot for capturing photos of the abundant waterfowl around Martin's Lake. Contact the park for information about when the photography blind will be set up.

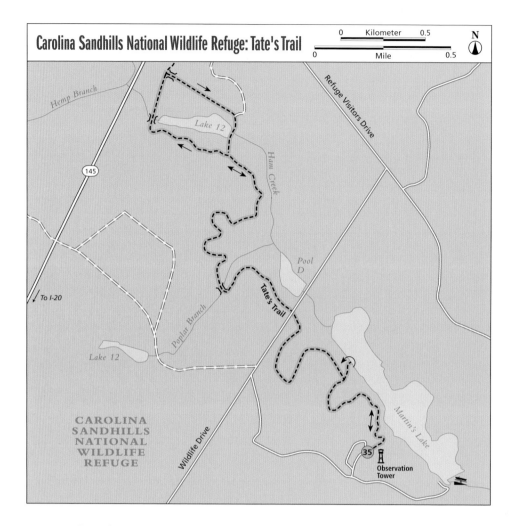

Tate's Trail crosses Wildlife Drive and continues on the other side of the road. The trail follows alongside Pool D, where you will have more opportunities to view wildlife and waterfowl as you hike along the edge of the pond, occasionally dipping back into the young forest. At the northern end of the hike, you reach Lake 12. Tate's Trail follows along the southern side of the lake, crossing over a large creek. Keep your eyes peeled for beaver activity around the bridge. At the northern tip of Tate's Trail, you reach a spur trail that will take you to the parking lot and trailhead at Lake Bee. If you want to make the trail shorter and don't want to hike back the way you came in, you can park a second car at this Lake Bee Trailhead.

To get back to the trailhead at Martin's Lake, follow the spur trail that loops around the north side of Lake 12 and then rejoins Tate's Trail. From here you can retrace your steps and follow Tate's Trail back to the parking lot and trailhead where you started.

Miles and Directions

0.0 Start from the gravel parking lot near the observation tower.

0.6 Arrive at a trail junction with a spur trail that leads 400 feet down to the edge of Martin's Lake. Turn right and follow the spur trail to the edge of the lake. After enjoying the view and hopefully seeing some wildlife, turn around and retrace your steps. Once back at the main trail, turn right and continue on Tate's Trail.

1.4 Follow the wooden steps to Wildlife Drive. Cross the road and continue on the trail on the other side of Wildlife Drive.

1.8 Cross the bridge over the small stream.

2.7 Arrive at a trail junction and stay straight on Tate's Trail, which follows along the west side of Lake 12. The other end of the loop trail that circles around Lake 12 is to the right.

3.1 Cross the bridge that spans a large creek.

3.3 A spur trail to the left leads to a parking lot, Wildlife Drive, and the trailhead at Lake Bee. Veer to the right on the loop trail around Lake 12, which continues to loop around the lake. After 200 feet you cross a wooden bridge spanning a small, seasonal stream.

3.8 Arrive at the end of the loop around Lake 12. Turn left, rejoining Tate's Trail. From here retrace your steps on Tate's Trail and return to the parking lot and trailhead where you started.

6.0 Arrive at the trailhead where you started.

Hike Information

Local Information: Chesterfield County Chamber of Commerce, 100 Main St., Chesterfield, SC 29709; (843) 623-2343

Local Events/Attractions: McLeod Farms, 29247 Highway 151, McBee; (843) 355-8611

Lodging: Camping at Sand Hills State Forest, 16218 Highway 1, Patrick; (843) 498-6478

Camping at Cheraw State Park, 100 State Park Rd., Cheraw; (843) 537-9656

Restaurants: Big's Meats and More Grill, 29241 Highway 151, McBee; (842) 355-6474; bigsmeatsandmore.com

The Company Store and Restaurant, 134 N. Seventh St., McBee; (843) 355-8834

Organizations: Carolina Sandhills NWR, 23734 Highway 1, McBee, SC 29101; (843) 335-8401

36 Cheraw State Park

This easy trail offers a great opportunity to see a large variety of birds and other wildlife while traversing a diversity of landscapes. Along this route, which follows the Turkey Oak Trail Long Loop, you will hike through pine forests as well as mixed forests of hardwood and pine, and journey through low-lying swamps. Bring your binoculars and search for a red-cockaded woodpecker in a managed nesting area along the trail.

Start: Gravel parking lot on the left side of the park road
Distance: 4.3-mile lollipop
Hiking time: About 2 hours
Difficulty: Easy due to level walking and length
Trail surface: Forested trail
Best seasons: Early spring and late fall for cooler temperatures and wildflowers
Other trail users: Hikers only
Canine compatibility: Leashed dogs permitted. Dogs not permitted in cabins or cabin area

Fees and permits: None
Schedule: Nov–Feb daily 7 a.m. to 6 p.m.; Mar, Sept, and Oct daily 7 a.m. to 8 p.m.; Apr–Aug daily 7 a.m. to 9 p.m.
Maps: TOPO! CD: North Carolina–South Carolina; USGS maps: Cheraw and Cash, South Carolina
Trail contacts: Cheraw State Park, 100 State Park Rd., Cheraw, SC 29520; (843) 537-9656; www.southcarolinaparks.com/cheraw

Finding the trailhead: From Charlotte take I-74 east for 25.5 miles. Turn right onto US 601 east and follow for 16 miles. Turn left onto SC 9 south and drive for 29.7 miles to Cheraw. Take a sharp right onto US 52 East and follow for approximately 4 miles. Turn right at the park entrance. Once you reach the T junction, turn right toward the golf course and clubhouse. Follow the park road 1.3 miles to the gravel parking lot and trailhead on the left side of the road. A kiosk marks the trailhead. GPS: N34 38.418′ / W79 55.566′

The Hike

If you are looking for a shorter hike, you can simply follow the Short Trail Loop for 1.5 miles and return back to the parking lot. This route follows the Long Loop Trail and passes by all the major features of the trails in the park. There are no restrooms or water at the trailhead, but you can purchase drinks and snacks and find restrooms at the park office. Towering pine trees are the hallmark of the beginning of this trail. It is nice to hike through the dense forest of pines in the morning hours when the dawn light cuts through the forest and the shadows of the tall trees create shafts of light. After nearly 1 mile on the Long Loop Trail, you reach a large sign marking the red-cockaded-woodpecker cavity trees to the right of the trail. These are trees that are used for nesting by the large endangered woodpeckers. All you have to do is listen for the loud knocking as these birds drill their large beaks into the trees in search of insects to eat. Once you hear them, pull out your binoculars and get an up-close look at these impressive and remarkably large woodpeckers.

A leaf-littered boardwalk crosses a creek on the Turkey Oak Trail.

Other birds found in this park are bald eagles, red-tailed hawks, ospreys, and Mississippi kites. Farther along the Long Loop Trail, you will take a spur trail that leads to the shore of Lake Juniper, a 360-acre lake that is 2.5 miles long. This portion of the lake is filled with beautiful cypress trees. Canoe rentals are available at the park office if you would like to explore the lake more by paddle after you have finished your hike. A small bench overlooks the lake at the end of the spur trail. During spring when the wildflowers are blooming, sweet pitcher plants and hunter's cups can be seen blossoming along the edge of the lake's shore. Around the lake is also a good place to spot fox squirrels that are commonly seen in this forest. Turn around at the bench overlooking the lake and continue on the Long Loop Trail.

During this next section of the trail, it is somewhat easy to get off the trail. There are many places where trail construction has taken place and it is easy to follow old trails. The park has also made a priority of blocking old roadbeds that intersect the trail in an effort to cut down on impactive walking and driving routes. Play close attention to the white-painted blazes on this next, long section of the trail to avoid getting lost. After 1.5 miles of pleasant and easy walking through the dense pine forest,

Cheraw State Park

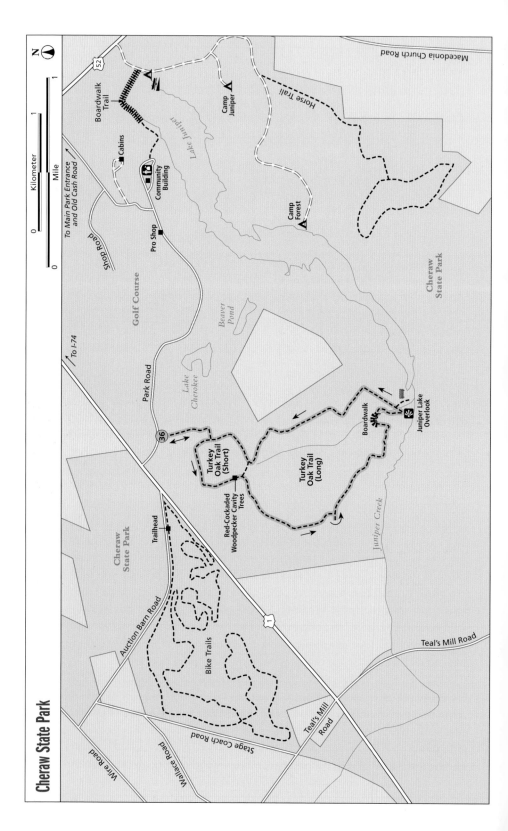

you arrive back at the end of the Long Loop and back at the junction with the trail that you hiked in on from the parking lot.

Turn right and follow the trail the 0.3 mile back to the trailhead and parking lot where you started. If you are up for a round of golf, you can always stop in and hit the links at the eighteen-hole golf course that you pass on the way out of the park.

Miles and Directions

0.0 Start from the trailhead at the gravel parking lot on the left side of the park road.

0.4 Reach a T junction. The short loop trail is to the left. Turn right onto the Long Loop Trail.

0.9 Look to the right of the trail and you will see the red-cockaded-woodpecker cavity trees. Continue 300 feet until you reach a split in the trail. The Short Loop Trail veers to the left. Stay to the right and continue on the Long Loop Trail.

2.3 Cross the boardwalk spanning the small stream.

2.5 Arrive at a trail junction. Follow the spur trail for 150 feet to Lake Juniper, a picturesque cypress swamp. A bench overlooks the swamp. Turn around, return to the trail junction, and continue on the Long Loop Trail.

4.0 Reach the junction with the Turkey Oak Trail. Turn right toward the parking lot and trailhead.

4.3 Arrive at the trailhead and parking lot where you started.

Hike Information

Local Information: Cheraw Chamber of Commerce, 221 Market St., Cheraw, SC 29520; (843) 537-7681

Local Events/Attractions: Cheraw Fish Hatchery, 433 Fish Hatchery Ln., Cheraw; (843) 537-7628. More than two million fish are raised and distributed from here each year. Free admission. Call to schedule a tour.

Old St. David's Church, 91 Church St., Cheraw. Visit the chamber of commerce for keys to the church, which was built in 1770 and was used in both the Revolutionary and Civil Wars.

Lodging: Cabins at Cheraw State Park, State Park Road, Cheraw; (843) 537-9656. Nightly cabin rates include a golf voucher during peak seasons (Sept 21 to Nov 4 and Mar 1 to May 19). Campsites also available

Spears Guest House, 228 Huger St., Cheraw; (843) 537-0302; spearsguesthouse.com

Restaurants: Rivers Edge Restaurant and Bakery, 162 Second St., Cheraw; (843) 537-1109; theriversedgecheraw.com

Fiesta Tapatia, 807 Market St., Cheraw; (843) 921-0200. Open daily 11 a.m. to 9 p.m.

37 Peachtree Rock

This short route is only a sample of the 4 miles of trails that the Peachtree Rock Heritage Preserve has to offer. Explore the mysterious, hilly landscape and see the peculiar rock formations along this trail, which takes you past all of the highlights in the park including the namesake Peachtree Rock, a waterfall, and Little Peachtree Rock.

Start: Dirt parking lot with kiosk and trailhead on SC 6

Distance: 2.1-mile lollipop

Hiking time: About 1 hour

Difficulty: Easy to moderate due to elevation gains

Trail surface: Forested trail

Best seasons: Early spring and late fall for cooler temperatures and wildflowers

Other trail users: Hikers only

Canine compatibility: Leashed dogs permitted

Fees and permits: None

Schedule: Open year-round from 1 hour before sunrise to 1 hour after sunset

Maps: TOPO! CD: North Carolina-South Carolina; USGS maps: Pelion East, South Carolina; USFS maps: Nature Conservancy brochure

Trail contacts: The Nature Conservancy, 2231 Devine St., Columbia, SC 29205; (803) 254-9049

Finding the trailhead: From Columbia take SC 302 / Edmund Highway south past Columbia International Airport. SC 302 will merge with SC 6. Veer left—toward Swansea—on SC 6 approximately 2 miles past the merge of SC 302 and SC 6. The preserve's parking lot is located on the left-hand side. A preserve sign is visible from the highway. GPS: N33 49.700' / W81 12.140'

The Hike

The scenery along this hike through the Peachtree Rock Heritage Preserve is unusual and interesting. The park is managed by the South Carolina chapter of the Nature Conservancy. They strive to keep the property in a wilderness state. As a result, there are no facilities at this 460-acre park, so be sure to pack your own water and food, and do not expect to find restrooms or trash cans along the trail. From the dirt parking lot just off SC 6, a trail ascends to the namesake Peachtree Rock. This first section is actually the steepest section of trail on the route. If you are looking for a very short hike outside of Columbia, you could hike to Peachtree Rock and the nearby waterfall and then turn around and head back to the parking lot for a half-mile hike. However, I highly recommend hiking this entire trail. The landscape changes very drastically as you ascend to a high point in the forest and then descend back down to the Peachtree Rock.

The trails throughout the park are sandy and surrounded by pine and oak forest. This area is part of the Sandhills region of South Carolina, which actually used to be the continent's eastern coastline. Just 0.3 mile from the trailhead, you reach Peachtree Rock, a strange-shaped rock of eroded sandstone that looks like an overturned pyramid that is precariously balancing on its tip. Look closely at the layers of rock that

Peachtree Rock

are clearly evident on the peculiarly shaped formation. These layers of rock explain the strange shape of the rock. The bottom layers of rock are composed of rock and sand that more easily erode than the upper layer of coarser and denser rock. A trail circles around Peachtree Rock and allows you to get a closer look at all sides of the interesting formation. Just north of Peachtree Rock is a small waterfall, which is the only cascade in the entire coastal plain of South Carolina. The waterfall may not be a torrent of water, but the cool water tumbling 20 feet over a limestone cliff is a welcome sight on a hot summer day.

From the waterfall the trail skirts around the front of the falls and in front of a steep wall of limestone and then gently ascends to a high point in the forest. Along this trail you may notice the presence of mountain laurel, which is more typically found in higher mountain elevations in the Appalachians but also grows in this area

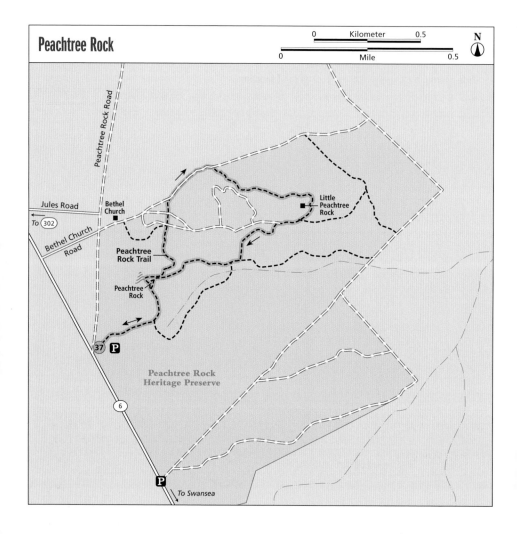

of the coastal plain region. Other plants you may see along the trail include crane-fly orchid, the endangered Rayner's blueberry, turkey oak, sparkleberry bushes, and woody goldenrod. Common animals seen in the preserve are deer, turkey, and northern red salamanders. If you're looking for birds, keep your eyes peeled for cardinals, chickadees, and red-cockaded woodpeckers.

The trail reaches a high point in the forest where there are several rock outcroppings along the trail that offer far-reaching views of the surrounding forest. From this high point you have to briefly navigate down some steep rock steps that lead down to Little Peachtree Rock on the right side of the trail. The rock formation bears the same upside-down pyramid formation as the larger Peachtree Rock. The trail skirts around the rock formation and then descends back past Peachtree Rock before returning to the parking lot and trailhead where you started.

Miles and Directions

0.0 Start from the dirt parking lot marked by a kiosk.

0.2 Turn left toward Peachtree Rock at the T junction.

0.3 Peachtree Rock is straight ahead. A trail circles around the rock. Stay straight toward the waterfall just 150 feet ahead. The trail veers to the right and runs directly in front of the rock wall. Continue for 250 more feet until you reach a split in the trail. Stay to the left.

0.4 The trail splits again. Stay to the right, heading toward Little Peachtree Rock.

0.6 Cross the dirt road, which is an old fire road. In 250 feet cross another dirt road. In just 200 more feet, you reach a trail junction. Turn right.

0.8 Reach another trail junction. Turn right toward Little Peachtree Rock.

1.2 Little Peachtree Rock is to your right. Continue on the trail that skirts to the left of Little Peachtree Rock. In 200 feet you reach a T junction. Turn right.

1.3 A dirt road continues straight. Follow the signs and turn left.

1.5 Reach a T junction. Turn right toward Peachtree Rock. In approximately 100 feet, stay right at the next junction.

1.8 Reach a split in the trail. Stay left toward Peachtree Rock. Follow the trail around the left side of Peachtree Rock and continue on the trail toward the parking lot.

1.9 The trail splits. Stay to the right and continue heading toward the parking lot and the trailhead where you started.

2.1 Reach the trailhead and parking lot where you started.

Hike Information

Local Information: Greater Lexington Chamber and Visitors Center, 321 S. Lake Dr., Lexington, SC 29072; (803) 359-6113; lexingtonsc.com

Local Events/Attractions: Lake Murray, South Carolina. Call (803) 781-5940 for information on 78-square-mile Lake Murray, or visit www.lakemurrayfun.com.

University of South Carolina, 945 Bull St., Columbia; (803) 777-0169; www.sc.edu

Lodging: Dreher Island State Park, 3677 State Park Rd., Prosperity; (803) 364-0756

Sesquicentennial State Park, 9564 Two Notch Rd., Columbia; (803) 788-2705

Restaurants: Café 403, 403 N. Lake Dr., Lexington; (803) 622-8141; cafe403.com

Hudson's Smokehouse BBQ, 4952 Sunset Blvd., Lexington; (803) 356-1070; hudsonsbbqsauce.com. Open Tues–Sun 10:30 a.m. to 9 p.m.

Organizations: DNR Heritage Trust Program, PO Box 167, Columbia, SC 29202; (803) 734-3886

38 Congaree National Park

This spectacular hike travels through much of the Congaree National Park. Hikers have the opportunity to explore one of the last remaining unlogged bottomland swamps in the United States. This pristine swamp features impressively large bald cypress, cherrybark oaks, and cedar trees, and the opportunity to view a great deal of wildlife along an exceptional trail that traverses a variety of low-lying terrains.

Start: From the trailhead for the Boardwalk Trail at the visitor center
Distance: 8.5-mile lollipop
Hiking time: About 5-8 hours
Difficulty: Easy
Trail surface: Boardwalk, forested trail
Best seasons: Late fall, winter, and spring to avoid the heat and insects
Other trail users: Hikers only
Canine compatibility: Leashed dogs permitted
Fees and permits: None

Schedule: 24 hours a day, 7 days a week
Maps: TOPO! CD: North Carolina-South Carolina; USGS maps: Gadsen and Wateree; South Carolina; USFS maps: Congaree National Park Trail Map available online at the park website or at the park office at the trailhead
Trail contacts: Congaree National Park, 100 National Park Rd., Hopkins, SC 29061; (803) 783-4241; nps.gov/cong

Finding the trailhead: From Spartanburg follow I-26 East (toward Charleston) to exit 116. At exit 116 turn onto I-77 North toward Charlotte (left exit). Continue on I-77 for approximately 5 miles to exit 5. At exit 5 turn off onto SC 48 East (Bluff Road), following the Congaree National Park directional signs. Travel southeast approximately 12 miles on SC 48 (Bluff Road) toward Gadsden and turn right onto Mountain View Road. Follow Mountain View Road for 0.8 mile. Turn right onto Old Bluff Road and travel 0.6 mile. At the large park entrance sign, turn left onto the park entrance road and proceed 1 mile to the Harry Hampton Visitor Center. GPS: N33 49.799' / W80 49.403'

The Hike

There are many opportunities to explore low-lying swamplands of South Carolina in this book, but few swamp hiking locations are as impressive as the Congaree Swamp, where you will discover the largest stand of old-growth river-bottom hardwood forest in the United States. However, before you hop in the car or hit the trail, call ahead to ensure the trails are open and to get an update on the mosquito forecast. Mosquitoes become especially thick and bothersome during the late spring through early fall, similar to any swamp or coastal area of South Carolina. Waters from the adjacent Congaree and Wateree Rivers also periodically sweep through the park's floodplain. This carries nutrients and sediments that nourish and rejuvenate the unique ecosystem. However, it also floods the trails and often leaves them impassable. And if you think you are ready to take on a trail after or during one of these flooding periods,

A bald cypress tree in Congaree Swamp at low water

simply visit the park website and view some of their photos of the trails submerged underwater and you might change your mind. That is unless you don't mind taking a canoe or kayak with you on the hike.

Located just 20 miles southeast of Columbia, the Congaree offers hikers more than 33 miles of excellent trails through varying low-lying terrain. The most popular of these trails is the elevated boardwalk that loops 2.4 miles from the visitor center. Raised nearly 6 feet off the forest floor, the elevated boardwalk traverses through a substantial area of intact old-growth forest and impressive stretches of swamp filled with cypress knees. If you only have a few hours in the park and want to get a feel for what you can experience in this wonderful gem, the best choice for a trail is this elevated boardwalk loop.

This swamp used to be even more impressive before Hurricane Hugo took out a substantial number of the old-growth trees in the area. During the storm the swamp lost a number of the record-setting trees, but you won't be disappointed while exploring this nearly 10-mile section of trails that introduces you to most of the highlights that you will find in the park. This hike combines the Boardwalk Trail, Weston Lake Loop Trail, Oakridge Trail, and the River Trail to form a dynamic out-and-back trail with a small loop at its southern end that follows along the Congaree River.

This area was first preserved as the Congaree Swamp National Monument in 1976 by the combined efforts of the Sierra Club and the National Park Service. A steep spike in timber prices put dollar signs in loggers' eyes and as a result threatened the remaining old-growth hardwoods in the swamp. In 1983 the astounding diversity

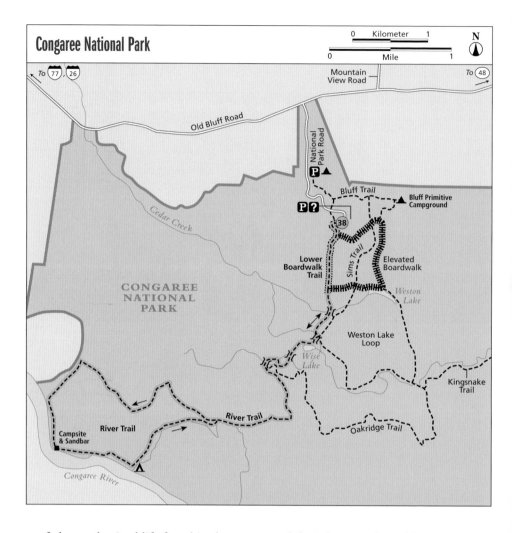

of plant and animal life found in the swamp and the inherent value of this rare ecosystem was fully recognized when the swamp was designated as an International Biosphere Reserve. In July of 2001 it was designated a Globally Important Bird Area, and on November 10, 2003, it was designated as the nation's fifty-seventh national park.

Along the hike the trees are the real stars of the show, but the area is also favored by birders. You will have the opportunity to spot a variety of wildlife along the trail. Look out for feral hogs, deer, opossums, and possibly an elusive bobcat if you're lucky and quiet. A great diversity of bird species are found in the park, including great blue herons, great horned owls (my favorite), and an impressive eight of the state's woodpecker species. You can create a variety of meandering loops and shortcuts through the park as you explore the network of trails. Anglers will enjoy the route proposed in the book as it passes by most of the major bodies of water in the park including Cedar Creek, Wise Lake, and the Congaree River.

Miles and Directions

0.0 Start from the visitor center and follow the Boardwalk Trail west.

0.1 Reach a T junction. The Bluff Trail is to the right. If you follow the Bluff Trail, it will take you toward the overnight parking area and the primitive campground. Turn left and continue on the Low Boardwalk Trail toward the Weston Lake Loop Trail.

0.2 Reach a split in the trail. To the left the Boardwalk Trail heads toward the east to complete a loop that returns to the visitor center. Stay to the right and continue on the Low Boardwalk Trail toward the Weston Lake Loop Trail.

0.6 The boardwalk splits again. Stay to the right.

0.7 Stay straight and join the Weston Lake Loop Trail.

1.1 Cross over Cedar Creek via the bridge. In 80 feet you reach the trailhead for the red-blazed Oakridge Trail. Follow the Oakridge Trail toward the River Trail.

1.2 The trail skirts by the shore of Wise Lake. This is a nice spot for a break or to do a little fishing if you came prepared.

1.4 Cross the short bridge over the small stream and continue on the red-blazed Oakridge Trail.

1.7 Cross the bridge over the small stream fed by Wise Lake. After the bridge you reach a split in the trail. Stay to the right and follow the white-blazed River Trail.

2.9 The River Trail splits. You can go either way and follow the loop back around to this junction. Stay to the right.

4.0 A spur trail takes you to a nice sandbar with excellent views of the river. There is an excellent campsite here if you are backpacking.

4.7 On the right side of the trail is a campsite that overlooks the Congaree River.

5.6 Arrive back at the junction that marks the beginning of the River Trail loop. From here follow the trail the way you came in. After 2.9 more miles you will be back at the visitor center.

8.5 Arrive back at the visitor center.

Hike Information

Local Information: Columbia CVB, 1101 Lincoln St., Columbia, SC 29201; (800) 264-4884; www.columbiacvb.com

Local Events/Attractions: Three Rivers Greenway, (803) 796-9020. Multiple trailheads in Cayce, South Carolina

Cayce Historical Museum, 1800 12th St., Cayce; (803) 739-5385; Small admission fee; discount for seniors and students. Open Tues–Fri 9 a.m. to 4 p.m., Sat–Sun 2 to 5 p.m.

Lodging: Inn at USC Wyndham Garden, 1619 Pendleton St., Columbia; (803) 779-7779

Camping at Congaree National Park, 100 National Park Rd., Hopkins; (803) 783-4241. A free camping permit is required and can be picked up at the visitor center.

Restaurants: Just Us Café, 1208 Knox Abbot Dr., Cayce; (803) 791-5162. Open Tues–Sun 6 a.m. to 3 p.m.

Kingsman Restaurant, 936 Axtell Dr., Cayce; (803) 796-8622; kingsmanrestaurant.com. Open Mon–Sat 11 a.m. to 10 p.m.

Hike Tours: Congaree National Park, 100 National Park Rd., Hopkins; (803) 783-4241. Park rangers provide guided programs.

39 Poinsett State Park Coquina Trail

This dynamic hike traverses a variety of terrains in a very short distance, making it one of the best and most highly recommended short day hikes in this collection of trails. Located west of Sumter in the east-central part of the state, hikers will skirt the 10-acre Old Levi Mill Pond and journey into an impressively hilly terrain with an interesting mix of mountain and coastal plants to discover along the way.

Start: From the trailhead at the park office
Distance: 1.3-mile loop
Hiking time: About 1-2 hours
Difficulty: Easy
Trail surface: Forested trail, boardwalk, gravel path
Best season: Year-round
Other trail users: Hikers only
Canine compatibility: Leashed dogs permitted. Dogs not permitted in cabin area

Fees and permits: None
Schedule: Daily from 9 a.m. until dark
Maps: TOPO! CD: North Carolina-South Carolina; USGS maps: Poinsett State Park; South Carolina; USFS maps: Poinsett State Park Trail Map available at the park office and online at southcarolinaparks.com
Trail contacts: Poinsett State Park, 6660 Poinsett Park Dr., Wedgefield, SC 29168; (803) 494-8177

Finding the trailhead: From Columbia take US 378/76 toward Sumter. After crossing over the Wateree River, proceed to the top of the hill and turn right onto SC 261 toward Wedgefield. Continue on SC 261 until you see signs for Poinsett. The park is on the right. GPS: N33 48.271' / W80 32.940'

The Hike

Poinsett Park is hands down one of the most interesting state parks in South Carolina, featuring 1,000 acres of extremely hilly terrain that incorporates part of the Wateree Swamp. The park is often referred to as the "Mountains of Midlands" and is found within an area of South Carolina known as the High Hills of the Santee, which is known for producing a large number of political and military leaders. The park offers hikers a variety of hiking trails that include the Coquina Trail, as well as the shorter Hilltop Trail and the Laurel Group Trail. Also nearby is the Wateree Passage of the Palmetto Trail.

The Wateree Trail is not a recommended trail for hikers due to the fact that an excessive amount of horse travel has left the trail extremely soiled with horse manure. The high amount of horse travel has also loosened and disturbed the surface of the trail to an excessive degree, to the point where hikers must trudge through very loose sand for most of the trail. If you are looking for a trail in this area, I highly recommend exploring the trails within Santee State Park, especially the Coquina Trail, which is easily the most popular trail in the park and in my opinion does not get the state-wide recognition that it deserves.

A spur trail skirts the small falls at the foot of the lake.

Santee State Park sits at a unique geographic location in South Carolina. About fifty million years ago, this was the location where the ocean met the coastal plain. This rare juxtaposition of mountain habitat with coastal plain has created a phenomenal diversity of plant and animal life as well as some of the most spectacular hiking in the midlands region of the state. The central location of the park makes this an excellent choice for interested hikers living in the Charlotte, Charleston, and Myrtle Beach areas, all of which are only 2 hours away. Along the trail you will discover the wonderful stonework that is the hallmark of Civilian Conservation Corps (CCC) crews who built many of the impressive cabins, picnic shelters, erosion walls, and canals throughout the park.

There is an astounding amount of wildlife and plant life to be found along the trails in the park including forty, yes forty, species of snakes. Six of these species are poisonous, so be sure to keep your eyes peeled for those pesky ankle-biters, which can quickly turn a pleasant hike into a frightening emergency. Along the trail you may also encounter alligators around the lake, as well as eastern fence lizards, bullfrogs, southern leopard frogs, squirrels, and white-tailed deer. Amateur and professional botanists will have their hands full on this hike while identifying more than sixty-five different species of trees and shrubs that include a host of pines, oaks, mountain laurel, and sassafras. In the spring the wildflowers put on quite a colorful show. You may find goldenrod, aster, strawberry bush, violets, and fairy wand all growing and blossoming along the forested trails in Poinsett Park.

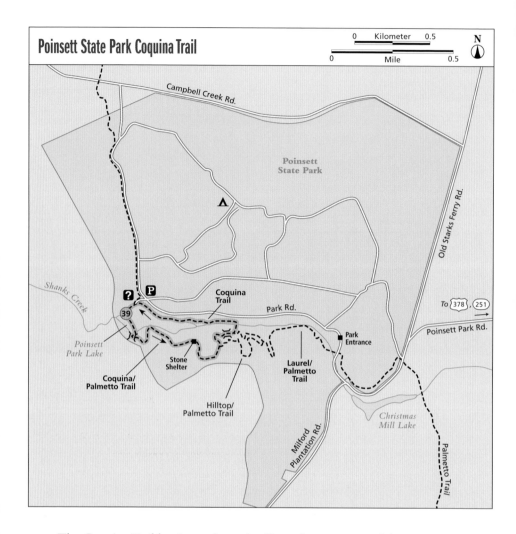

0   Kilometer   0.5

0   Mile   0.5

N

Campbell Creek Rd.

Poinsett
State Park

Old Starks Ferry Rd.

Shanks Creek

Coquina
Trail

Park Rd.

To 378, 251

Poinsett Park Rd.

Poinsett
Park Lake

Stone
Shelter

Park
Entrance

Coquina/
Palmetto Trail

Laurel/
Palmetto
Trail

Hilltop/
Palmetto Trail

Christmas
Mill Lake

Milford Plantation Rd.

Palmetto Trail

The Coquina Trail begins at the park office, where you can pick up an interpretive brochure about the trail. The trail was named after a form of limestone that is commonly found throughout the park. This coquina is evidence of the park's distant connection with the sea. The trailhead is not well marked but it's easy to find. Just head toward the lake and then walk to the left. The trail starts at the small bridge that crosses the pond spillway. This was the site of Singleton's Mill, an important meeting place for British sympathizers during the Revolutionary War. You can either cross the bridge here or follow the short spur trail that leads past a small but impressive multitiered waterfall. The trail follows along the northern shore of the pond and offers impressive views of the tranquil Old Levi Mill Pond, with the reflection of the park office often looking like a perfect bucolic oil painting.

From here you continue on the pleasant and level trail, following alongside the lake. The trail crosses another small bridge before curving around to the south and paralleling the west side of the lake. At this point the trail begins to climb and absolutely redefines your idea of what it means to walk around a South Carolina lake. This isn't your average hike around a lake—you are in the Mountains of the Midlands, my friend. After a 0.5-mile climb, you reach an impressive shelter that looks down toward the lake. This is an excellent and peaceful place to stop and rest or enjoy a leisurely lunch. A spur trail leads down to the lake from here. However, stay straight and follow the Coquina Trail around, then descend to a delightful swamp where if you're lucky, you'll get to see your first alligator in the "mountains." What a trail! This place has it all!

After crossing the bridge spanning a small sandy-bottom stream, the trail rejoins the lake and emerges out of the forest back at the parking lot where you started this wonderful hike. This is the perfect introduction to the extreme diversity of landscapes that you will find in this state filled with natural treasure and beauty.

Miles and Directions

0.0   Start from the Poinsett Park Visitor Center. Walk to the stone bridge to the right of the visitor center. This is the start of the Coquina Trail.

0.1   You can either cross the stone bridge or follow the short spur trail that leads down to the right of the bridge, passing a 5-foot waterfall to the left of the trail.

0.2   Cross the bridge that spans a small outlet of the lake.

0.6   Reach an impressive stone shelter on the right side of the trail that was built by the CCC. A spur trail to the left leads down to the lake. Stay straight on the Coquina Trail.

0.8   Reach a trail junction. The Red Trail is to the right. Stay straight on the Coquina Trail.

0.9   Cross the wooden bridge over a small stream. In 100 feet you reach a split in the trail. The Laurel Group Trail is to the right. Veer to the left and stay on the Coquina Trail.

1.3   Reach the end of the loop trail. You can see the visitor center where you started and the parking lot straight ahead.

Hike Information

Local Information: Sumter City Hall, 21 N. Main St., Sumter, SC 29150; (803) 436-2500; sumtersc.gov

Local Events/Attractions: Iris Festival at Swan Lake Iris Gardens, 822 W. Liberty St., Sumter. Held annually on Memorial Day weekend

Fantasy of Lights at Swan Lake Iris Gardens, 822 W. Liberty St., Sumter. Begins Dec 1 annually, with more than one million lights on display

Lodging: Cabins at Poinsett State Park, 6660 Poinsett Park Dr., Wedgefield; (803) 494-8177. One- and two-bedroom cabins available

Camping at Poinsett State Park, 6660 Poinsett Park Dr., Wedgefield; (803) 494-8177. Water and electrical hookups

Restaurants: Simply Southern Bistro, 67 W. Wesmark Blvd., Sumter; (803) 469-8502. Open Mon–Tues 11 a.m. to 3 p.m., Wed–Sat 11 a.m. to 9 p.m., Sun 11 a.m. to 3 p.m.

Lucky Corner Thai, 110 W. Wesmark Blvd., Sumter; (803) 773-7450. Open Mon–Fri 11:30 a.m. to 3 p.m. and 4 to 9 p.m., Sun noon to 4 p.m.

40 Santee State Park Mountain Bike and Hiking Trail

This easy day hike introduces you to the forests within Santee State Park, the second-most visited state park in South Carolina. Highlights of the trail include traversing through a beautiful mixed pine-hardwood forest draped with Spanish moss, occasional views of Lake Marion, and stretches of boardwalk spanning low-lying sections of the trail.

Start: From the Cleveland Road Trailhead
Distance: 6.0-mile loop
Hiking time: About 3-5 hours
Difficulty: Easy
Trail surface: Forested trail, boardwalk
Best season: Early spring, fall, winter
Other trail users: Mountain bikers
Canine compatibility: Leashed dogs permitted. Dogs not permitted in cabin area.
Fees and permits: Free for kids under age 16; small fee for age 16 and over; senior discount available

Schedule: Year-round daily from 6 a.m. to 10 p.m.
Maps: TOPO! CD: North Carolina-South Carolina; USGS maps: Summerton and Vance; South Carolina; USFS maps: Santee State Park Trail Map at the park office and online at southcarolinaparks.com
Trail contacts: Santee State Park, 251 State Park Rd., Santee, SC 29142; (803) 854-4834

Finding the trailhead: From Columbia take I-26 to SC 6 / Bridge Street, exit 136, travel through St. Matthews, continue on SC 6 for approximately 15 miles to Elloree, and follow the signs to Santee State Park. Turn left on State Park Road. The park is on the left after 4 miles. GPS: N33 31.060' / W80 28.626'

The Hike

Santee State Park may be best known for its fishing, but the network of trails found throughout the park is definitely worth exploring. There are many options for hiking in the park. This hike traverses the longest trail in the park and offers the most dynamic hiking in the state park. Other hikes to consider are the 1-mile Limestone Nature Trail, the 1-mile Oak Pinolly Nature Trail, and the 0.5-mile Sinkhole Pond Nature Trail. Although this trail is featured as a mountain bike trail, hiking is also encouraged along this path. The mostly level and firm trail makes this route exceptionally popular with runners. In recent years the state park has hosted several adventure triathlons that have included the Mountain Bike Trail as part of the running and biking components of the race. Be cautious when hiking this trail and give mountain bikers the right-of-way. Some mountain bikers ride extremely fast on these trails and a collision with one of

A view of the Mountain Bike Trail ▶
in Santee State Park

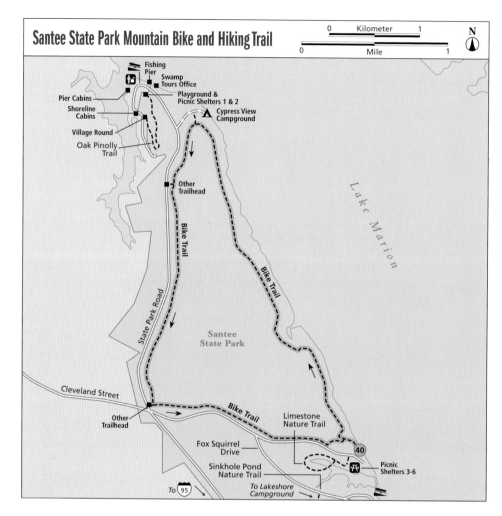

0   Kilometer   1

0   Mile   1

N

Fishing Pier

Swamp Tours Office

Pier Cabins

Playground & Picnic Shelters 1 & 2

Shoreline Cabins

Cypress View Campground

Village Round

Oak Pinolly Trail

Other Trailhead

Bike Trail

State Park Road

Lake Marion

Bike Trail

Santee State Park

Cleveland Street

Other Trailhead

Bike Trail

Limestone Nature Trail

Fox Squirrel Drive

40

Sinkhole Pond Nature Trail

Picnic Shelters 3-6

To 95

To Lakeshore Campground

them would definitely take the enjoyment out of this hike. Also be sure to bring plenty of water along with you, especially during the hot summer months.

One of the first things you will notice along this trail is the prevalence of Spanish moss hanging from the many oak trees along the route. During the warmer months you may also notice a great number of impressively large spiderwebs spanning the trail and blocking the route. Most of these webs are spun by the colorful golden silk spiders that spin strong, golden webs. These spiders and their webs may be intimidating but don't worry: They are nonpoisonous and can be easily avoided by skirting around them.

Most visitors come to this state park to fish, and for good reason. Santee State Park has an excellent fishing pier on Lake Marion where you can reel in largemouth bass, striped bass, bream, crappie, and catfish. A valid South Carolina fishing license is required. Before you leave the park, drive down to the park office and check out the impressive cabins they rent on Lake Marion. Twenty cabins are on the lakeshore and ten are located on a dock that extends over the lake. They all offer their own fish-cleaning stations and are fully furnished and have fully equipped kitchens. They are air-conditioned and a great getaway for anglers and outdoors lovers looking for an escape in the south-central part of the state.

There are two trailheads to this trail. You can start your hike at the trailhead along the State Park Road near the campground right before you arrive at the lakeshore. However, for the route described here, you will start from the other trailhead on Cleveland Road near the swimming area. The trailhead and parking area are well marked. The trail has been largely expanded since the last edition of this book was published in 1999. The trail used to simply run from this trailhead to the other trail-head near the campground for a nearly 4-mile hike. The trail has more than doubled in length and is now a loop trail that begins from the Cleveland Road Trailhead, parallels the shore of Lake Marion, and then circles around to the south, paralleling Santee State Road before returning to the Cleveland Road Trailhead where you started your hike. There are several spur trails that lead down to the lake, but the trail is very easy to follow, well maintained, and well marked. Simply follow the directions below and keep your eyes open for the blue blazes along the way.

The trail is wide in many places and exposed to the sun, which can make for an exceptionally hot hike during the summer. A wide-brimmed hat reminiscent of the antebellum era is recommended for shade and style, as are plentiful amounts of water and sunscreen for the fair-skinned folks among us. If you're lucky, a light breeze will be blowing across Lake Marion to cool off the trail and stir up the roselike scent of the wax myrtles along the route. Throughout your walkabout you see impressive-size loblolly pines and a variety of oaks. Wildlife lovers may spot squirrels, snakes, opossums, raccoons, and bird species such as Carolina wren, osprey, and wild turkeys along this excellent trail that explores the shore of Lake Marion and the surrounding moss-filled forest.

Miles and Directions

0.0 Start from the trailhead near the end of Cleveland Road. A kiosk marks the start of the Bike Trail.

0.1 Reach a split in the Bike Trail. This is the start of the Bike Trail Loop. Stay to the right and head toward the Cypress View Campground.

2.6 Reach a trail junction. To the right a spur trail leads to the Cypress View Campground. Stay to the left and continue on the Bike Trail.

3.1 Arrive at another trail junction. The trail splits, and to the right a spur trail leads to a trail-head on Oak Pinolly Road. Stay to the left and continue on the Bike Trail.

4.6 Reach a T junction. To the right a spur trail leads to State Park Road. Turn left and continue on the Bike Trail.

5.9 Arrive at the end of the loop. Turn right to return to the trailhead where you started.

6.0 Arrive at the trailhead on Cleveland Road where you started and the end of this hike.

Hike Information

Local Information: Santee Tourism Office, 176 Brooks Blvd., Santee, SC 29142; (803) 854-2152; santeetourism.com

Local Events/Attractions: Elloree Trails, Elloree Training Center, 170 Wishbone Circle, Elloree; (803) 897-2616. This fifty-year tradition of thoroughbred and quarter-horse racing in South Carolina takes place annually in March. Admission fee; free for children 12 and under

Santee Cooper Country Club, 9069 Highway 6, Santee; (803) 854-2554; santeecoopergolf .com. Enjoy one of more than fifteen golf courses in the area.

Lodging: Camping at Santee State Park, 251 State Park Rd., Santee; (803) 854-4834. Water and electrical hookups

Cabins at Santee State Park, 251 State Park Rd., Santee; (803) 854-4834. Two-bedroom cabins available

Clarks Inn, 114 Bradford Blvd., Santee; (803) 854-2141; clarksinnandrestaurant.com

Restaurants: Lone Star BBQ and Mercantile, 2212 State Park Rd., Santee; (803) 854-2000; www.lonestarbbq.net. Open Thurs–Sat 11:30 a.m. to 8 p.m., Sun 11:30 a.m. to 3 p.m.

Craig's Place Deli and Café, 190 Plaza Cir., Santee; (803) 854-4601. Open daily 8:30 a.m. to 5 p.m.

Honorable Mentions

☾ The Jungle Nature Trail

Don't let the name of this very easy hike deter you from exploring this route. I assure you that there is no jungle in South Carolina. This hike is actually located right in the heart of Aiken's famous horse country. This easy 2.6-mile loop hike explores the Aiken State Natural Area. You don't have to worry about any difficult elevation along this route. This midland trail only has 30 feet of elevation change along a route that explores the botanically diverse forest found in this preserve on the banks of the Edisto River. The preserve was created to protect the spring-fed ponds and rare plants found throughout the South Edisto River Valley. Highlights of the hike include a trek along the Edisto River and stops at an impressive freshwater pond and spring.

After entering the Aiken State Natural Area, follow the signs to the Nature Trail, which leads to the trailhead for the Jungle Nature Trail. At the trailhead you will find a beautiful and shady picnic area on a lakeshore. The picnic pavilions offer excellent views of the lake and are an excellent destination for a picnic. The trail leaves the picnic area and enters into a thick pine-and-hardwood forest. You quickly reach a junction. To the left is a spur trail that leads to the campground. Stay to the right and continue on the Jungle Nature Trail. In just a few feet, you will reach another junction. This is the split for the loop trail. Stay to the right and cross the short boardwalk section over a small stream that flows into the Edisto River.

After 0.6 mile from the trailhead, the path crosses the paved park road and passes through the Cypress Stump Picnic Area. After 1.3 mile you reach a four-way junction. Straight ahead the trail leads to Fishing Lake. To the left the Jungle Nature Trail heads south and back toward the trailhead. Turn right and follow the spur trail to the Edisto River and the River Dock and Spring. A well-maintained boardwalk leads to the edge of the Edisto River, where you may see paddlers enjoying a day of fishing or exploration on the beautiful river. If you are interested, the park rents canoes that you can take out on the Edisto. Also along the river you find a natural freshwater spring bubbling out from an artfully constructed stone fountain.

After enjoying the river and the fascinating freshwater spring, turn around and head back to the four-way junction. At the junction turn right and follow the spur trail to Fishing Lake. If you brought your pole along for the hike, you can try your best to reel in a few catfish, bream, or bass from the spring-fed pond. After exploring the lake, turn around and return once again to the four-way junction. At the junction turn right and follow the Jungle Nature Trail, which leads to the south and back to the trailhead and picnic area where you started this excellent and interesting hike.

AIKEN'S HORSE COUNTRY

Take a short drive through downtown Aiken and you will quickly understand what the main attraction is in this town: horses and the people who love to ride them. The signs that mark the roads are engraved with the stately images of horse heads. There are life-size horse statues along the sidewalks. Even some of the roads downtown are unpaved so that they may be easier on those lucky enough to own a good set of hooves. There are murals of riders dressed in swanky riding clothes engaging in a spirited game of polo. The talk at teatime is often about horses, recent or upcoming horse events, or how to manage and care for horses and stables, and everything else that goes along with the posh and pastoral lifestyle of owning a ranch as a mere hobby or even as one's livelihood. Aiken is horse country, and the easy rolling hills and open pastures attract equestrian lovers and trainers from all over the world.

Several of the trails in this book may take you through Aiken. Take the time to take a slow drive through the horse farms, polo fields, and equestrian centers that surround the city. After a nice hike you will find several excellent sandwich shops and cafes in the historic district of town. If you are looking for somewhere to ride, stop by the 2,000-acre Hitchcock Woods Park, located just a few blocks from the historic district—it is filled with dogwoods, pines, and azaleas.

The history of Aiken's transformation into one of the most recognized destinations for horse lovers in the Southeast dates back to the 1800s. The area was originally known as the site of a popular health resort. Northerners would travel down in the winter to escape the cold, and in the summer folks from Charleston would head to Aiken for a cool break from the heat and humidity of the coast. Travelers quickly realized that the sandy soil hardly ever froze and that the soil was nearly free of rocks. This was perfect for riding horses. By 1882 Aiken held its first polo match. There were more than 10,000 spectators in attendance to watch the sport, which had just been introduced in the United States six years earlier. Polo dominated the scene during this period, and by the 1930s Aiken had sixteen polo fields, more than one hundred players, and games occurring nearly every day during the winter season. Fox hunting and horse racing are also favorite pastimes of Aiken citizenry. If you want a first glance at one of the future winners of the Kentucky Derby, you may have to look no further than the Training Track, located in the middle of the historic district.

D Stevens Creek

Explore this spectacular 11.3-mile trail during the months of April and May for some of the most wonderful displays of jack-in-the-pulpit wildflowers found in this region. Although this is a long hike that requires you to hike to the trail's end and then turn around and return to the trailhead, there is very little elevation gain along the route. That makes this a trail that can easily be completed in around 5 to 6 hours and one that can certainly be hiked in a single day. This well-maintained trail is located just north of Augusta, Georgia, in the Long Cane District of Sumter National Forest. Highlights include an exploration of the steep bluffs and scenic banks of Stevens Creek and several smaller tributary crossings, as well as enjoyable jaunts through some very impressive bottomland forests. Be mindful that this trail has definitely become increasingly popular with mountain bikers in recent years. Stay alert while hiking and give mountain bikers the right-of-way.

The trail begins from the trailhead and parking area on SC 23, near the bridge over Stevens Creek. It travels into a rich and lush forest that is blanketed with a thick understory of green ferns. A forest filled with hardwoods such as maple, oak, and beech towers above the lush forest floor. On the first section of the trail, you cross many wooden footbridges spanning small tributaries that feed Stevens Creek. No need to carry a ton of water on this hike. Save the weight and take a water purifier with you and just refill as you go. However, during dry years or periods of drought, I recommend that you bring at least two liters of water on this hike. You will reach several crossings on this trail where you will have to cross the stream by jumping from rock to rock, but no need to worry. The stream crossings are easy and can be made easier with a set of trusty hiking poles, which I highly recommend buying if you do not already own a good, sturdy pair.

Along this route you will notice that the trail is marked every 0.5 mile so that you can track your progress as you hike north. The trail curves to the west and away from the creek before turning toward the east and back in the direction of Stevens Creek. After 2.0 miles you reach a trail junction. A spur trail to the left leads to another parking area located off FR 632. Stay to the left and continue on the Stevens Creek Trail. The trail traverses a series of bluffs before reaching its highest elevation of around 300 feet at about 3.7 miles from the trailhead. The trail then descends to some beautiful bottomland forest before climbing back onto a ridge where you are offered excellent views of the rapids of Stevens Creek below. After 5.6 miles you reach the official end of the Stevens Creek Trail, which is marked by a trail marker. A small, thin path continues forward, and another trail that leads to an old road is to the left. Turn around and return to the trailhead and parking area along SC 23 where you started.

E Turkey Creek Trail Day Hike

This 9.3-mile hike explores a 4.5-mile section of the Turkey Creek Trail, located in the Long Cane District of Sumter National Forest. The route described here travels from the trailhead of the Turkey Creek Trail to Key Bridge, where you will turn around and return to the trailhead. If you enjoy backpacking, this is an excellent choice for an overnight hike. From Key Bridge you can continue exploring the remaining 7 miles of the Turkey Creek Trail. This will provide you with 23 miles of trail to backpack and discover. There are many excellent campsites along this route, especially along Wine Creek and Turkey Creek.

To find the trailhead from Edgefield, drive down US 25 North for 4 miles. Turn left onto SC 283 and continue for 10 more miles. Don't be confused by the fact that you will pass Turkey Creek on your way to the trailhead—the trail actually begins along Wine Creek.

From the trailhead and parking area, the trail travels through a pine forest to the banks of Wine Creek. You will follow along the pleasant, meandering creek and cross several small tributary streams until you arrive at a bluff with an excellent view of Turkey Creek below.

You descend down into the flats, which are thick with brush and blooming wild-flowers during the spring and fall, before climbing up steeply again onto the bluff. Once you are up on the bluff again, you will gently descend back down to Turkey Creek. During this next section you will cross several bridges spanning small tributaries and continue to follow Turkey Creek as it winds through thick brush and along the streambed, where large cypress trees can be observed. After 3.3 miles the trail crosses a swath clearing and travels through a patch of very healthy forest before arriving at a section of forest that is noticeably decimated by a recent pine-beetle infestation that ravaged this part of the Sumter National Forest. The forest gradually becomes healthy again before you arrive at a kiosk near Key Bridge. From here turn around and retrace your steps back to the trailhead where you started this hike, or you can continue to explore the remaining 7 miles along the Turkey Creek Trail. Another option is to leave a vehicle at the dirt road near Key Bridge.

Coastal Plain and Southern Region

If you are looking for the easiest hiking in the state, then you want to come down south to the Lowcountry and hike the coastal plain. Here you will find miles and miles of undeveloped beaches as well as thousands of acres of stunningly beautiful marshland, wetlands, and tidal creeks that flow into the Atlantic Ocean. This part of the state is by far the most popular and populated area of the state with population centers in Hilton Head and Beaufort on the southern coast, Charleston on the central coast, and Myrtle Beach in the north. The hiking in these areas may be easy as far as the steepness of the terrain is concerned, but the coastal plain presents its own unique challenges. During periods of heavy rainfall, the trails that explore the marshlands and wetlands are often flooded and impassable. During the summer the heat and insects, particularly mosquitoes, can be nearly intolerable. Alligators and poisonous snakes are also of concern, but they are less likely to give you trouble than the aforementioned challenges.

While the swamps and wetlands may at first seem daunting and foreboding to hikers who are less familiar with such subtropical terrains, I encourage you to put your fears aside and give them a wholehearted chance. The best

Dwarf palmettos crowd the drier areas of the forest understory (hike 48).

A view of the Atlantic Ocean from a boardwalk along the trail in Huntington Beach State Park (hike 60)

introductions to these environments are found at the Caw Caw Interpretive Center and along the most impressive network of trails at Huntington Beach State Park. For the more adventurous, you can embark on a three-day backpacking trip along the Swamp Fox Trail and likely become more intimately familiar with swamps and alligators than you may feel necessary.

The coastal plain is also the best place in South Carolina for bird watching. Hundreds of varieties of birds call the coastal plain their home, and hundreds more pass through each year during the spectacular annual migrations that occur during the fall and spring. While in the area be sure to sample some of the excellent seafood, especially at the old Seewee Restaurant along US 17 in Awendaw close to the South Tibwin, I'on Swamp, and Seewee Shell Mound Trails, which is an excellent place to stop for some fried shrimp and sweet tea after a long day adventuring around the surrounding beautiful swamps and marshes.

41 Savannah National Wildlife Refuge

This excellent half-day hike explores a large segment of the Savannah National Wildlife Refuge, located at the southern tip of the state just north of Savannah. Highlights include beautiful marshland, a network of extensive canals, maritime forest, and a visit to Kingfisher Pond at the end of the hike.

Start: The trailhead at the Tupelo Trail parking area on SC 170
Distance: 7.2-mile out and back
Hiking time: About 2–3 hours
Difficulty: Easy
Trail surface: Gravel road, old roadbed, forested path, dirt road
Best seasons: Winter, early spring, late fall
Other trail users: Mountain bikers
Canine compatibility: Dogs not permitted
Fees and permits: None
Schedule: Dawn–dusk daily; visitor center hours Mon–Sat. 9 a.m. to 4:30 p.m.

Maps: TOPO! CD: North Carolina–South Carolina; USGS maps: Limehouse and Savannah; South Carolina; USFS maps: Savannah National Wildlife Refuge Map available at the trailhead, online at fws.gov, and at the Savannah National Wildlife Refuge Visitor Center located on US 17 in Jasper County, South Carolina, approximately 6 miles north of downtown Savannah, Georgia
Trail contacts: Savannah National Wildlife Refuge, 694 Beech Hill Ln., Hardeeville, SC 29927; (843) 784-2468

Finding the trailhead: From I-95, take SC exit 5 (Hardeeville/Savannah), US 17 South (right off exit ramp if on I-95 South; left off exit ramp if on I-95 North) toward Savannah, Georgia. After about 6 miles, you'll come to an interchange with SC 170 West. Stay on US 17 up over the overpass, as if you're going to Savannah, and the Savannah NWR Visitor Center entrance is approximately 0.5 mile past the overpass on your right. There is a sign at the interchange with SC 170 West indicating to exit right for the Savannah NWR, however, this will take you to another part of the refuge, not the visitor center. GPS: N32 10.393' / W81 05.830'

The Hike

There is a wide variety of roads and hikes for exploring the refuge. This hike starts from the parking lot across the road from the eastern end of Wildlife Drive, the most popular driving route through the refuge. You can create a wide variety of loops and out-and-back hikes by following any number of routes across the many dikes that crisscross the ponds, pools, and marshes in the 29,000-acre refuge, which features freshwater marshes, tidal rivers, creeks, and bottomland hardwoods. Opened in 1927, the refuge is composed of a low band of land bordered by sandhill ridges to the west and the Atlantic Ocean on the east. The refuge stretches from St Mary, Georgia, to Georgetown, South Carolina.

During the winter the refuge is a prime spot to observe migrating birds as they make their way south along the Atlantic Flyway. Birds you may see during this time

The Tupelo Trail

of high activity include thousands of ring-necked, teal, pintails, and as many as ten other species of ducks. In the spring and fall, birders will enjoy identifying the many songbirds that make a stop at the refuge during their journey to and from the nesting grounds to the north. Along the trail you are likely to see alligators, turtles, snakes, salamanders, great horned owls, ospreys, bald eagles, deer, feral hogs, and, if you're lucky, the wood stork, which has made an excellent recovery in the refuge in recent years.

The primary objective of the refuge is to provide habitat for migratory waterfowl, therefore portions of the 34 miles of canals, trails, and roadways open to hikers and bikers are periodically closed. Call ahead to check on what closures may affect your visit to the refuge. The 4-mile-long Wildlife Drive is open all year long. Fishing is allowed year-round in the creeks and rivers throughout the refuge so pack a pole and reel in some dinner along the hike, which offers several excellent fishing opportunities along the route. The refuge is also open for hunting during hunting season, which generally extends from October 1 through January 1. Check with the refuge beforehand to see if there will be any trail closures during this time, and be sure to stay safe and wear bright-orange-colored clothing and a bright-orange-colored hat if you choose to hike during this time of the year.

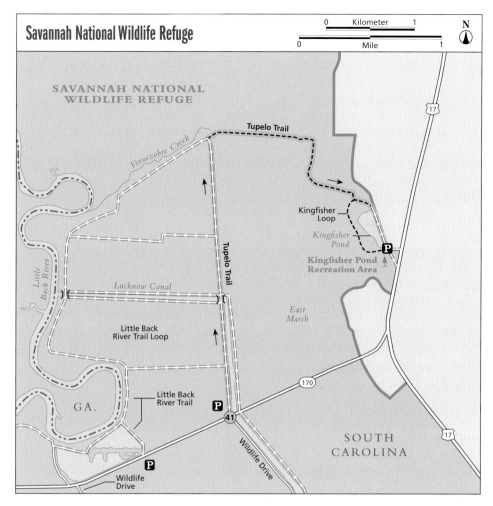

SAVANNAH NATIONAL
WILDLIFE REFUGE

Tupelo Trail

Vernezobre Creek

Kingfisher Loop

Kingfisher Pond

Kingfisher Pond Recreation Area

Tupelo Trail

Little Back River

Lucknow Canal

Little Back River Trail Loop

East Marsh

Little Back River Trail

GA.

41

Wildlife Drive

SOUTH CAROLINA

Wildlife Drive

The first section of the trail runs straight alongside the refuge's main diversion canal. You shouldn't have a problem spotting plenty of alligators of all sizes in the canal. Some of them are impressively large and can be more than 10 feet long. This main diversion canal is where you will most likely see the largest alligators along this route. You cross several bridges and enjoy the expansive views of the surrounding wetlands, which were used for old rice-field operations dating back to the 1700s. After 1.8 miles you reach the junction with the Tupelo Trail and follow the forested path through a rare coastal bald cypress-tupelo swamp. You walk alongside a tributary of the Vernezobre Creek and explore the wetland until you emerge at a dirt road that takes you down to Kingfisher Pond and the end of this hiking route.

From the Kingfisher Recreation Area, you can either turn around and hike back the way you came, walk along the highway back to the parking lot, or arrange a shuttle to take you back to where you started this adventurous hike through a segment of the Savannah Wildlife Refuge.

Miles and Directions

0.0 Start from the trailhead at the Tupelo Trail Parking Area on SC 170. The Kingfisher Trail follows the dirt road starting from the northern side of the parking lot.

0.3 Reach a trail junction. The Little Back River Trail is to the left. Stay straight on the Kingfisher Trail.

0.7 Reach a trail junction with the north end of the Little Back River Trail to the left. Stay straight on the Kingfisher Trail. In 100 feet you cross a bridge spanning the Diversion Canal. Continue straight on the Kingfisher Trail.

1.1 Arrive at a trail junction. To the left is a road that follows alongside a dike. Stay straight on the Kingfisher Trail.

1.8 Reach the junction with the Tupelo Trail. Turn right onto the forested path that follows alongside a canal.

3.2 Reach a trail junction. Turn left.

3.3 Arrive at a trail junction with a dirt road. Turn right and head south toward the Kingfisher Pond Recreation Area. In 200 feet you reach another junction with a dirt road. Stay straight.

3.6 Reach the parking area for the Kingfisher Pond Recreation Area and the northern end of this hike. Turn around to head back the way you came. (**Option:** To shorten your hike, this is a good spot to leave a car or arrange for someone to pick you up here.)

3.9 Stay straight at the first junction with another dirt road, then in 200 feet turn left off the dirt road and onto the forested path.

4.0 Turn right at the trail junction.

4.4 Turn left onto the Kingfisher Trail.

5.1 To the right is a road that follows alongside a dike. Stay straight on the Kingfisher Trail.

5.5 Cross a bridge spanning the Diversion Canal. In 100 feet you reach a trail junction with the Little Back River Trail to the right. Stay straight on the Kingfisher Trail.

5.9 Arrive a junction with the Little Back River Trail to the right. Stay straight on the Kingfisher Trail.

7.2 Arrive back at the Tupelo Trail Parking Area and trailhead on SC 170 where you started this hike.

Hike Information

Local Information: City of Hardeeville, 205 E. Main St., Hardeeville, SC 29927; (843) 784-2231; cityofhardeeville.com

Local Events/Attractions: Sergeant Jasper County Park, 1458 Red Dam Rd., Hardeeville; (843) 784-5130. Open daily 8 a.m. to 6 p.m.; free admission

Newhall Audubon Nature Preserve, Palmetto Bay Rd., Hilton Head; (843) 842-9246. Open dawn–dusk; free admission

Lodging: Inn at Harbour Town-Sea Pines Resort, 32 Greenwood Dr., Hilton Head Island; (866) 561-8802; seapines.com/accommodations/inn-at-harbour.asp

Main Street Inn, 2200 Main St., Hilton Head Island; (843) 681-3001; mainstreetinn.com

Restaurants: Chicken Lickin' Hickory House, 16161 Whyte Hardee Blvd., Hardeeville; (843) 784-5141

The Pink Pig, 3508 S. Okatie Hwy., Hardeeville; (843) 784-3635; the-pink-pig.com. Open Tues–Sat 11 a.m. to 3 p.m., Thurs–Fri 5 to 7 p.m.

42 Sea Pines Forest Preserve

Enjoy this short and easy day hike on one of South Carolina's most popular barrier islands. The trek explores the dynamic maritime forests and marshlands of the 605-acre preserve within the Sea Pines Plantation, the oldest development on Hilton Head Island.

Start: From the Greenwood Entrance parking area

Distance: 2.0-mile lollipop

Hiking time: About 1–2 hours

Difficulty: Easy

Trail surface: Forested path, boardwalk, paved path

Best season: Year-round

Other trail users: Horses, bicycles, and vehicles on designated trails. Hiking trails are for hikers only.

Canine compatibility: Dogs not permitted

Fees and permits: Small fee per car for non-residents or guests of Sea Pines Plantation

Schedule: Dawn–dusk daily

Maps: TOPO! CD: North Carolina–South Carolina; USGS maps: Tybee Island; South Carolina; USFS maps: Sea Pines Forest Map available at the trailhead and entrance station

Trail contacts: Sea Pines Forest Preserve Foundation, Community Services Associates Inc., Hilton Head Island, SC 29928; (843) 671-7170

Finding the trailhead: From Charleston proceed on US 17 South for 53 miles. Turn right onto SC 170 West for 18 miles. Merge onto SC 278 East toward Hilton Head Island. From the entrance to Hilton Head Island, drive on SC 278 and turn right onto the Cross Island Parkway (toll). Continue to the traffic circle on Palmetto Bay Road and turn right onto Greenwood Drive. The Sea Pines gate is 0.2 mile farther and the preserve is 1 mile from the gate on the left. GPS: N32 08.795' / W80 46.903'

The Hike

Starting in the 1700s the land that now comprises the Sea Pines Forest Preserve was used to grow rice, indigo, and cotton. However, the shell mound in the southwest section of the preserve is evidence that Native Americans enjoyed this land long before the Europeans began using the property for agriculture, hunting, and timber harvesting. The shell mound here is listed on the National Register of Historic Places and makes an excellent side trip with the hike listed in this book or a short extra hike if you start from the Lawton Entrance accessed from Lawton Drive. Evidence of Native American habitation on this 11-mile-long, 3-mile-wide barrier island actually dates back 4,000 years. Today, Hilton Head Island sees more than two million visitors a year. Fortunately, in 1956 developers set aside 605 acres as a preserve, which was recognized by the Audubon Society as an Important Bird Area in 1998.

There are three entrances and trailheads to the preserve and ample opportunities to create interesting and fun hiking loops and out-and-back hikes to suit your time

An anhinga suns itself in the Sea Pines Forest Preserve.

frame, hiking abilities, and interests. There are more than 6 miles of trails found in the preserve, and I strongly encourage you to go out and explore more of this beautiful preserve. The most popular segment of trails start from the Greenwood Entrance. The route described here takes you through most of the highlights in the preserve and offers a sampling of all of the diverse ecosystems that you can encounter in the preserve, which include maritime forest, old agricultural rice fields and canals, several freshwater ponds and lakes, and plenty of wetlands and marshes along the way. The area is very popular with birders, who may see bald eagles, ospreys, egrets, herons, red-winged blackbirds, anhinga, owls, and a wide variety of ducks and waterfowl along the trail. Other wildlife found in the preserve includes alligators, deer, raccoons, marsh rabbits, squirrels, opossums, and turtles. In the lakes and ponds, you can fish for bass, crappie, and bream.

After passing through the entrance gate and paying the steep fee to get into the Sea Pines Plantation, you will find the parking area and trailhead for the Greenwood Entrance approximately 1 mile further on the left side of the road. The trailhead is easy to miss so keep your eyes open. A paved path winds through a beautiful maritime forest bordered by marshland and a small pond before reaching the Boggy Gut Trail. This unpaved path to the left will take you to the foot of the Rice Field Boardwalk. The boardwalk crosses the Old Lawton Rice Field, where you are offered impressive views of the surrounding marshes and wildlife from three observation decks along the way.

At the foot of the boardwalk, you briefly follow the Bridle Trail through a maritime forest of large oak trees and pines before turning right onto the Vanishing Swamp Trail. There, you cross another boardwalk and enjoy stunning views of a secluded forest where surface levels rise and fall seasonally. A combination of dirt roads and

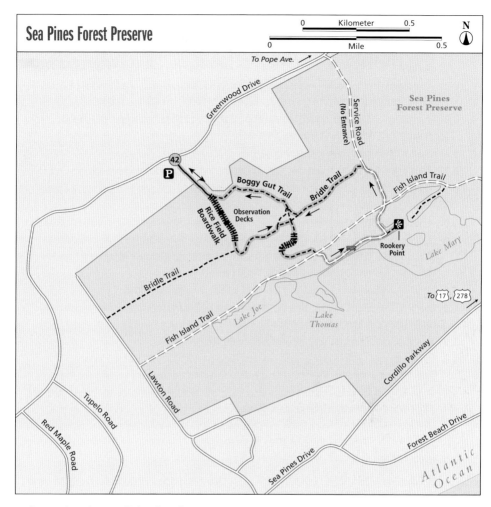

Sea Pines Forest Preserve

forested paths parallel Lake Thomas and Wood Duck Pond and then take you out to the Rookery Point where you can sit at the benches atop the observation deck and enjoy the picturesque views of Rookery Island and Mary Lake. This is also an excellent place to see a variety of waterfowl, especially ducks, anhinga, and herons. From here a connector road takes you back to the Bridle Trail, which traverses through more high-ground forest, before rejoining the Boggy Gut Trail, which treks alongside an old rice field canal. You reach the junction with the paved path and turn right to return to the parking lot and trailhead where you started this easy hike filled with a variety of forested and wetland terrain.

Miles and Directions

0.0 Start from the Greenwood Entrance parking area approximately 1 mile from the entrance gate to Sea Pines and located on the left side of the road. The kiosk marks start of trail. Follow the paved Boggy Gut Trail south toward the Rice Field Boardwalk.

0.1 The trail splits. The paved path continues to the right. Veer left onto the unpaved Boggy Gut Trail. In 20 feet turn right onto the Rice Field Boardwalk.

0.2 Arrive at the first of two observation decks along the boardwalk. The second is 150 feet down the trail.

0.3 After leaving the boardwalk and rejoining the unpaved trail, you arrive at a T junction. Turn left toward Vanishing Swamp.

0.5 The trail splits. Stay right toward the Vanishing Swamp. In 220 feet you arrive at a four-way junction. Turn right toward Vanishing Swamp.

0.6 The boardwalk over Vanishing Swamp begins.

0.7 Arrive at the end of the boardwalk. At the T junction turn left toward Rookery Point.

0.8 Arrive at a T junction with a dirt road. The golf course is to the left. Stay to the right toward the Rookery Point Trail.

0.9 Arrive at an observation bench on the right side of the trail. Continue straight on the dirt road.

1.0 Reach a split in the trail. Veer right onto the Rookery Point Trail. In 250 feet you arrive at the Rookery Point Overlook with excellent views of Rookery Island and Lake Mary. From here turn around and follow the spur trail back to the Rookery Point Trail

1.1 Arrive at the Rookery Point Trail and turn right toward the Fish Island Trail.

1.2 Reach a T junction. Turn right onto the dirt road, the Fish Island Trail. In 100 feet you reach a split in the road. Veer left onto Pit Road.

1.3 Reach a split in the trail. Veer left onto a dirt path, the Bridle Trail.

1.6 Arrive at a split in the trail. Veer right onto the Boggy Gut Trail. In 160 feet you arrive at another split in the trail. Stay straight toward the Greenwood Entrance parking area.

1.9 Arrive back at the paved portion of the Boggy Gut Trail. Turn right and follow the paved path back to the Greenwood Entrance parking area.

2.0 Arrive at the end of the trail back at the Greenwood Entrance parking area where you started.

Hike Information

Local Information: Hilton Head Island–Bluffton Chamber of Commerce, 1 Chamber of Commerce Dr., Hilton Head Island, SC 29928; (843) 785-3673

Local Events/Attractions: Hilton Head Food and Wine Festival, Coastal Discovery Museum. Contact the Hilton Head Chamber of Commerce for tickets and more information.

Coastal Discovery Museum at Honey Horn, 70 Honey Horn Dr., Hilton Head Island; (843) 689-6767; coastaldiscovery.org

Lodging: Inn at Harbour Town—Sea Pines Resort, 32 Greenwood Dr., Hilton Head Island; (866) 561-8802; seapines.com/accommodations/inn-at-harbour.asp

Main Street Inn, 2200 Main St., Hilton Head Island; (843) 681-3001; mainstreetinn.com

Restaurants: A Lowcountry Backyard, 32 Palmetto Bay Rd., Hilton Head Island; (843) 785-9273; hhbackyard.com. Open for lunch and dinner Tues–Sun. Brunch served beginning at 8 a.m. Sat–Sun

Bistro 17, 17D Harbourside Dr., Shelter Cove Marina, Hilton Head Island; (843) 785-5517; bistro17hhi.com. Open daily from 11:30 a.m.

43 Pinckney Island National Wildlife Refuge

Discover the salt marshes and freshwater ponds of this coastal island just west of Hilton Head Island on an easy day hike that traverses most of the trails on the island. Highlights include Ibis and Osprey Ponds, abundant bird-watching and wildlife-viewing opportunities, and a trek out to White Point on Port Royal Sound.

Start: From the parking lot and trailhead 0.5 mile from the park entrance
Distance: 7.7-mile lollipop
Hiking time: About 4–6 hours
Difficulty: Easy
Trail surface: Grass trail, forested path, gravel path
Best seasons: Fall, winter, spring
Other trail users: Mountain bikers
Canine compatibility: Dogs not permitted
Fees and permits: None

Schedule: Dawn–dusk daily
Maps: TOPO! CD: North Carolina-South Carolina; USGS maps: Bluffton, Spring Island, and Paris Island; South Carolina; USFS maps: Pinckney Island National Wildlife Refuge brochure and trail maps available online at fws.gov
Trail contacts: Pinckney Island National Wildlife Refuge, 694 Beech Hill Ln., Hardeeville, SC 29927; (843) 784-2468

Finding the trailhead: From Hilton Head, exit the island via US 278 West, and the refuge entrance is approximately 0.5 mile farther on the right. GPS: N32 14.041'/W80 46.722'

The Hike

Bounded by Skull Creek (the Intracoastal Waterway) on the east, Mackay Creek on the west, and Port Royal Sound to the north, Pinckney Refuge is the largest of the islands that are a part of the larger Pinckney Island Refuge complex and the only one open for public use. There are many route options for hikers interested in exploring this 4,000-acre island, which is popular with birders. Sixty-seven percent of the island consists of saltwater marshland and tidal creeks. However, a diversity of coastal ecosystems can be explored on the island including salt marsh, forestland, brushland, fallow fields, and freshwater ponds that support a wide variety of plant and animal life. While trekking on the island, you may spot waterfowl, shorebirds, wading birds, raptors, neotropical migrants, white-tailed deer, and American alligators, with large concentrations of white ibis, herons, and egrets.

The island not only has an interesting and storied past, but it is considered an archaeological gem in South Carolina. More than 115 prehistoric and historic sites have been identified on the island, including prehistoric sites that indicate human occupation dating from the Archaic period (8000–1000 BC), with intensive use during the Mississippian period (AD 1000–1500). The French made impermanent settlements on the island during the sixteenth and seventeenth centuries, and the first

permanent settlement was made by Alexander Mackay, an Indian trader who obtained title to 200 acres of Pinckney Island. In 1734 the island was passed to Charles Cotesworth Pinckney, a signer of the US Constitution, member of the prominent aristocratic planting family in Charleston, a Revolutionary War hero, and twice a candidate for the US presidency in the elections of 1804 and 1808. The Sea Island plantation that Pinckney ran on the island was very successful until the Civil War arrived and the island was taken over by Union troops. Today evidence of the war can be found on the island at the five US Colored Infantry headstones, located in a cemetery on the northwest side of Pinckney Island, that indicate the possibility that slaves living on the plantation during the Civil War were recruited by the US Army. The island was maintained as a hunting preserve after the war until 1975 when it was handed over to the US Fish and Wildlife Service to be managed exclusively as a National Wildlife Refuge.

Starting from the parking area, you are met with a picturesque view of large live oaks draped in Spanish moss. Follow the main gravel trail north toward Ibis Pond. Throughout the hike you will encounter many grass trails that are as wide as roads and intersect and spur off from the main gravel path that bisects the island. The trails on the island are nearly devoid of forest canopy for much of the way, and I highly recommend that you bring a stylish wide-brimmed hat on your hike to keep you cool and free from sunburn, especially during the warmer summer months. The gravel path is very easy to follow. Continue north, passing Ibis Pond and the narrow spur trail that leads to the pond that supports a rookery for ibises and egrets. Turn when you reach the grass trail that loops around Osprey Pond. The trail is well marked and explores the pond, where in the summer months you may see an impressive number of ibises and egrets nesting.

The trail loops back around and rejoins the gravel path, continuing 2 more miles to the north to Clubhouse Pond, where visitors often encounter alligators. The gravel path ends and you will follow the grass path the rest of the way to White Point at the northern tip of the island. There, you will be met with excellent views of Port Royal Sound, a perfect spot to watch dolphins and other aquatic life found in the productive sound.

Take the grass path back to the gravel road and left to follow the grass trail around Clubhouse Pond. This trail intersects several spur trails that will reconnect you back to the gravel road for an easier walk if you prefer at any point to return to the trailhead faster. You can take a side trip out to Bull Point, with views of Skull Creek and the Intracoastal Waterway, and follow the grass trail around the freshwater Wood Stork Pond before returning to the gravel trail that leads to the south and back to the trailhead and parking area where you started this hike.

◀ *A view to the west toward Mackay Creek*

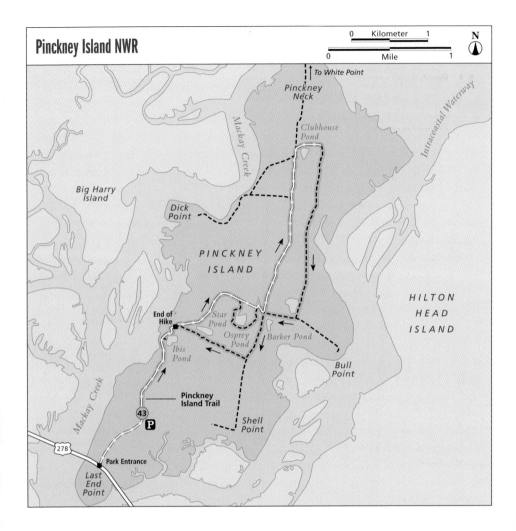

Pinckney Island NWR

0 — Kilometer — 1
0 — Mile — 1

N

To White Point

Pinckney
Neck

Clubhouse
Pond

Mackay Creek

Big Harry
Island

Dick
Point

PINCKNEY
ISLAND

HILTON
HEAD
ISLAND

Intracoastal Waterway

End of
Hike

Star
Pond

Osprey
Pond

Barker Pond

Ibis
Pond

Bull
Point

Mackay Creek

Pinckney
Island Trail

43

P

Shell
Point

278

Park Entrance

Last
End
Point

Miles and Directions

0.0 Start from the parking lot and trailhead 0.5 mile from the park entrance.

0.7 Arrive at a trail junction. To the right is a spur trail that leads to Ibis Pond. Stay straight toward Star Pond.

0.9 Arrive at a trail junction with a grass trail. Stay to the left on the gravel road.

1.6 Reach a trail junction. Turn right onto the grass trail that loops around Osprey Pond.

2.3 Arrive back at the gravel road. Turn right. In 300 feet you reach a four-way trail junction. Turn left and stay on the gravel road.

3.2 Arrive at a trail junction with the grass trail that leads out toward Dick Point Pond. Stay straight toward Clubhouse Pond.

3.6 Reach a trail junction. To the left is the grass trail that leads out toward Dick Point. Stay straight toward Clubhouse Pond.

3.7 Arrive at a trail junction. To the north, a grass trail leads out to White Point. Follow the gravel road to the east then, in approximately 0.2 mile the gravel road curves sharply to the right and becomes a grass trail. Follow the grass trail south toward Barker Pond.

5.4 Reach a trail junction. To the left a grass trail leads toward Bull Point. Turn right.

5.7 Reach a trail junction with a grass trail. Turn left onto the grass trail.

6.1 Reach a trail junction. Straight ahead a grass trail leads toward Shell Point. Turn right toward Star Pond.

6.8 Arrive back at the gravel road. Turn left onto the gravel road.

7.0 Arrive at the spur trail on the left that leads to Ibis Pond. Stay straight on the gravel road.

7.7 Arrive back at the parking lot and trailhead where you started.

Hike Information

Local Information: Hilton Head Island–Bluffton Chamber of Commerce, 1 Chamber of Commerce Dr., Hilton Head Island, SC 29928; (843) 785-3673

Local Events/Attractions: Hilton Head Food and Wine Festival, Coastal Discovery Museum. Contact the Hilton Head Chamber of Commerce for tickets and more information.

Coastal Discovery Museum at Honey Horn, 70 Honey Horn Dr., Hilton Head Island; (843) 689-6767; coastaldiscovery.org

Lodging: Inn at Harbour Town—Sea Pines Resort, 32 Greenwood Dr., Hilton Head Island; (866) 561-8802; seapines.com/accommodations/inn-at-harbour.asp

Main Street Inn, 2200 Main St., Hilton Head Island; (843) 681-3001; mainstreetinn.com

Restaurants: A Lowcountry Backyard, 32 Palmetto Bay Rd., Hilton Head Island; (843) 785-9273; hhbackyard.com; Open for lunch and dinner Tues–Sun. Brunch is served beginning at 8 a.m. Sat–Sun.

Bistro 17, 17D Harbourside Dr., Shelter Cove Marina, Hilton Head Island; (843) 785-5517; bistro17hhi.com. Open daily from 11:30 a.m.

LOWCOUNTRY SHRIMP AND GRITS

1 cup quick-cooking or traditional hominy grits

1¼ tablespoons olive oil

4 slices bacon, chopped

1 small onion, chopped

1 small green bell pepper, chopped

1 clove garlic, minced

⅓ cup dry white wine

⅓ cup chicken broth

¾ teaspoon cornstarch

¼ cup low-fat half-and-half

1 pound large shrimp, peeled and deveined

Chopped scallion tops for serving

1. Start cooking the grits according to the directions on the package.

2. In a large skillet, heat olive oil over a medium-high temperature. Combine the chopped bacon, onion, and bell pepper to the oil and cook. Be sure to stir the mixture often and cook the mixture until the vegetables are soft. This usually takes about 4 to 6 minutes. Add the garlic to the mixture and cook for another 45 seconds. Next, add the white wine and let it bubble for about 1½ minutes or until most of it is evaporated.

3. In a small mixing bowl, combine 1 tablespoon chicken broth with cornstarch and stir them together until the cornstarch is dissolved. Pour the rest of the chicken broth, the half-and-half, and the cornstarch mixture into the skillet. Bring to a light boil and cook for about 4 minutes, or until the mixture is thickened just a little. Next, add the shrimp and cook them for about 4 more minutes.

4. Serve the shrimp and sauce over the top of a bed of grits, and then top with the dark green ends of scallions. This can be served in bowls or on plates. For a special event, serve the shrimp and grits in martini glasses.

44 Edisto Nature Trail

This short and sweet hike explores the site of an old phosphate mine along a trail that passes through a variety of forested terrain. A spur trail along the route leads to an observation deck on the Edisto River. Other highlights of this well-maintained trail include man-made canals and the site of old rice-growing operations.

Start: Trailhead and parking area off US 17
Distance: 1.4-mile loop
Hiking time: About 1 hour
Difficulty: Easy due to level walking and short distance
Trail surface: Forested path, boardwalk
Best seasons: Early spring and late fall for cooler temperatures and bird watching
Other trail users: Hikers only
Canine compatibility: Leashed dogs permitted

Fees and permits: None
Schedule: Dawn–dusk daily
Maps: TOPO! CD: South Carolina–North Carolina; USGS maps: Edisto Beach, South Carolina; USFS maps: Edisto Nature Trail brochure, available at trailhead
Trail contacts: MeadWestvaco, Forestry Division, PO Box 118005, Charleston, SC 29423; (843) 871-5000

Finding the trailhead: From Charleston follow US 17 south for approximately 30 miles toward Beaufort. The trailhead is on the right, just after a bridge over the Edisto River and immediately before the town of Jacksonboro. GPS: N32 46.142' / W80 27.140'

The Hike

The forest that this trail passes through was once the site of quite a bit of industry. The trail takes you past areas of forest that were once mined for phosphate, the site of an old phosphate mine, canals that were used to haul goods to the Edisto River, old rice fields, and the site where a railroad tram transported material to a phosphate factory. This was a bustling place. Eventually the land was bought by the Westvaco Company, which owns large amounts of forested tracts in the Carolina coastal plains. Today, an interpretive trail guides hikers through a quiet and peaceful forest where the only sounds of industry you are likely to hear are the sounds of speeding cars down nearby US 17. Interpretive signs along the trail identify more than fifty varieties of plants and trees found in the forest and describe the details of the historical significance of the area. Along the way you may encounter deer, rabbits, and the ubiquitous squirrels that have turned the forest into their own industrious epicenter for acorn collection.

A kiosk marks the start of the trail from the parking area just off US 17. The trail enters into a mature pine-and-hardwood forest. By the looks of the tall pines and large oaks, it is hard to believe that this area was once heavily logged and farmed. The forest is a testament to the speed at which nature can reclaim a deforested region. This first section of the trail briefly joins with the old roadbed of the Old King's Highway, which once served as a major transportation route for the area. After 0.2 mile you

The boardwalk parts for a tree along the Edisto Nature Trail.

reach a junction. The Short Trail to the left cuts through the middle of the forest and provides a route for hikers who would like a shorter walk. Stay straight and continue on the Long Trail toward the Edisto River. In 0.1 mile you reach another trail junction. Continue straight to follow the Pon Pon Spur Trail toward the Edisto River. Along this section the trail follows over a series of boardwalks and traverses through a low-lying cypress swamp. At the end of the boardwalk, you reach an observation deck that overlooks a large tributary that flows into the Edisto River. Benches on the deck provide a great spot to watch birds and other wildlife that you can observe wading in the slow-moving water of the river and the surrounding swamp. Turn around and return to the Long Trail.

At the trail junction turn right and continue along the forested path, passing the Sawmill Water Hole and a phosphate-mining area before reaching a canal that was once used as a barge channel to the Edisto River. The trail turns sharply to the left and briefly follows along the canal. In 400 feet you reach the site of the old phosphate factory. The trail loops around and begins to head south again, passing a railroad tram site and then reaching an area of the forest that was once used for rice-growing operations. An interpretive plaque marks the site and explains some of the history of rice-growing operations in South Carolina. Continue on the trail and follow the wooden steps up to an outdoor amphitheater on the right side of the trail. From the amphitheater, hike 0.1 mile before returning to the trailhead and the parking area where you started.

Miles and Directions

0.0 Start from the parking lot just off US 17.

0.2 Reach a trail junction. To the left the blue-blazed Short Trail cuts through the middle of the park. Stay straight and continue toward the southeast corner of the forest.

Edisto Nature Trail

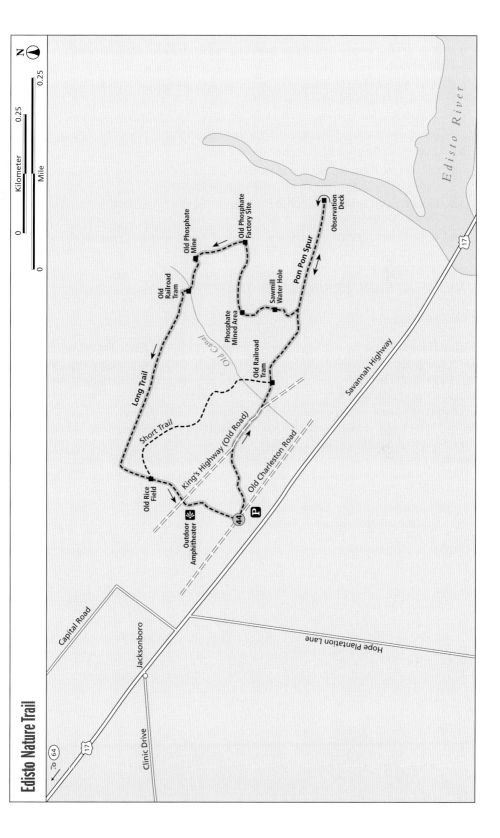

0.3 Arrive at a trail junction. Stay straight to walk the Pon Pon Spur Trail that leads to the Edisto River.

0.5 Reach the end of the boardwalk at an observation deck overlooking the Edisto River. Turn around and head back to the Long Loop Trail.

0.7 Arrive back at the start of the Pon Pon Spur Trail. Turn right and head north toward the old phosphate mine. In 200 feet you reach the Sawmill Water Hole.

0.8 A sign marks the site of the old phosphate mine area.

0.9 Cross the Old Canal. The trail turns to the left, and in 400 feet you arrive at the site of the Old Phosphate Factory. Here the trail veers sharply to the left.

1.0 Reach the old Railroad Tram. Again, the trail veers to the left and leads past an exceptionally large oak tree.

1.3 An interpretive sign beside the trail marks the site of the old rice fields to your left. Walk up the wooden steps toward the parking lot. After 300 feet you pass an outdoor amphitheater on the right side of the trail.

1.4 Arrive at the trailhead and parking lot where you started.

Hike Information

Local Information: Walterboro-Colleton Chamber of Commerce, 109 Benson St., Walterboro, SC 29488; (843) 549-9595

Local Events/Attractions: Charleston Tea Plantation, 6617 Maybank Hwy., Wadmalaw Island; (843) 559-0383; charlestonteaplantation .com. Open Mon–Sat 10 a.m. to 4 p.m., Sun noon to 4 p.m.

Magnolia Plantation and Gardens, 3550 Ashley River Rd., Charleston; (843) 571-1266; magnoliaplantation.com. Open daily 9 a.m. to 4:30 p.m. Admission fee; discounted for kids 6–12

Lodging: Camping at Edisto Beach State Park, 8377 State Cabin Road, Edisto Island; (843) 869-2156. Cabins and campsites available

Seaside Plantation Bed and Breakfast, 400 Highway 174, Edisto Island

Restaurants: The SeaCow Eatery, 145 Jungle Rd., Edisto Island; (843) 869-3222; thesea coweatery.com. Open daily at 7 a.m.

Edisto Waterfront Restaurant, 136 Jungle Rd., Edisto Island; (843) 869-1400

45 Edisto Beach State Park

This wonderful trail traverses a variety of terrain including bottomland forest and saltwater marsh. An easy and level hike takes you along extremely well-maintained trails, through beautiful pine and oak forest, past an old Native American shell mound, and to the Bache Monument. Along the way you can take a break and explore the exhibits at the Interpretive Center, which hosts displays on the history and natural features of the area.

Start: From the trailhead just past the park office on the right side of State Cabin Road
Distance: 5.4 miles out and back
Hiking time: About 3 hours
Difficulty: Easy due to level walking and distance
Trail surface: Forested trail, paved path, boardwalk
Best seasons: Early spring and late fall for cooler temperatures and bird watching
Other trail users: Hikers only
Canine compatibility: Leashed dogs permitted. Dogs not permitted in cabins or cabin areas

Fees and permits: Free for kids under age 6; small fee for everyone 6 and over; senior discount available
Schedule: Daily 8 a.m. to 6 p.m.; extended hours during daylight saving time
Maps: TOPO! CD: South Carolina–North Carolina; USGS maps: Edisto Beach, South Carolina; USFS maps: Edisto Beach State Park brochure
Trail contacts: Edisto Beach State Park, 8377 State Cabin Rd., Edisto Island, SC 29438; (843) 869-2156; www.southcarolinaparks.com/edistobeach

Finding the trailhead: From Charleston take US 17 South to SC 174 and proceed 28 miles to the entrance of the town of Edisto Beach. As you enter the town limits, the entrance to the park is on your left. GPS: N32 30.713'/W80 18.156'

The Hike

First things first, this a great candidate for a trail to hike during the cooler months. When it's hot out, you're probably going to want to be on the beautiful beaches that are just feet away from the trail. The hot months are also the time of the year when ticks and mosquitoes thrive in this park. The mosquitoes can become thick, aggressive and downright as unbearable as the heat for many months of the summer. Also during this time of the year, if you hike the trail and don't get a tick on you, you should go and buy a lottery ticket because your luck is running high! During the cooler months it is advisable to wear light, long pants and shirts to protect yourself from the ticks and stray mosquitoes that are still lingering around the trail here and there.

The trail starts at the parking lot on the right side of State Cabin Road just past the park office. A large kiosk marks the start of the trail, which enters into a dense maritime forest of live oaks draped in Spanish moss with an understory of palms and dwarf palmetto. There is a large network of trails to experience in the park. Another

popular route is to hike on the Spanish Mount Trail to the Scott Creek Trail and follow the Edisto Bike Trail to the beach and back. This route combines the Spanish Mount Trail, the Big Bay Trail, and the Bache Monument Trail to take hikers past the Spanish Mount, along Big Bay Creek, and to the Bache Monument.

You follow the red-blazed Spanish Mount Trail for the first 1.7 miles as the trail winds through the picturesque forest. Along the way a spur trail leads down to a bench with excellent views of Scott Creek to the south. The trail traverses over mostly level terrain until you reach a trail junction with the Big Bay Trail. Turn left and follow the trail down to a boardwalk that extends along the edge of Scott Creek. To the right of the boardwalk you get an up-close look at the Spanish Mount, a Native American shell mound and pottery refuse pile left behind by the early inhabitants of the area. From the Spanish Mount, turn around and return to the trail junction, then follow the Big Bay Trail to a parking lot for the boat launch. Cross the parking lot. The boat launch is to the left. You pass a fee station on the right and then rejoin the trail that enters back into the forest on the other side of the parking lot. After crossing a wooden bridge that offers excellent views of a small section of marshland on the eastern edge of Big Bay Creek, you arrive at the Interpretive Center.

Behind the Interpretive Center you join the Bache Trail and follow it to the Bache Monument. At the end of the trail, you find a small stone column in the forest, and several interpretive signs along the trail explain the historical and scientific significance of the monument. Bache Monument is actually a marker that was constructed by Alexander Bache, great grandson of Benjamin Franklin and director of a survey that measured the coastline from the Gulf of Mexico to Maine for the first time. From the monument, turn around and retrace your steps back to the trailhead on State Cabin Road.

Miles and Directions

0.0 Start from the trailhead just past the park office on the right side of State Cabin Road. After 375 feet the trail splits. The Forest Loop Trail is to the right. Stay to the left on the red-blazed Spanish Mount Trail.

0.4 The trail splits again. To the right is the end of the Forest Loop Trail that heads back toward the parking lot to the east. Stay left on the Spanish Mount Trail.

0.7 The trail splits. To the left the yellow-blazed Scott Creek Trail leads to the Edisto Bike Trail. Stay to the right on the Spanish Mount Trail.

0.9 Cross the wooden bridge that spans a marsh pond.

1.3 At the trail junction take the spur trail to the left, which leads to a bench overlooking the marsh. Turn around and return to the Spanish Mount Trail. Turn left and continue toward the Spanish Mount.

◄ *A soft wind blows Spanish moss over a bridge that spans a marsh.*

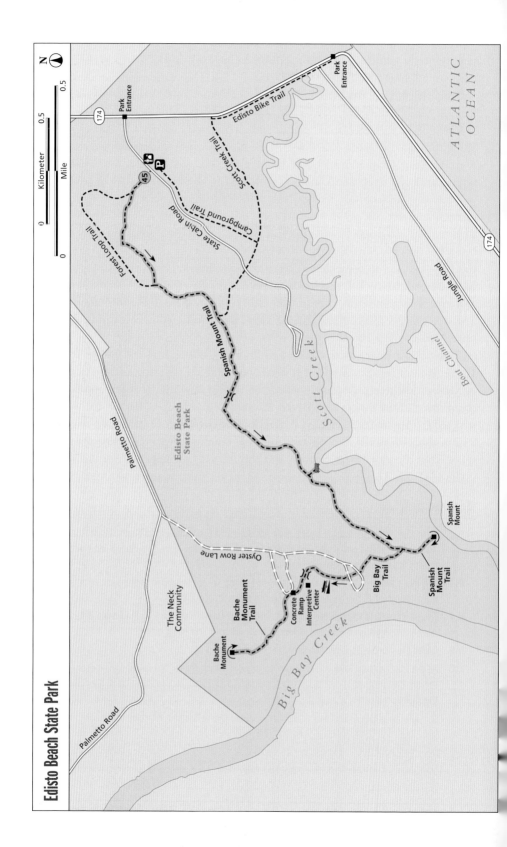

1.7 The trail splits. To the right the Big Bay Trail leads to the Interpretive Center. Turn left and follow the trail toward Spanish Mount.

1.8 Arrive at the Spanish Mount. Turn around and hike back to the junction with the Big Bay Trail. Stay straight on the Big Bay Trail.

2.1 Arrive at the boat launch parking lot. Walk across the parking lot and continue on the Big Bay Trail that enters back into the forest.

2.3 Cross the bridge spanning the small marsh area.

2.4 Arrive at the Interpretive Center. Walk through the breezeway and past the entrance to the center. Follow the concrete ramp down to the paved trail. About 75 feet from the concrete ramp, you arrive at a trail junction. A paved path leads to the left toward the edge of the Big Bay Creek. Turn right onto the unpaved Bache Monument Trail.

2.7 Arrive at the Bache Monument, a stone column in the forest. Turn around and retrace your steps back to the trailhead on State Cabin Road where you started.

5.4 Arrive back at the trailhead.

Hike Information

Local Information: Charleston County Chamber of Commerce, 4500 Leeds Ave. #100, North Charleston, SC 29405; (843) 577-2510

Local Events/Attractions: Charleston Tea Plantation, 6617 Maybank Hwy., Wadmalaw Island; (843) 559-0383; charlestonteaplantation.com. Open Mon–Sat 10 a.m. to 4 p.m., Sun noon to 4 p.m.

Magnolia Plantation and Gardens, 3550 Ashley River Rd., Charleston; (843) 571-1266; magnoliaplantation.com. Open daily 9 a.m. to 4:30 p.m. Admission fee; discount for kids 6–12.

Lodging: Camping at Edisto Beach State Park, 8377 State Cabin Road, Edisto Island; (843) 869-2156. Cabins and campsites available

Seaside Plantation Bed and Breakfast, 400 Highway 174, Edisto Island.

Restaurants: The SeaCow Eatery, 145 Jungle Rd., Edisto Island; (843) 869-3222; theseacoweatery.com. Open daily at 7 a.m.

Edisto Waterfront Restaurant, 136 Jungle Rd., Edisto Island; (843) 869-1400; edistowaterfrontrestaurant.com

46 Hunting Island State Park

Take a long day hike along this hilly and dynamic trail that travels through many of the diverse coastal ecosystems found in South Carolina's most popular state park. The trail starts with a lengthy trek through a rolling maritime forest before exploring Fripp Inlet, a picturesque lagoon, and a wide stretch of sandy beach leading to the Atlantic Ocean.

Start: From the Maritime Forest Trailhead
Distance: 4.5-mile lollipop
Hiking time: About 2-3 hours
Difficulty: Easy
Trail surface: Forested trail, paved road, gravel road
Best seasons: Winter, early spring, late fall
Other trail users: Equestrians and mountain bikers
Canine compatibility: Leashed dogs permitted
Fees and permits: Small fee; kids under 6 free; senior discount. Lighthouse admission extra.

Schedule: Daily 6 a.m. to 6 p.m.; hours extended to 9 p.m. during daylight saving time
Maps: TOPO! CD: North Carolina-South Carolina; USGS maps: Fripp Inlet, Saint Helena Sound; South Carolina; USFS maps: Hunting Island State Park Trail map available at the park office and online at southcarolinaparks.com
Trail contacts: Hunting Island State Park, 2555 Sea Island Pkwy., Hunting Island, SC 29920; (843) 838-4263

Finding the trailhead: From Charleston take US 17 South toward Beaufort. After 53 miles take the second left in the roundabout to Trask Parkway, which turns into US 21. Continue onto Sea Island Parkway for 16.3 miles. Turn left onto Hunting Island Drive and enter Hunting Island State Park. After 24 feet you reach a split in the road. Stay to the left. Follow Hunting Island Drive for about 0.3 mile; then take the first right toward the Maritime Forest Trail trailhead. The trailhead and parking lot are on the right side of the road. GPS: N32 22.114' / W80 26.653'

The Hike

Hunting Island State Park is located south of Charleston in Beaufort County. A favorite destination for camping, fishing, and outdoor adventure, the park draws millions of visitors each year. If you're searching for seclusion and serene solitude, I suggest avoiding the summer months, when the park is the most crowded. However, during the winter the park and trails are often quiet and at their most enjoyable. Apart from the excellent hiking trails and beaches found in the park, I strongly suggest you take a visit to the Hunting Island Lighthouse, one of the park's main attractions and the only lighthouse in all of South Carolina that is open for exploration. Take a climb to the top of the 130-foot lighthouse for stunning and sweeping views of

The Maritime Forest Trail has a bed of soft pine needles. ▶

Look toward the horizon over the Atlantic Ocean along the Nature Trail.

the surrounding complex coastal landscape. Also worth visiting is the park's Nature Center and museum. The Nature Center, located near the park's fishing pier, offers exhibits with live reptiles, amphibians, and aquatic creatures that are found throughout the park and is a great choice for families with children. The museum, located at the park's visitor center, focuses on the history of the Hunting Island Lighthouse and highlights the park's ongoing battles with erosion.

The park also offers excellent camping, with some of the sites located directly on the edge of the beach with wonderful views of the lighthouse off to the west. The 200 campsites in the drive-up section of the campground are fairly close together and offer little in the way of privacy or buffers for noise, making these sites more suitable for RVs and trailer campers. However, the white noise of the waves from the nearby Atlantic Ocean often mask much of the noise and makes this campground an adequate, yet less than ideal, choice for tent campers. A better option for those looking to tent camp is to reserve one of the ten walk-in tent sites in the north section of the campground. The walk is short to the sites and they offer a much better wilderness camping experience than your other options at this campground.

The park boasts more than 5 miles of undeveloped beaches and other highlights such as thousands of acres of marsh and maritime forest, saltwater lagoon, and ocean inlet, all of which are explored on this 8-mile nature trail, which is open to hikers as well as bikers. The summertime brings swarms of pesky mosquitoes to the southern coast of South Carolina, so be sure to pack a strong selection of bug spray if you are bothered by these bloodsucking bugs. While hiking on the well-marked and exceptionally well-maintained trails in the park, you may encounter alligators, raccoons, osprey, owls, squirrels, bald eagles, and deer in the marshes and maritime forests. There are several species of snakes found in the park including the poisonous rattlesnake and even the coral snake. Along the beaches and around the lagoon and inlet, you may observe sea turtles, dolphins, sea horses, stingrays, seagulls, herons, and a variety of fish including barracudas and sharks.

The trail begins at the trailhead directly across from the park office that houses the museum. You start on the Maritime Forest Trail and enjoy a walk through an exceptionally hilly maritime forest dotted with low-lying marsh in areas. Along this section you pass through a dense forest of oaks covered in Spanish moss, with a thick understory of palmettos. The trail is exceptionally easy to follow. There are many opportunities along the next 1.8 miles as you make your way toward Fripps Inlet to take the various side trails and create shorter loops back to the trailhead. Once you reach the Nature Center Scenic Trail, turn left and follow the trail that parallels the inlet. You cross the sturdy bridge that offers excellent views of the saltwater lagoon before reaching the end of a dirt road at the beach. Explore and enjoy the coastline before turning around and crossing the saltwater lagoon. At the junction with the Lagoon Access Recreation Trail, turn right and follow the winding trail that parallels the lagoon. Along this section of trail, you have many opportunities to stop at benches along the way and enjoy impressive views of the lagoon.

This is the best stretch of trail for bird watching and wildlife viewing, so take it slow and enjoy the trek as you pass through more rolling maritime forest on your way back to the trailhead where you started this excellent and superbly scenic hike through the most popular state park in South Carolina.

Miles and Directions

0.0   Start from the trailhead to the Maritime Forest Trail located in the parking lot for the park office.

0.5   Reach a trail junction. To the left a connector trail leads to the Lagoon Access Trail. Stay straight and continue on the Maritime Forest Trail.

1.0   Arrive at a trail junction. To the left is the Palmetto Pine Pass Trail. Stay straight and continue on the Maritime Forest Trail.

1.5   Reach a four-way junction. To the left and right is the Marsh Boardwalk Crossover. Stay straight and continue on the Maritime Forest Trail.

1.9   Arrive at a T junction with the Nature Center Scenic Trail. Turn left onto the Nature Center Scenic Trail.

2.0   Reach a split in the trail. To the left is the Lagoon Access Recreation Trail. Stay straight on the Nature Center Scenic Trail. In 100 feet cross the large bridge spanning an arm of the Fripp Inlet.

2.2   Arrive at the beach. Enjoy the beach and then turn around and head back across the bridge and to the junction with the Lagoon Access Recreation Trail.

2.4   Turn right at the junction with the Lagoon Access Recreation Trail.

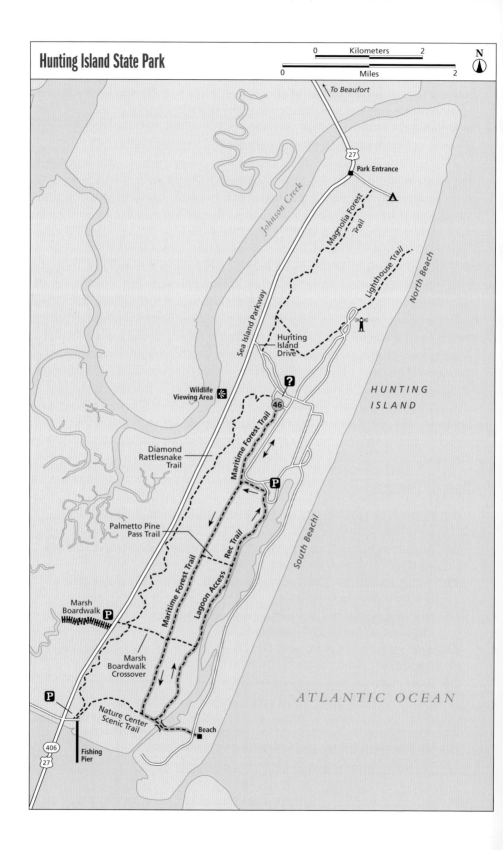

2.8 Reach a trail junction. To the left is the Marsh Boardwalk Crossover Trail. Stay straight on the Lagoon Access Trail.

3.3 To the left is the Palmetto Pine Pass Trail. Stay straight and continue on the Lagoon Access Recreation Trail.

3.8 Arrive at a trail junction. Turn left onto the connector trail toward the Maritime Forest Trail.

4.0 Reach a trail junction. To the left and right is the Maritime Forest Trail. Turn right onto the Maritime Forest Trail.

4.5 Arrive at the parking lot and trailhead where you started.

Hike Information

Local Information: Beaufort Visitors Center, 713 Craven St., Beaufort, SC 29902; (843) 525-8500; beaufortsc.org

Local Events/Attractions: Shrimp Festival Beaufort, Henry C. Chambers Waterfront Park in Downtown Beaufort. This festival takes place annually in October. Free admission

Lodging: The Beaufort Inn, 809 Port Republic St., Beaufort; (843) 379-4667; beaufortinn.com

Camping at Hunting Island State Park, 2555 Sea Island Pkwy., Hunting Island; (843) 838-4263. Water and electric sites available

Restaurants: Breakwater Restaurant, 203 Carteret St., Beaufort; (843) 379-0052; breakwater sc.com. Open Mon–Sat 5 to 9:30 p.m.

Bricks on Boundary, 1420 Boundary St., Beaufort; (843) 379-5232. Open Sun–Mon 11 a.m. to 9 p.m., Tues–Sat 11 a.m. to 10 p.m.

CLASSIC LOWCOUNTRY BOIL

No trip to South Carolina is complete without a taste of the classic Lowcountry Boil.

   2 teaspoons crab boil per quart of water

   2 pounds smoked sausage, cut into 2-inch or longer sections

   10 new red potatoes

   6 ears corn, shucked and broken in half or cut into shorter sections

   3 pounds fresh South Carolina shrimp, unpeeled

1. Fill a large pot with plenty of water to cover all the ingredients.

2. Add the crab boil. Bring the water to a boil and cook to taste.

3. As the water continues to boil, add the sausage and potatoes and cook over medium-high heat for about 20 minutes.

4. Add the corn and boil for 10 more minutes.

5. Add the shrimp and boil for 3 minutes. If you cook the shrimp longer, it will become rather chewy.

6. Drain the water from the pot and serve.

47 Kiawah Island: Marsh Island Park

This hike across a central portion of Kiawah Island explores all of the diverse landscapes that make the island unique and fascinating. Along this mostly flat path, you will venture through scrub maritime forests, walk beneath picturesque canopies of massive arching oaks, and pass several brackish-water ponds where alligators are commonly spotted. The trail leads to a lookout tower at Marsh Island with sweeping views of the surrounding salt marsh. The end of the trek includes a walk along the beach through wind-sculpted sand dunes beside the Atlantic Ocean.

Start: At the eastern edge of the Sanctuary Golf Resort parking lot (Sanctuary Beach Drive)

Distance: 5.8-mile lollipop hike with a spur trail in the middle

Hiking time: About 2–3 hours

Difficulty: Moderate due to length

Trail surface: Paved trail, boardwalk, dirt path, sandy beach

Best seasons: Feb–June when the temperature is cooler, Sept–Nov before the cold of winter arrives

Other trail users: Bikers, runners, and golf carts. All users share the same paved path.

Canine compatibility: Leashed dogs permitted

Fees and permits: No fee. Call the resort at least 24 hours in advance of your visit to reserve a permit that will allow you access to the hiking trails and nature center. Your name will be added to a list at the entrance station, allowing you access to the trails.

Schedule: Year-round 24 hours a day. Not recommended at night due to the presence of alligators and poisonous snakes.

Maps: TOPO! CD: North Carolina–South Carolina; USGS maps: Wadmalaw Island and Kiawah Island, South Carolina

Trail contacts: Kiawah Island Golf Resort, 5480 A Sea Forest Dr., Johns Island, SC 29455; (843) 768-2121; kiawahresort.com

Special considerations: Be on the lookout for rattlesnakes, moccasins, and copperheads along the trail as the island does have a healthy population of poisonous snakes.

Finding the trailhead: From downtown Charleston take US 17 South to Folly Road Boulevard and continue for 1.2 miles. Turn right (west) onto Maybank Highway and follow it for 7.2 miles. Turn left (south) onto Bohicket Road and continue for 10.4 miles until its end at roundabout. Follow the roundabout to the third exit onto Kiawah Island Parkway and follow for 4.2 miles. When you reach the gate entrance station, inform them that you are visiting the nature center and hiking the trails. Continue straight through the gate, drive 3.4 miles, then turn right (south) onto Sanctuary Beach Drive. Follow the road for 0.1 mile until you reach the guest parking lot on your right. The trail begins by following the paved path on the east side of the parking lot north toward Kiawah Island Parkway. GPS: N32 36.179' / W80 05.584'

The Hike

Nestled in the heart of the Lowcountry, Kiawah Island has become synonymous with exclusivity and prestige. It is home to the Kiawah Island Golf Resort and some of the most massive and impressive mansions along the South Carolina coast. Along

Boardwalks leading to a lookout tower at Marsh Island Park provide stunning views of the expansive salt marsh.

this 5.8-mile hike, you will get to experience the salt marshes, brackish ponds, maritime forests, and ocean beaches that define the environment of Lowcountry barrier islands. Several interpretive plaques give glimpses into the rich history of the island's plantation-era roots.

Kiawah is named after the Native American tribe that occupied the island until measles, smallpox, and fighting with European settlers nearly wiped out the entire tribe in the late 1600s. Ironically, the Kiawahs were the ones who originally led European settlers to establish the colony at Charleston Landing. Today the island is considered one of the premier private developments in the country. A mixture of residential and resort development, the island has five golf courses, and the Ocean Course, considered one of the most challenging courses on the East Coast, was the host for the 2012 PGA Tournament.

The island community is devoted to preserving the natural integrity of the barrier island and protecting the unique wildlife that inhabits the diverse landscape. The Heron Park Nature Center, located just west of the sanctuary at Kiawah Island Golf Resort on Sea Forest Drive, offers interpretive programs and exhibits on the wildlife and natural world found on Kiawah Island. A community-run organization called the Kiawah Conservancy monitors the wildlife and ecosystem of the island, initiates natural science research, conducts educational and awareness programs in

▶ The Kiawah Island Ocean Course hosted the 2012 PGA Championship as well as the Ryder Cup in 1991, plus the World Cup in 1997 and 2003. The course was designed by the famous course architect Pete Dye.

the community, and purchases land on the island to be protected from development. You are likely to see plenty of alligators in the brackish ponds and salt marshes along this hike. White-tailed deer, turtles, egrets, herons, ibis, and a variety of other migrating birds are also common sightings on the island. Elusive bobcats, owls, and minks are occasionally seen as well. In the estuaries and around the river, you can spot manatees slowly drifting through the waters. In and near the ocean, a variety of shorebirds and seagulls, dolphins, sharks and other fish, and sea turtles can be found.

The trail begins on a paved walking and biking trail that departs from the sanctuary parking lot. The paved path follows along Sanctuary Beach Drive and then turns right (northeast) onto Kiawah Island Parkway. You pass your first brackish pond on your right, where you will most likely have your first alligator sighting. The trail passes alongside the Turtle Point Golf Course before you turn right (east) onto Governor's Drive and venture over small rolling hills under the canopy of large arching oaks. On this trail section you pass through a stretch of impressive residential development that is broken up with the entrance to the historic Vanderhorst Mansion. The paved path leads to the entrance of Marsh Island Park, a preserved section of the resort property where you are most likely to encounter wildlife. Cross the road and turn left (north) onto a boardwalk that passes over the salt marsh and leads to a lookout tower with stunning views of the expansive marsh that surrounds the island.

Sandy footpaths can be explored throughout Marsh Island Park. From here you turn around (south) and head back to the entrance of the Vanderhorst Mansion and turn left (south), following the Avenue of the Oaks, an exceptionally intriguing collection of old-growth oaks that arch over the walkway that leads all the way to the

VALUABLE REAL ESTATE

The island was originally titled to George Raynor in 1699 and then passed on to General Arnoldus Vanderhorst, a hero of the Revolutionary War. The Vanderhorst family was so successful at farming island cotton here that they built a mansion on the river side of the island just west of Marsh Island. The first shots of the Civil War at Fort Sumter could be heard on Kiawah Island, and during the war the Vanderhorsts abandoned Kiawah and then returned after the war was over. The Vanderhorst family owned the island for more than 200 years, until a lumberman named C. C. Royal purchased the entire island for only $125,000. Now are you ready to hear the real estate deal of a lifetime? Just twenty-three years later, the heirs of C. C. Royal sold the island to a real estate developer for $18.2 million.

Alligators are easy to spot in the brackish ponds along this hike across Kiawah Island.

ocean. The trek ends with a walk along the Atlantic Ocean through the sand dunes of the Vanderhorst Plantation Beach, which leads back (west) to the Sanctuary Resort and the parking lot where you started.

Miles and Directions

0.0 Start from the northeastern corner of the guest parking lot at Kiawah Island Golf Resort's sanctuary.

0.1 Cross Sanctuary Beach Drive and follow (north) the paved walking and biking path alongside Sanctuary Beach Drive, passing the Roy Barth Tennis Center on the right.

0.2 Turn right (northeast) onto Governor's Drive. Continue to follow the paved path past the brackish pond and alongside the Turtle Point Golf Course.

0.4 Cross Surf Song Road and continue following the paved path alongside Governor's Drive.

0.6 Follow the paved path around to the right (east) and continue along Governor's Drive until you reach the entrance of the Vanderhorst House.

1.7 Reach the entrance to the Vanderhorst House on the left. Turn right (south) and follow the signs toward Marsh Island. After 300 feet follow the paved path to the left (east) and cross Flyway Drive. The paved path leads back alongside Governor's Drive.

2.3 Turn left (north), crossing Governor's Drive into the entrance of Marsh Island Park. Follow along boardwalks crossing the salt marsh.

Kiawah Island: Marsh Island Park

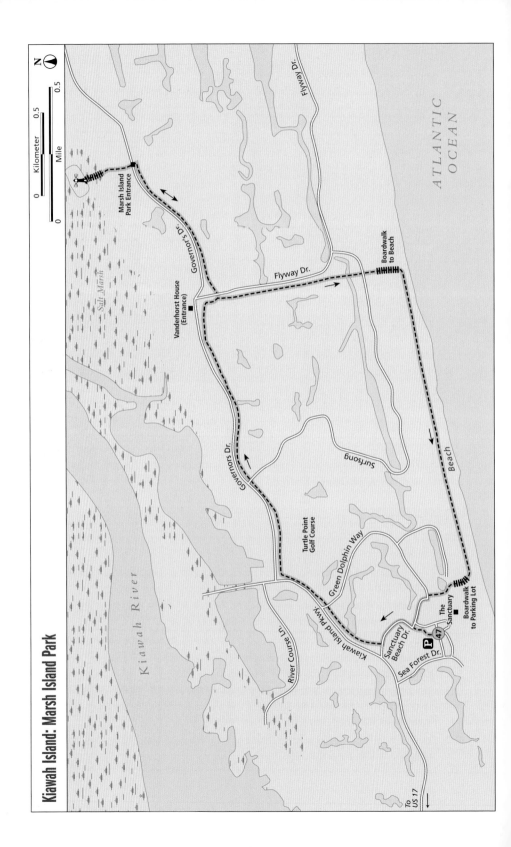

2.5 Climb the lookout tower for awesome views of the surrounding marsh. From here sandy footpaths loop around the outer edges of the island to the east and west. You can add 0.4 mile to your hike if you want to explore these trails, which always return to the lookout tower. From the tower turn around and follow the boardwalk (south) back out to Governor's Drive. Turn right (west), heading back the way you came, and follow Governor's Drive back to the Vanderhorst Mansion entrance.

3.3 Turn left (south) onto Flyway Drive and follow the paved path under the impressive Avenue of the Oaks. Toward the end of the paved path, the trail crosses Canvasback Pond via a wooden boardwalk.

4.0 Follow the boardwalk (south) that leads to the beach. Turn right (west) and walk along the beach back to the sanctuary resort where you started.

5.2 Turn right (north) and exit the beach, following the boardwalk back to the parking lot where you started your hike.

5.8 Arrive back at the parking lot where you started.

Hike Information

Local Information: Town of Kiawah Island, 21 Beachwalker Dr., Kiawah Island, SC 29455; (843) 768-9166; kiawahisland.org

Local Events/Attractions: The Ocean Course at Kiawah, 1 Sanctuary Beach Dr., Kiawah Island; (843) 266-4085; www.kiawahresort.com/golf/the-ocean-course. The Ocean Course at Kiawah is located on the eastern end of the island.

Lodging: The Sanctuary at Kiawah Island Golf Resort, 5480 A Sea Forest Dr., Johns Island; (843)768-2121; kiawahresort.com

Restaurants: The Atlantic Room at Kiawah Island Ocean Course Clubhouse, 1 Sanctuary Beach Dr., Kiawah Island; (843) 266-4085; www .kiawahresort.com/dining/the-atlantic-room. Seafood and steak with views of the Ocean Course

The Ocean Room at the Sanctuary, 1 Sanctuary Beach Dr., Kiawah Island; (843) 266-4085; www.kiawahresort.com/dining/the-ocean-room. Kiawah's signature steakhouse

Organizations: Kiawah Conservancy, 80 Kestrel Ct., Kiawah Island, SC 29455; (843) 768-2029; kiawahconservancy.org. Land trust and community conservation group

48 Francis Beidler Forest

This fun and easy hike explores the cypress swamp and lake along a wide, wooden boardwalk. A great trail for all ages, highlights include an elevated observation deck at the lake and many remarkably large cypress trees. One cypress tree beside the trail is so large that you can climb inside of the hollow trunk. Along the trail many interpretive plaques describe the natural history and wildlife of the forest.

Start: The boardwalk behind the Nature Center
Distance: 1.5-mile lollipop
Hiking time: About 1 hour
Difficulty: Easy due to level walking and short distance
Trail surface: Boardwalk
Best seasons: Early spring and late fall for cooler temperatures and wildflowers. Great in winter for cool temperatures, fewer insects, and bird watching
Other trail users: Hikers only

Canine compatibility: Dogs not permitted
Fees and permits: Free for kids under age 6; fee for everyone 6 and over; senior discount available
Schedule: Tues–Sun 9 a.m. to 5 p.m.; closed Mon
Maps: TOPO! CD: South Carolina–North Carolina; USGS maps: Harleyville, South Carolina
Trail contacts: Audubon Center & Sanctuary at Francis Beidler Forest, 336 Sanctuary Rd., Harleyville, SC 29448; (843) 462-2150

Finding the trailhead: From Charleston take I-26 West and drive for 32 miles. Take exit 187 toward Ridgeville / St. George. At the end of the ramp, turn left onto SC-27 / Ridgeville Road and follow it for 1.2 miles. Turn right onto US 78 and follow it for 2.8 miles. Turn right onto US 178 and drive for 3.7 miles. Turn right onto Taylor Pond Road and drive for 2.6 miles. Taylor Pond Road becomes Bishop Road. Continue on Bishop Road for 0.5 mile. Once you reach Mims Road, turn left and drive for 0.7 mile. Take the third right onto Beidler Forest Entrance Road. Follow the park road back to the Nature Center. Enter the Nature Center and pay the entrance fee. The trail starts at the boardwalk behind the Nature Center. GPS: N33 13.209' / W80 21.213'

The Hike

The 10,728-acre forest is the largest tract of remaining bald cypress–tupelo swamp in the world. Now managed by the Audubon Society, the Francis Beidler Forest was originally preserved in the 1800s by Francis Beidler, a visionary lumberman who was able to foresee the importance of preserving forest in this unique region. Located within the Four Holes Swamp, the forest also has historical significance. General Francis Marion, also known as "The Swamp Fox," and General Nathanael Greene both used the Four Holes Swamp to conduct guerrilla operations during the Revolutionary War. Today the forest is a peaceful and beautiful place to hike, and some of the ancient trees that you will encounter along the well-maintained and extensive boardwalk that loops through the virgin forest are more than 1,000 years old.

Author Joshua Kinser peeks out from inside a cypress tree.

You have to walk through the Nature Center and pay a small fee before hiking the boardwalk trail. Inside the Nature Center is a small museum with exhibits on the history, wildlife, and flora of the forest. The boardwalk trail starts from the back door of the Nature Center. Although this is a swamp, you will still find wildflowers growing in the forest. The highlight of these wildflowers is the rare Carolina trillium. The population in this forest is South Carolina's only known occurrence of this plant. Other wildflowers found in the forest include swamp azalea, greenfly orchid, and cardinal flowers. The fact that the swamp has been bought by the Audubon Society should hint at the fact that there are a great deal of birds to be seen here. In fact, more than 140 species of birds have been identified in the forest, including warblers, prothonotaries, and northern parulas. There are also more than fifty reptile species in the park, which may give you extra incentive to stay on the elevated boardwalk and keep your hide safe and out of the dark tannic waters of the swamp. Lurking in the swamp you may see alligators, turtles, nonvenomous snakes, and water moccasins. Also keep your eyes peeled for the red foxes, flying squirrels, minks, otters, deer, and bobcats that call the swamp home.

Starting from the Nature Center, the entire trail is elevated boardwalk. After 0.1 mile the trail splits at the beginning of the loop. Stay to the left and follow the loop trail to the edge of Goodson Lake at the eastern end of the trail. Since the swamp and the lake are fed by rainwater, the water levels change drastically during the year. The

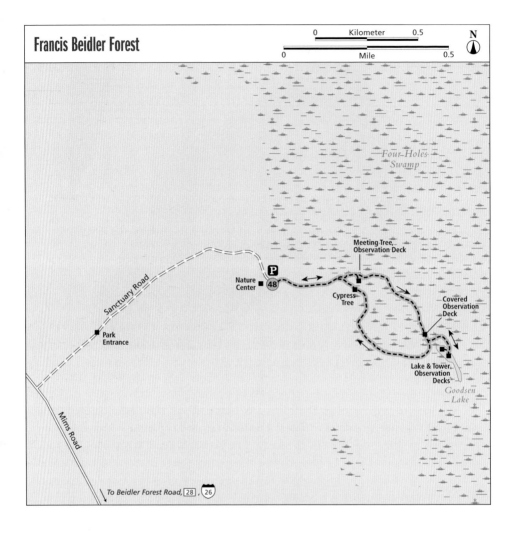

Francis Beidler Forest

best time to visit the area is during the cooler months when the water levels are highest and the bird populations are the largest. During low-water months and periods of drought, the lake will be the best spot to view wildlife. A spur trail 0.6 mile from the start of the boardwalk leads to the first of two observation decks along the route. The second observation deck is the best. An elevated observation deck gives you an excellent view of the surrounding lake. Benches atop the elevated deck give you the chance to observe the tranquil lake and the surrounding wildlife in comfort and quietly for extended periods of time, which are often required for bird viewing and photography. The trail is very popular, and its relatively close proximity to Charleston means that there are often considerable numbers of people on weekends and holidays. For the best bird watching, visit the forest in the early morning on weekdays during the early spring.

From the lake the trail loops around through the swamp and forest that is in some places blanketed with a dense understory of bright-green dwarf palmetto. On the way back to the Nature Center, a half mile from the elevated observation deck, you reach my favorite part of the trail. To the right side of the trail is a short wooden staircase that leads down to a large cypress tree with a hollow trunk that you can climb inside. Crawl in, look up, and enjoy the view from inside of a giant cypress. It is a very interesting and remarkable experience. From here, simply follow the boardwalk back to the Nature Center where you started.

Miles and Directions

0.0 Start from the trailhead at the boardwalk behind the Nature Center.

0.2 The trail splits. Stay to the left toward the lake. In 300 feet take the spur trail to the left that leads to the observation deck and the meeting tree. At the observation deck that overlooks the cypress swamp, turn around and retrace your steps back to the main boardwalk trail.

0.5 Arrive at the covered observation platform with benches that overlook the cypress swamp. In 100 feet you reach a trail junction. Take the spur trail to the left toward the lake.

0.6 Reach a trail junction. Take the spur trail to the right, which leads 150 feet to an observation deck on the lake. Once you reach the observation deck, turn around and return to the main trail, then turn right toward the next observation deck on the lake.

0.7 Arrive at the observation deck with an elevated viewing platform on the lake. Turn around and retrace your steps back to the main trail.

0.8 At the trail junction stay straight and head toward the Nature Center.

1.2 On the right side of the trail, there is a short set of wooden stairs that lead down to a cypress tree that you can climb into. In 350 feet from the cypress tree, you arrive at a trail junction. Stay straight toward the Nature Center.

1.5 Arrive at the Nature Center where you started.

Hike Information

Local Information: Dorchester County Chamber of Commerce, 402 N. Main St., Summerville, SC 29483; (843) 873-2931; greater summerville.org

Local Events/Attractions: Cooper River Bridge Run, (843) 856-1949; bridgerun.com. This 10K across the Cooper River Bridge into downtown Charleston takes place in late March / early April.

Middleton Place Plantation and Gardens, 4300 Ashley River Rd., Charleston; (843) 556-6020. Middleton features a museum, an inn, gardens, and a restaurant.

Lodging: Woodlands Inn Resort, 125 Parsons Rd., Summerville; (843) 875-2600; woodlands inn.com

Gihvans Ferry State Park (camping), 746 Gihvans Ferry Rd., Ridgeville; (843) 873-0692

Restaurants: Coastal Coffee Roasters Coffeehouse and Café, 108 E. Third North Street, Summerville; (843) 376-4559; coastalcoffee roasters.com. Open Mon–Sat from 8 a.m.

The Red Pepper Italian Eatery, 709 N. Main St., Summerville; (843) 873-8600; thered pepper.com

Organizations: Audubon Center at Francis Beidler Forest, 336 Sanctuary Rd., Harleyville, SC 29448; (843) 462-2150

CARRY YOUR OWN WATER AND BE SURE TO DRINK IT

Even in frigid conditions, a human body needs at least two quarts of water a day to function efficiently.

When you are hiking, your body's rate of fluid loss depends on the outside temperature, humidity, altitude, and your activity level. On average, a hiker walking in warm weather will lose a gallon of fluid a day. That fluid loss is easily replaced by normal consumption of liquids and food. However, if you're walking briskly in hot, dry weather and hauling a heavy pack, you can lose one to three quarts of fluid an hour. It's important to always carry plenty of water and to stop often to drink nonalcoholic fluids regularly, even if you aren't thirsty.

What if you don't? Symptoms of dehydration can include a headache, fatigue, and decreased coordination and judgment. It can be dangerous.

Now, where do you plan on getting the water when you're on the trail?

The easiest solution is to bring water with you. Natural water sources can be loaded with intestinal disturbers, such as bacteria, viruses, and fertilizers. Giardia lamblia, the most common of these disturbers, is a protozoan parasite that lives part of its life cycle as a cyst in water sources. The parasite spreads when mammals defecate in water sources. Once ingested, Giardia can induce cramping, diarrhea, vomiting, and fatigue within two days to two weeks after ingestion. If you believe you've contracted giardiasis, see a doctor immediately, as it is treatable with prescription drugs. If you're hiking too far to bring all the water you'll need, carry a lightweight water filter so you can get water from streams and lakes.

Pine saplings growing beneath mature pine along the Santee Coastal Reserve Woodlands Trail (hike 59). ▶

49 Palmetto Trail: Lake Moultrie Passage

This two- to three-day backpack located north of Charleston in the state's central coastal plain traverses a segment of the Palmetto Trail along varied terrain. The trail mostly follows along the top of the Lake Moultrie dike system and explores lush wetlands, loblolly pine savannas, and dense lowland forests.

Start: From the northwest trailhead at the Diversion Canal
Distance: 24.4-mile shuttle
Hiking time: About 2-3 days
Difficulty: Easy to moderate due to length and lack of shade for much of the way
Trail surface: Gravel road, forested path, boardwalk
Best seasons: Winter, early spring, late fall
Other trail users: Mountain bikers
Canine compatibility: Leashed dogs permitted

Fees and permits: None
Schedule: Open year-round
Maps: TOPO! CD: North Carolina–South Carolina; USGS maps: Bonneau, St. Stephens, and Pineville; South Carolina; USFS maps: Lake Moultrie Passage Map available from the Palmetto Trail Conservation Foundation online at palmettoconservation.org
Trail contacts: Palmetto Conservation, 722 King St., Columbia, SC 29205; (803) 771-0870; palmettoconservation.org

Finding the trailhead: *To the northwestern trailhead:* From Santee drive southeast on US 6 for 10.3 miles to Eutawville. US 45 joins US 6; continue on US 6/45 for about 6.7 miles until 6 and 45 split, then stay to the left and keep north on US 45. The trailhead is about 1.8 miles on the right just after you cross the Diversion Canal. GPS: N33 22.981'/W80 08.107'

To leave a car at the eastern trailhead: From Harleyville take I-26 east toward Charleston for about 22 miles. Take exit 199 and follow US 17-A north through Monks Corner for about 17 miles to where US 17A and US 52 split. Stay to the left and continue on US 52. The trailhead is 3.6 miles on the left at the USDA Forest Service Canal Recreation Area. GPS: N33 16.467'/W79 57.859'

The Hike

Much of the trail travels across the service roads that top the dike system for the 40,000-acre lake. The trail is easily one of the most popular and therefore populated stretches of trail along the Palmetto Trail, especially with mountain bikers. The trail offers excellent views of expansive Lake Moultrie, which was constructed between 1939 and 1941 as part of a massive federal project to provide electricity to South Carolina. The lake and dam system originally diverted an enormous amount of water from the Santee River, which empties into the ocean just south of Georgetown. However, a Rediversion Canal now diverts much of this water back into the Santee River.

The Pinopolis Dam on the south end of the dam near Monks Corner generates hydroelectric power. While you're hiking the trail, you will be able to see the smokestacks of coal-fired power plants on the south side of the lake beside the Pinopolis Dam. Also in this area is an impressive and huge lock that allows boaters to pass from

The Lake Moultrie Passage is carpeted with a thick layer of pine straw.

Lake Moultrie onto the Cooper River and on down to Charleston, one of the most beautiful cities in the south. A visit to historic downtown Charleston is well worth the trip if you want a break from the trail. Be sure to take a walk on the battery downtown, and for the best pizza, stop by Paisano's Pizza on James Island . . . but I digress.

Along the trail you will see a variety of birds including osprey, bald eagles, herons, egrets, sparrows, and red-winged blackbirds. The wetlands support a diversity of waterfowl as well as raccoons, deer, frogs, toads, salamanders, snakes, turtles, and alligators. In the wetlands bald-cypress trees provide shade for the abundant water lilies. In the forests you will find pickerel weeds, trumpet honeysuckles, and incredibly stunning passionflowers, daisies, and dandelions.

You can start your hike from either the northwest trailhead at the diversion canal or at the southern trailhead at the Canal Recreation Area. In recent years there has been talk of closing the trailhead down at the Canal Recreation Area and redirecting the trail slightly. Call ahead to get details on this trail before you plan your route. No matter where you start your hike, I highly recommend either leaving a vehicle at the opposite end, arranging a shuttle back to where you started, or preparing for a long four- to six-day hike that is nearly 50 miles long if this trail is hiked out and back.

The route in this book begins at the northwestern trailhead and parking lot at the diversion canal. You follow the road from the parking lot for 0.7 mile until

Hikes along the Lake Moultrie Passage of the Palmetto Trail start from this octagonal kiosk.

you reach an unpaved road where the trail turns sharply to the left and follows the unpaved road to a primitive campsite. After crossing the railroad tracks, you traverse on a forested path through marshy bottoms, shrub forest, and pines before crossing a wooden footbridge spanning Quattlebaum's Canal. You continue on a forested path through a mixed forest of hardwoods and pines, crossing footbridges and in low-lying marshy sections of trail. An old roadbed that parallels the canal takes you through a pine forest. You cross the wooden railroad trestle spanning the canal and are offered excellent views of the dark waters of the canal before following the top of the dike on the other side. You walk along the dike for much of the rest of the trail, crossing the Rediversion Canal, and continuing on the dike for 6.2 miles until you reach General Moultrie Road. The next section navigates through a series of paved commercial and residential roads through historic Bonneau Beach, easily the least appealing section of the hike.

You briefly return to the dike for another 3.5 miles until you reach the Pinopolis East Dike where you are rewarded with stunning views of the expansive and stunningly beautiful Lake Moultrie. From here you descend a series of steps to a short stretch of trail that ventures through a pine forest before reaching the trailhead and parking area at the Canal Recreation Area.

Miles and Directions

0.0 Start from the parking lot and western trailhead for the Fort Moultrie Passage located just off 45 adjacent to the Diversion Canal. The trail begins at the southern end of the parking area.

0.7 Arrive at a trail junction with an unpaved road. Turn left and follow the unpaved road to the east.

1.6 Arrive at a primitive campsite.

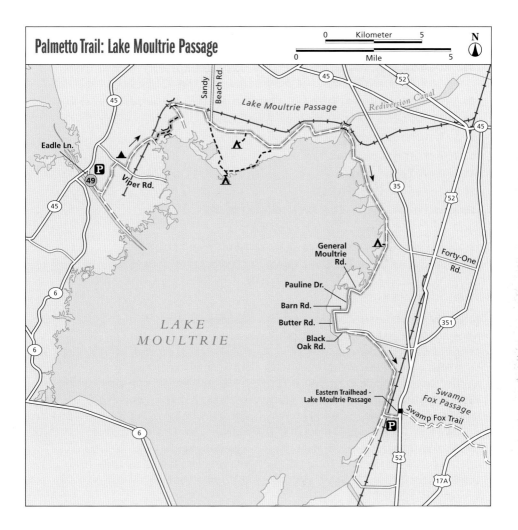

Palmetto Trail: Lake Moultrie Passage

1.8 Turn right onto Viper Road.

2.2 Turn left onto the unpaved road.

3.5 Cross the railroad tracks and continue on the forested trail on the other side.

4.2 Cross the wooden footbridge spanning the canal and continue on the forested trail. Along this next section you encounter many sections of the boardwalk that traverses over low-lying marshland.

5.0 Reach a trail junction. Turn left onto the unpaved road that runs parallel to the canal.

5.5 Cross the wooden railroad trestle spanning the canal and continue on the sandy top of the dike on the other side.

7.0 Reach a trail junction. To the right is the Sandy Beach Spur Trail, which leads to a campsite right on Lake Moultrie and then loops back to rejoin the Lake Moultrie Passage. Stay straight on the Lake Moultrie Passage. In 150 feet you reach a junction with Sandy Beach Road. Stay straight.

8.3   To the right is a spur trail to a campsite on Lake Moultrie.

9.2   The Sandy Beach Spur Trail rejoins the Lake Moultrie Passage.

12.2   Cross the bridge over the Rediversion Canal. On the other side of the bridge, turn right, follow the gravel road back to the dike, and continue to follow the dike to the east.

16.5   Arrive at a trail junction. To the right is a spur trail that leads to a campsite 0.4 mile away.

18.2   Turn left off the dike and onto General Moultrie Road.

18.5   Turn left onto Pauline Drive.

19.2   Turn right onto Barn Road.

19.6   Turn left onto Butter Road.

20.2   Turn left onto Black Oak Road.

20.5   Veer left onto the top of the dike. Follow along the dike.

24.0   Turn left off the dike and onto the unpaved road.

24.1   Cross the railroad tracks and continue east toward the eastern trailhead.

24.4   Arrive at the eastern trailhead of the Lake Moultrie Passage on the west side of US 52.

Hike Information

Local Information: Berkeley Chamber of Commerce, 1004 US 52, Moncks Corner, SC 29461; (843) 761-8238; berkeleysc.org

Local Events/Attractions: Mepkin Abbey, 1098 Mepkin Abbey Rd., Moncks Corner; (843) 761-8509; mepkinabbey.org. Open Tues–Sat 9 a.m. to 4 p.m., Sun 1 to 4 p.m.

Old Santee Canal Park, 900 Stony Landing Rd., Moncks Corner; (843) 899-5200. Open daily 9 a.m. to 5 p.m. Small fee

Lodging: Peach Tree Inn, 111 Conners Dr., Saint George; (866) 539-0036

Restaurants: Music Man's BBQ, 112 E. Railroad Rd., Moncks Corner; (843) 899-7675; musicmansbbq.com. Wed–Sat 11 a.m. to 8:30 p.m., Sun 11 a.m. to 2 p.m.

Barony House, 401 Altman St., Moncks Corner; (843) 761-7600; Mon–Wed 11 a.m. to 2 p.m., Thurs–Fri 11 a.m. to 2 p.m. and 5:30 to 8:30 p.m., Sun 11 a.m. to 2:30 p.m.

Organizations: Palmetto Conservation, 722 King St., Columbia, SC 29205; (803) 771-0870; palmettoconservation.org

50 Palmetto Trail: Swamp Fox Passage

This three-to-four-day backpacking trip traverses mostly level paths through a typical coastal pine forest and swampy wetlands. Located north of Charleston along the state's central coast, this popular segment of the Palmetto Trail crosses a large number of creeks and seasonal streams as it makes its way through various swamps and mostly pine forests. Abundant footbridges, mounted split-plank logs, and boardwalks make easy work of trekking through the low-lying swampy areas along the trail.

Start: From the northwestern trailhead at the Canal Recreation Area off US 52
Distance: 46.8-mile shuttle
Hiking time: About 3-4 days
Difficulty: Easy to moderate due to length
Trail surface: Forested path, boardwalk, gravel and dirt roads, old roadbeds
Best seasons: Winter, early spring, late fall
Other trail users: Mountain bikers
Canine compatibility: Leashed dogs permitted
Fees and permits: None

Schedule: Open year-round
Maps: TOPO! CD: North Carolina-South Carolina; USGS maps: Bonneau, Cordesville, Bethera, Huger, Ocean Bay, and Awendaw; South Carolina; USFS maps: Francis Marion Hiking Trails Map available at the Francis Marion Ranger District office and at the Sewee Environmental Education Center
Trail contacts: Sewee Visitor & Environmental Education Center, 5821 Highway 17 N., Awendaw, SC 29429; (843) 928-3368

Finding the trailhead: From Charleston drive north on US 17 to Steed Creek Road (Charleston County Road S-10-1032) in Awendaw. Look for the trailhead parking area on US 17 just beyond Steed Creek Road. GPS: N33 16.388' / W79 57.810'

To park a car or be picked up at the end of the shuttle: From the parking lot at the start of the trail off US 52, drive south on US 52 East for 3.8 miles. Turn left onto SC 402 East and drive for 15.6 miles. Cross SC 41 and stay straight onto Steed Creek Road. Follow Steed Creek Road for 11.9 miles. Turn left onto US 17 North and follow for 2.5 miles. Make a U-turn and follow US 17 South for 0.2 mile until you reach the southern trailhead for the Swamp Fox Trail on the right side of the road.

The Hike

You can begin your hike from either the southern trailhead in Awendaw or as I suggest from the northwestern trailhead at the Canal Recreation Area. Wherever you decide to start your hike, you should either arrange a shuttle to pick you up at the end of your hike, leave a second vehicle at the opposite trailhead, or prepare for a six- to eight-day out-and-back hike. The trail becomes flooded and often is impassable during times of excessively heavy rainfall. Call the Francis Marion Ranger District office to check on trail conditions before you pack your bags and lace up your boots. The trail is shared with bikers so exercise caution when hiking on the narrow sections of the trail and around blind curves, where it may be difficult for mountain bikers to see you when they are riding fast.

The Swamp Fox Passage

The southernmost 27 miles of trail was originally built by Boy Scouts in 1968 and local Boy Scout Troops still regularly contribute to the maintenance of the Swamp Fox Trail. Both the Swamp Fox Trail and the Francis Marion National Forest are named for General Francis Marion, a local hero of the Revolutionary War who is particularly remembered for his cunning tactics in guerrilla warfare. He gained fame and his elusive name "Swamp Fox" as a result of his ability to continually evade capture and counterattack by the British by escaping and disappearing into the dense and foreboding swamps throughout the South Carolina coastal plains.

Along the trail you will encounter predominantly longleaf-pine forest with a variety of hardwoods scattered throughout. The trail is particularly attractive in the fall when the leaves are changing and the hardwoods put on a colorful display for the long-distance hikers passing through. During the spring you will find an abundance of blooming wildflowers. The swamps are excellent fishing grounds for bass, catfish, and brim. Alligators are especially abundant in the bald-cypress wetlands, where deer and otters are also found.

The nearly 47-mile-long trail is generally level for easy walking and can easily be completed in four days. However, the trail crosses so many roads that hikes of shorter sections of the trail can easily be planned if you're not up for a backpacking trip of this length. To thru-hike the trail, begin at the Canal Recreation Area and traverse through a drier pine forest for the first 3 miles of trail until you cross US 17. This is where the swamp really begins. You cross through the Wadboo Swamp, which is exceptionally challenging after periods of rain, and cross the Wadboo Creek. After crossing SC 97 you trudge through the Cane Gully Branch Swamp and cross the main channel of the creek, where you will find several excellent campsites. You briefly climb onto high ground and arrive at the Witherbee Trailhead at the Witherbee Ranger Station, where you will find designated campsites and facilities including restrooms and water.

▷ **Francis Marion, aka the Swamp Fox, is well regarded as one of the fathers of modern guerrilla warfare. Marion was originally stationed with General Horatio Gates, however, Gates had very little confidence in him and sent him away to command the Williamsburg Militia in the Pee Dee region.**

The trail then meets up with an extremely straight railroad bed that is often shared with equestrians to traverse the Jericho Swamp. The trail then takes a sharp turn to the southeast and crosses Witherbee Road near the junction with Conifer Road before crossing Nicholson Creek, where you will find exceptional campsites along the creek's northern bank. You will cross SC 41 and Turkey Creek before traversing Dog Swamp and hiking through a section of the trail that traverses the largest variety of habitats in the shortest length of trail. Along this section you walk through scattered wetlands, forests of pines at varying stages of growth, and broom-straw savannas. You cross SC 133 and traverse through the wetlands of Harleston Dam Creek and Deep Branch before crossing 2 miles of pine forest to arrive at the Halfway Creek Campground, which has potable water. Cross Cooter Creek and pass through pine forests and mixed hardwood sections, then traverse an old rail bed through wetlands of Willow Hall Swamp before crossing Steed Creek Road, turning sharply to the right at the junction with the Awendaw Passage, and hiking back to the trailhead and parking lot on US 17.

Miles and Directions

0.0   Start from the parking lot and trailhead at the Canal Recreation Area off US 52.

0.4   Cross US 52.

2.0   Cross Bonneau Road.

2.8   Cross an unpaved road.

3.4   Cross US 17.

4.6   Cross the bridge over Wadboo Creek and Swamp.

5.5   Cross the unpaved road.

7.7   Cross Cane Gully Road.

9.0   Cross the bridge over Cane Gully Branch. In 400 feet you reach a campsite on the left side of the trail.

9.2   Cross the unpaved Cane Gully Road.

10.4   Cross the unpaved road.

11.3   Cross unpaved road.

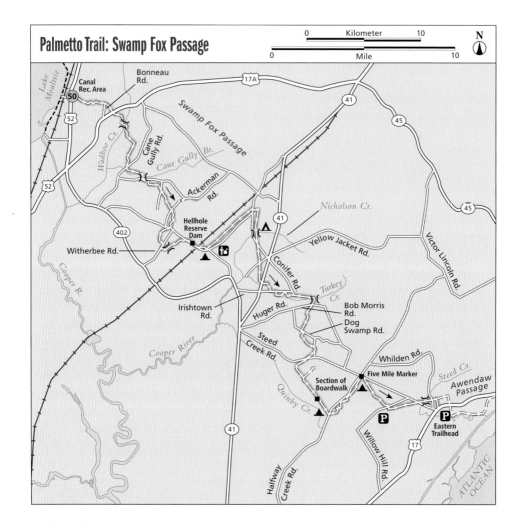

Palmetto Trail: Swamp Fox Passage

11.8 Cross the unpaved Ackerman Road.

13.0 Cross Witherbee Road.

14.7 Cross Cordesville Road.

14.9 Cross the bridge over Alligator Creek.

16.2 Cross Witherbee Road again.

16.7 Reach the Hellhole Reserve Dam on the left side of the trail.

17.1 Cross the railroad tracks.

17.3 Arrive at the Witherbee primitive campground.

18.1 Reach the Witherbee Ranger Station Trailhead, a trailhead and parking area.

20.5 Cross an unpaved road.

21.1 Cross Witherbee Road.

22.8 Arrive at Nicholson Creek Camp.

23.0 Cross the bridge spanning Nicholson Creek.

23.1 Cross Conifer Road. Over the next 0.7 mile, you will cross Conifer Road two more times.

24.5 Cross Yellow Jacket Road.

25.7 Cross SC 41.

26.5 Cross Irishtown Road.

28.4 Cross Conifer Road.

29.6 Reach the bridge at Turkey Creek.

30.1 Cross Bob Morris Road.

31.7 Cross Dog Swamp Road.

33.1 Cross the unpaved road.

33.3 Cross the unpaved road.

34.0 Cross Steed Creek Road.

35.4 Cross the unpaved road.

36.8 Arrive at the boardwalk that crosses the Harleston Dam Creek and the surrounding marsh.

37.5 Arrive at Harleston Dam Camp.

38.1 Cross Halfway Creek Road.

40.9 Arrive at Halfway Creek Camp.

41.7 Reach a sign marking the 5-mile point on the trail. It is 5 miles to the Steed Creek Bridge.

43.7 Arrive at the parking lot on Willow Hall Road. This is an excellent point to arrange a shuttle if you want to cut the last 3 miles off this trail. To continue on the Swamp Fox Trail, cross Willow Hall Road.

45.3 Cross Steed Creek Road.

46.0 Cross the bridge spanning Steed Creek. You have less than a mile to go.

46.2 Cross Whilden Road.

46.3 Arrive at a trail junction. The Awendaw Passage begins straight ahead. Turn right and continue on the Swamp Fox Trail toward the trailhead and parking lot.

46.8 Arrive at the trailhead and parking lot at the end of this hike.

Hike Information

Local Information: Berkeley Chamber of Commerce, 1004 US 52, Moncks Corner, SC 29461; (843) 761-8238; berkeleysc.org

Local Events/Attractions: Mepkin Abbey, 1098 Mepkin Abbey Rd., Moncks Corner; (843) 761-8509; mepkinabbey.org. Open Tues–Sat 9 a.m. to 4 p.m., Sun 1 to 4 p.m.

Old Santee Canal Park, 900 Stony Landing Rd., Moncks Corner; (843) 899-5200. Open daily 9 a.m. to 5 p.m. Small fee for adults; senior discount available

Lodging: Peach Tree Inn, 111 Conners Dr., Saint George; (866) 539-0036

Restaurants: Music Man's BBQ, 112 E. Railroad Rd., Moncks Corner; (843) 899-7675; musicmansbbq.com. Open Wed–Sat 11a.m. to 8:30 p.m., Sun 11 a.m. to 2 p.m.

Barony House, 401 Altman St., Moncks Corner; (843) 761-7600. Open Mon–Wed 11 a.m. to 2 p.m., Thurs–Fri 11 a.m. to 2 p.m. and 5:30 to 8:30 p.m., Sun 11 a.m. to 2:30 p.m.

Organizations: Palmetto Conservation, 722 King St., Columbia; (803) 771-0870; palmetto conservation.org

SWEETGRASS BASKETS

While traveling through the Lowcountry of South Carolina, especially along US 17 through Mount Pleasant, you will notice small, ramshackle booths lining the roadside. Beautiful woven baskets hang from hooks and cover every inch of free space around the booths. Be sure to take some time to stop at some of these booths and discover the artistry and cultural legacy of the Lowcountry sweetgrass baskets that are sold from these roadside stands. The coiled baskets are woven by members of the Gullah community, the descendants of the slaves that originated from Africa and were brought to South Carolina to work on the cotton and rice plantations of the region.

The sweetgrass baskets were originally woven by the Gullahs to carry rice and cotton on the plantations. Today, the coiled basket designs are widely respected and sought after as some of the finest examples of Gullah folk art and crafts. The exact process used in weaving these baskets is surrounded by a great deal of mystery. There are very few instructional books and classes on the subject of sweetgrass baskets, and all indications point to the fact that the Gullah would like to keep it this way. The art of weaving these baskets has been passed down from one generation to the next through oral instruction. This has not only preserved the knowledge of this beautiful skill and craft, but has also kept the knowledge exclusive to the Gullah community and as a result preserved the cultural integrity of the art form and secured the livelihood of the Gullahs who choose to carry on this widely respected and valued tradition.

The actual shape and form of the baskets are often compared to the baskets that are traditionally found in the historical record of the Wolof people in Senegal, West Africa. It is believed that the original makers of sweetgrass baskets in the United States originated from this region of Africa. However, the language spoken by the Gullah, known as Sea Island Creole, is a dynamic and rhythmic combination of Jamaican Patois, Barbadian Dialect, Bahamian Dialect, and the Krio language of Sierra Leone in West Africa. While the Gullah language, cuisine, music, and art can be found throughout the Charleston area, the sweetgrass baskets have become the most well-recognized symbol and representation of the interesting culture and rich heritage of the Gullah people.

51 Battery Warren Trail

Explore the Battery Warren, a Civil War–era earthen fort, along this short and easy day hike that leads down to the Santee River and an observation deck overlooking the battery. Just 15 minutes from McClellanville, this trail is a great choice for hikers with children or dogs, as well as history lovers looking to explore nature or the past.

Start: From the trailhead at the end of Echaw Road, FS 5032
Distance: 1-mile out and back
Hiking time: About 1 hour
Difficulty: Easy
Trail surface: Forested trail, old roadbed
Best seasons: Spring, fall, winter
Other trail users: Equestrians and mountain bikers
Canine compatibility: Leashed dogs permitted
Fees and permits: None

Schedule: Dawn–dusk daily
Maps: TOPO! CD: North Carolina–South Carolina; USGS maps: Cedar Creek; South Carolina; USFS maps: Battery Warren Trail Map and Francis Marion Ranger District Map available at the Francis Marion National Forest park office and the Sewee Visitor Center
Trail contacts: Francis Marion National Forest, Sewee Visitor Center, 5821 Highway 17 N., Awendaw, SC 29429; (843) 928-3368

Finding the trailhead: From Charleston drive northeast on US 17 to McClellanville and turn left onto SC 45. Drive to Honey Hill and turn right onto Chicken Creek Road (Berkeley County S-8-103). Drive 0.7 mile and turn right onto Echaw (FS Road 204). Drive 1.4 miles and keep right where the gravel road splits. Drive another 2.2 miles and turn left onto FS Road 204-A. Drive 1 mile and stay to the right at the fork in the road. The trailhead is another 0.5 mile farther, at the end of the road. GPS: N33 14.616' / W79 32.193'

The Hike

The Battery Warren was built in 1862 at this strategic sharp turn in the Santee River. As Union boats traveled up the Santee, they would come around this blind curve and be met with gun and cannon fire from Confederate forces camped out at the battery. When you look at the battery from an aerial perspective, it looks like a large L on the high bluff along the Santee River. The earthen walls that protected confederate soldiers are known as parapets. Six openings were built into these parapets to enable cannons to be fired from behind the parapets while the gun crews operated from behind large mounds.

The battery is named after Revolutionary War hero Colonel Samuel Warren and was built to protect the railroad that ran between Charleston and the Confederate capital in Richmond, Virginia, and to keep Confederate forces from moving inland down the Santee River. The battery is near Blake's Plantation, which is where the Confederate soldiers stationed at Battery Warren camped. A great resource for further exploring what life was like at the battery during the Civil War is a compendium

Battery Warren
Construction of an Earthen Fortification

Fort Hudson, LA. (National Archives)

Built in 1862, Battery Warren is made of two earthen parapets coming together in an L-shape on the banks of the Santee River. The parapets contain six gun embrasures.

Parapets
Embrasures

Fort Fisher, NC (Chicago Historical Society)

Parapet: a wall or bank of earth, along the edge of the fortification giving protection to the troops.

Embrasure: an opening made through a parapet, to enable a cannon to fire through the wall of thick earth.

Francis Marion National Forest

of letters written by James M. Barr and compiled into a book titled *Let Us Meet in Heaven: The Civil War Letters of James Michael Barr* (2004). In one letter in the book, he describes the difficult conditions that the soldiers lived through when stationed at the battle: "Looking around the place where we are is enough to make anyone have a long face and I assure you there is many a long face here." He describes the prevalent illnesses and the deaths that affected the soldiers at Battery Warren in his detailed letters, which are widely considered some of the best documentations recounting life at the Battery Warren during this violent period.

Start from the grass-and-dirt parking lot at the end of Echaw Road. A kiosk marks the start of the trail that begins on an old doubletrack dirt roadbed and traverses through a mixed hardwood-pine forest dotted with dogwood trees. The trail is short and very easy to follow. However, be sure to avoid the trail during periods of recent heavy rainfall as the trail has a tendency to become flooded and impassable. During the late spring and throughout the summer, mosquitoes can be especially bothersome. Call the Francis Marion Ranger District and inquire about flooding and mosquito conditions on the trail before you navigate the lengthy and extensive network of dirt roads to the trailhead.

Near the beginning of the trail, if you look to the left, you will see the first evidence of parapets. However, the main battery is farther ahead on the high bluff of the Santee River. You cross a dirt road twice as the trail winds toward the battery, and along the way several interpretive plaques provide information on the battery and natural history of the forest you are exploring. After 0.4 mile you reach an observation deck that allows you to get a good view of the battery from above. A small spur trail leads down to the bank of the Santee River, where you can enjoy excellent views of the river and get a closer look at the blind curve that gave Confederate soldiers the element of surprise. From here simply turn around and return to the trailhead of this excellent trail rich in Civil War history.

Miles and Directions

0.0 Start from the parking lot at the end of Echaw Road. A kiosk marks the start of the Battery Warren Trail, which follows an old roadbed for most of the way to Battery Warren.

0.4 Reach the first evidence of the battery at the first parapet along the trail. An interpretive plaque recounts a diary entry that relates to the battery.

0.5 You arrive at the Battery Warren, where you can still see the earthen mound that was built as part of the original fort here along the Santee River. A narrow path leads past the battery and up to an observation deck, where you have an excellent view of the entire battery. A very narrow trail leads 60 feet from the observation deck to the river for an impressive view of Santee. After exploring the battery and the river, turn around and retrace your steps back toward the parking lot and trailhead where you started.

1.0 Arrive at the trailhead and parking lot where you started this hike.

A view of the Battery Warren

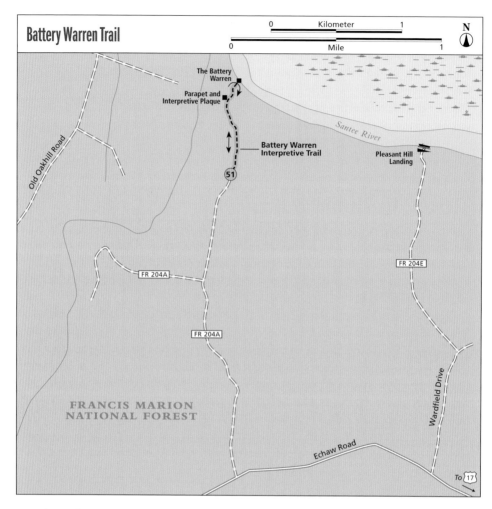

Battery Warren Trail

Hike Information

Local Information: Awendaw Town Hall, 6971 Doar Rd., Awendaw, SC 29429; (843) 928-3100; awendawsc.org

Local Events/Attractions: Center for Birds of Prey, 4872 Seewee Rd., Awendaw; (843) 971-7474. Open Thurs–Sat 10 a.m. to 5 p.m. Admission fee; discount for kids 6–18

Blue Crab Festival, Camp Seewee 7407 Doar Rd., Awendaw; (843) 928-3100. This festival occurs annually in October.

Lodging: McClellanville Rentals, (843) 606-0622; mcclellanvillerentals.com. Long- and short-term rentals are available.

Shem Creek Inn, 1401 Shrimp Boat Ln., Mount Pleasant; (843) 881-1000; shemcreek inn.com

Restaurants: Seewee Restaurant, 4804 N. Highway 17, Awendaw; (843) 928-3609

52 Palmetto Islands County Park

Enjoy this quick day hike that treks through the lush forest and marshlands surrounding the Splash Island Waterpark in one of Charleston County's most popular parks. This easy and level trail takes you along paved paths through a tropical setting before crossing a long boardwalk over the Wando River marshland to an undeveloped island, making this an excellent choice for hikers with children and dogs.

Start: From the trailhead at the Park Center
Distance: 1-mile loop
Hiking time: About 1 hour
Difficulty: Easy
Trail surface: Paved path, boardwalk, gravel trail, forested path
Best season: Year-round
Other trail users: Mountain bikers
Canine compatibility: Leashed dogs permitted
Fees and permits: Small per-person fee

Schedule: Daily 8 a.m. to 5 p.m.
Maps: TOPO! CD: North Carolina–South Carolina; USGS maps: Fort Moultrie; South Carolina; USFS maps: Palmetto Islands County Park Trail Map available at the entrance station and Park Center
Trail contacts: Palmetto Islands County Park, 444 Needlerush Pkwy., Mount Pleasant, SC 29464; (843) 884-0832

Finding the trailhead: From Charleston take US 17 North toward Mount Pleasant. Cross over the bridge toward Mount Pleasant. Veer left toward US 17 North / Johnnie Dodds Boulevard. Merge to a slight right onto I-526 West toward North Charleston. Take exit 28 for Long Point Road and turn right onto Long Point Road. Continue 1.5 miles to Needlerush Parkway, turn left onto Needlerush Parkway. The park is located on the right. GPS: N32 51.811' / W79 49.985'

The Hike

You have a myriad of options for hiking within this 943-acre park. The best options for hiking are found at either end of the park. This trail explores the western end of the park, starting near the Splash Island Waterpark and following the long boardwalk out to Nature Island. The water park is the most popular attraction here so be prepared for lots of loud kids splashing in the pools and screaming at the tops of their lungs as they zip down the 200-foot-tall slide at incredible speeds. Once you get out onto the boardwalk and onto Nature Island, you will have left most of the noise of the crowds behind. However, on summer weekends and holidays, the crowds will extend throughout every inch of the park as droves of Charlestonians looking for outdoor adventure, fishing, and a spot to beat the heat fill the place to capacity. Take one look at the massive parking lots at this park and you'll get an idea of how many visitors enjoy this park during the summer. The water park thankfully is closed during the winter, and this is an excellent time to visit the park for hiking. Also, early mornings are an excellent time to explore the trails before the kids show up.

The boardwalk to Nature Island

If you're looking for a little more solitude, try the trails that zigzag around the eastern section of the Palmetto Islands County Park. An excellent route is to park your vehicle at the last parking lot just past the Sweet Gum Picnic Shelter and walk across the long boardwalk that connects you to the complex of trails on the east side. Several fishing docks and picnic areas along Horlbeck Creek make this an excellent choice for anglers who want to pack their pole and reel in some bass, catfish, crappie, and bream. Once again, there are plenty of options to make loops and out-and-back routes as you explore the eastern peninsula of the park that juts out toward the curving tidal creek. And before you leave be sure to visit the 50-foot observation tower and enjoy impressive picturesque views of the surrounding marshes and tidal ecosystem.

This hike stops by the Park Center, where you can partake of the snack bar or rent kayaks, bicycles, and even paddleboats if you want to explore the pond on the west side of the park. From here you also have an excellent view of the 2-acre pond to the west. Follow the steps down from the Park Center deck and join a paved path that circles around the pond and leads to the start of the boardwalk. You emerge from

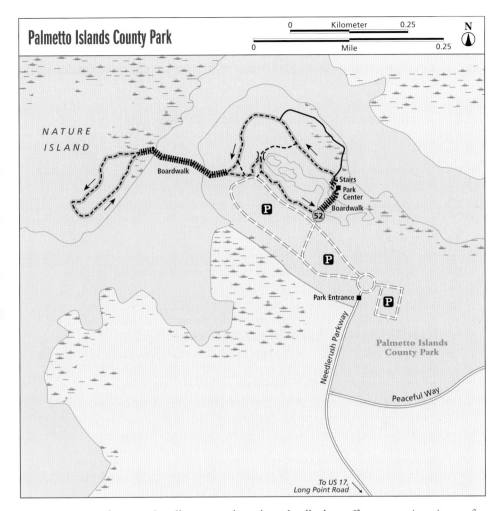

Palmetto Islands County Park

NATURE
ISLAND

Boardwalk

Stairs
Park
Center
Boardwalk

52

P

P

Park Entrance

P

Palmetto Islands
County Park

Needlerush Parkway

Peaceful Way

To US 17,
Long Point Road

0   Kilometer   0.25
0   Mile   0.25

N

the maritime forest and walk across a long boardwalk that offers expansive views of the surrounding marshland bordering Horlbeck Creek and the Wando River. At the split in the boardwalk, veer left and follow the boardwalk to the start of the network of forested trails that explore Nature Island. The trail complex on the island is best approached in a casual and informal way. None of the trails is named or marked, and they are easily explored without getting disoriented. Still, I highly recommend taking a compass with you, especially if you are new to navigating and hiking. Throughout the island you find a mix of forest and marshland and you can often spot alligators and a variety of birds on the island including osprey, owls, herons, and egrets.

After exploring the island return to the boardwalk and cross the marsh back to the paved trail that leads behind the water park and then parallels the pond. You cross several arching bridges with excellent views of the pond that make great stops for spotting gators before returning to the trailhead at the Park Center where you started your hike.

Miles and Directions

0.0 Start from the front of the Park Center. A large sign that reads Park Center marks the start of the trail. Follow the boardwalk up to the Park Center, walk behind the building, and follow the steps down to the paved trail.

0.1 Turn left at the paved trail.

0.2 Splash Island Waterpark is to the left. Stay straight toward Nature Island.

0.3 The trail splits. To the left is the parking lot. Stay right toward Nature Island. In 80 feet you reach the boardwalk to Nature Island. Cross the boardwalk over the saltwater marsh.

0.4 Reach a split in the boardwalk. Stay to the left toward Nature Island. In 150 feet you arrive at the end of the boardwalk. Follow the dirt trail into the forest.

0.5 The trail splits. Stay to the right. In 300 feet you reach another split in the trail. Stay to the left.

0.6 Arrive at a T junction. Turn left back toward the marsh. In 230 feet you reach a split in the trail. Veer to the right.

0.7 You are back at the boardwalk. Follow the boardwalk across the marsh and back to the paved trail.

0.8 After you reach the paved trail, the trail splits again. Stay to the right. In 120 feet the paved trail ends at a dirt road. Stay straight and follow the dirt road to the boardwalk on the left. In 80 more feet turn left onto the boardwalk. The water park is to your left.

0.9 You reach a T junction in the trail. Turn right and walk over the pair of bridges. In 75 feet you reach a junction in the trail on the other side of the bridges. Turn left and follow the dirt path alongside the pond back toward the trailhead where you started.

1.0 Arrive at the trailhead and parking lot where you started in front of the Park Center.

Hike Information

Local Information: Charleston Visitors Center, 375 Meeting St., Charleston, SC 29403; (843) 724-7174. Open daily 8:30 a.m. to 5 p.m.

Local Events/Attractions: Lowcountry Oyster Festival, Boon Hall Plantation, 1235 Long Point Rd., Mount Pleasant; (843) 884-4371. Eighty thousand pounds of oysters are roasted annually in January at this festival.

Patriots Point Naval Museum, 40 Patriots Point Rd., Mount Pleasant; (843) 884-2727; patriotspoint.org. Open daily 9 a.m. to 6:30 p.m. Admission fee; discount for seniors and kids 6–11

Lodging: Charleston Harbor Resort and Marina, 20 Patriots Point Rd., Mount Pleasant; (888) 856-0028; charlestonharborresort.com

Shem Creek Inn, 1401 Shrimpboat Ln., Mount Pleasant; (843) 881-1000; shemcreekinn.com

Restaurants: Page's Okra Grill, 302 Coleman Blvd., Mount Pleasant; (843) 881-3333; pagesokragrill.com. Mon–Sat 6:30 a.m. to 3 p.m. and 5 to 9 p.m., Sun 8 a.m. to 2 p.m.

Red Drum, 803 Coleman Blvd., Mount Pleasant; (843) 894-0313; reddrumrestaurant.com. Open Tues–Sat 5:30 to 10 p.m., Sun brunch 10:30 a.m. to 2 p.m.

53 Sewee Shell Mound

A pleasant walk through a bottomland forest leads to the edge of a picturesque marsh. You may be surprised by the beautiful views from the boardwalk that travels along the edge of the expansive marshland and passes by an ancient shell mound. Benches and an observation deck along the boardwalk give you the opportunity to enjoy the views, look for birds in the wetlands, and fish in the water below. On the hike back to the parking area, a spur trail leads to a clam-shell mound, evidence of the early Native American inhabitants that once called this land home.

Start: Gravel parking lot on left side of Salt Pond Road
Distance: 1.1-mile lollipop
Hiking time: About 1 mile
Difficulty: Easy due to distance and level walking
Trail surface: Dirt path, boardwalk
Best seasons: Early spring and late fall for cooler temperatures and bird watching
Other trail users: Hikers only
Canine compatibility: Leashed dogs permitted

Fees and permits: None
Schedule: Daily dawn to dusk
Maps: TOPO! CD: South Carolina–North Carolina; USGS maps: Sewee Bay, South Carolina; USFS maps: Francis Marion National Forest Map available at Francis Marion Ranger Stations and Sewee Environmental Education Center
Trail contacts: Francis Marion National Forest, Sewee Visitor and Environmental Education Center, 5821 US 17 N., Awendaw, SC 29429; (843) 928-3368

Finding the trailhead: From Charleston follow US 17 north for approximately 18 miles and turn right (northeast) onto Doar Road (Charleston County S-10-432). Drive 2.5 miles and turn right (east) onto Salt Pond Road (FS 243), which is one lane with a turnaround loop at the end. After 0.5 mile look for a sign on the right that marks the trailhead. GPS: N33 00.068' / W79 36.555'

The Hike

The forest is recovering nicely after Hurricane Hugo made direct landfall just near this forest. Two years later a fire ravaged through the area and devastated what was left of the mature pines and large oak trees, and most of the forest along the edge of this large salt marsh is now dense scrub oak and very young bottomland hardwood forest. The main historical features of the trail that have placed this area on the National Register of Historical Places are the two shell mounds along the route. These large mounds of shells are actually refuse piles left behind by the Native Americans who inhabited the area for thousands of years. These large mounds of shells are evidence of their presence and also of their seemingly insatiable appetite for oysters and clams, which they harvested from the salt marsh. Shell mounds can be found all up and down the Atlantic coast and Florida, and the mounds here are considered some of the best preserved examples of shell mounds in this region. These mounds are believed to be more than 4,000 years old, and along this route you get the chance to get very

A boardwalk offers beautiful views of the salt marsh.

close to these historical relics of Native American history. The first of the mounds that you encounter is considered a shell ring. Native Americans lived in huts that surrounded a shell mound. The center of the mound was left open and it is believed this area was used for ceremonial purposes.

From the trailhead a forested path leads through the young, dense forest. After 400 feet you reach a split in the trail. This is the beginning of a loop trail to both of the shell mounds. To the right the loop trail leads to the marsh and the clam mound. Stay to the right and follow the path toward the shell ring. The trail continues through the forest for 0.3 miles until you reach a T junction. Turn right and continue on the spur trail to the shell ring. Right after the junction the forest abruptly opens up into a

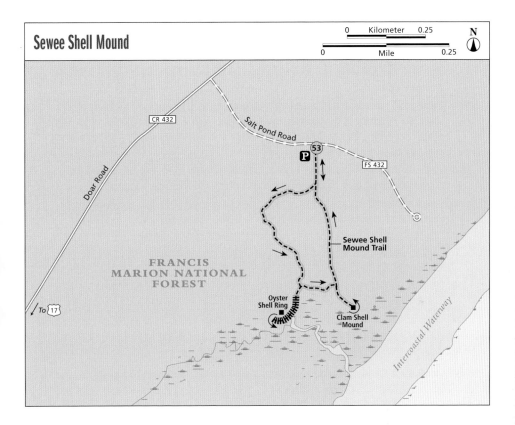

Sewee Shell Mound

beautiful and expansive marsh. The shade of the forest ends and a boardwalk leads the way over the saltwater marshland. A network of slow-flowing channels cut through the thick marsh grass where you can see schools of fish darting in the water below. Look past the surface of the water and notice the clusters of oysters that make up the marsh bottom. The boardwalk is particularly pleasant during the cooler months of the year, and when the weather is nice and cool, the place is as close to coastal perfection as glossy copy of *Coastal Living* magazine. Fifty feet from the start of the boardwalk, you will find the oyster-shell mound on the right side of the boardwalk and an interpretive plaque that describes the historical significance of the mound. Continue on the boardwalk to the end, where you reach an observation deck with several benches where you can sit and watch for the enormous variety of birds that frequent this location. In the early spring mornings, when bird watching is best, you are likely to see herons, osprey, woodpeckers, and warblers in and around the marsh.

From the end of the boardwalk, turn around and walk back to the forested looping path. This will take you to another spur trail that leads to a clam mound on the edge of the marsh and more excellent views of the creek, marsh, and Bulls Bay in the distance. From here, the trail loops around and rejoins the forested trail that returns to the trailhead and parking area where you started.

Miles and Directions

0.0 Start from the gravel parking lot on the left side of Salt Pond Road. Follow the forested trail 400 feet to a split in the trail. The trail straight ahead leads to the clam mound. Turn right toward the shell ring.

0.4 Arrive at a T junction and turn right toward the shell ring. Continue for 250 feet until you reach the beginning of the boardwalk and excellent views of the surrounding marsh. Fifty feet from the beginning of the boardwalk, on the right side of the trail, is the shell mound and an interpretive plaque.

0.5 Arrive at an observation deck at the end of the boardwalk. From here turn around and retrace your steps back to the forested path that follows alongside the marsh.

0.6 Reach the junction at the beginning of the boardwalk again. Turn right and follow the forested path alongside the marsh.

0.7 The trail splits. Stay to the right and follow the spur trail to the clam mound 200 feet away on the edge of the marsh. Turn around and retrace your steps back to the main trail and continue on the loop back toward the parking area.

1.0 Arrive at the beginning of the loop trail. Stay straight and follow the trail back toward the parking area.

1.1 Reach the parking lot and trailhead where you started.

Hike Information

Local Information: Charleston County Chamber of Commerce, 4500 Leeds Ave. #100, North Charleston, SC 29405; (843) 577-2510

Local Events/Attractions: Cooper River Bridge Run, (843) 856-1949; bridgerun.com. This 10K run across the Cooper River Bridge into downtown Charleston takes place in late March / early April.

Middleton Place Plantation and Gardens, 4300 Ashley River Rd., Charleston; (843) 556-6020. Middleton features a museum, an inn, gardens, and a restaurant.

Lodging: Inn at Middleton Place, 4300 Ashley River Rd., Charleston; (843) 556-6020; middletonplace.org

Meeting Street Inn, 173 Meeting St., Charleston; (843) 723-1882; meetingstreetinn.com

Restaurants: 39 Rue de Jean, 39 John St., Charleston; (843) 722-8881; 39ruedejean .com. Open daily at 11 a.m.

Fleet Landing, 186 Concord St., Charleston; (842) 722-8100; fleetlanding.net. Open daily at 11 a.m.

Paisano's Pizza, 1246 Camp Rd., Charleston; (843) 762-1135; paisanosji.com. Open daily at 11 a.m.

Organizations: Francis Marion National Forest, Sewee Visitor and Environmental Education Center, 5821 US 17 N., Awendaw, SC 29429; (843) 928-3368

54 Caw Caw Interpretive Center

This hike explores a large complex of trails that traverse a network of canals and old rice fields that now harbor an abundant diversity of waterfowl and wildlife. Observation decks along the route provide ample viewing areas and offer spectacular views of the marshland and surrounding forest. The trail explores a bottomland forest with impressive-size live oaks with Spanish moss hanging from their massive limbs. At the end of the route, you are treated to an elevated boardwalk that cuts through a tranquil cypress swamp. Halfway through the cypress swamp, you arrive at an observation deck with rocking chairs that look over the swamp.

Start: From the connector trail behind the Nature Center near Kiosk 2
Distance: 2.1-mile loop
Hiking time: About 1 hour
Difficulty: Easy due to length and level
Trail surface: Dirt path, forested trail, boardwalk
Best seasons: Early spring and late fall for cooler temperatures and bird watching

Other trail users: Hikers only
Canine compatibility: Dogs not permitted
Fees and permits: Small fee
Schedule: Wed-Sun 9 a.m. to 5 p.m.
Maps: TOPO! CD: South Carolina-North Carolina; USGS maps: Ravenel, South Carolina
Trail contacts: Caw Caw Nature and History Interpretive Center, 5200 Savannah Hwy., Ravenel, SC 29470; (843) 889-8898

Finding the trailhead: From Charleston take US 17 south for 14 miles to the entrance of the park on the right-hand side of the road. Follow the park road back to the interpretive center and park at the parking lot in front of the center. Walk into the center and pay the entrance fee. The trail starts at Kiosk 2 behind the center. GPS: N32 47.511'/W80 11.875'

The Hike

Every trip to Charleston should include five events: a walk along the Battery and past Rainbow Row, dinner at 39 Rue de Jean, a day at Folly Beach, a night listening to Chris Crosby at Smokey Oak, and an early morning hike through Caw Caw. Before you start your hike, be sure to visit the Caw Caw Interpretive Center. Wander through the impressive exhibits that explore the historical significance of the area and give you an insight into the abundant birds and wildlife that you are likely to see along the trail. You might be detoured by the admission fee before you start your hike, but after you finish exploring the park, you will realize that the fee is one of the best deals in town. I can't say enough about how well maintained these trails are and how impressive of an experience you can have at the 654-acre preserve.

It is an understatement to say that this park is a hot spot for birders on the Carolina coast. More than 250 species of birds have been sighted in this park. Bring your binoculars and camera and look out for the wood storks, herons, bald eagles, warblers, swallowtail kites, egrets, ibises, buntings, and hundreds of other migratory waterfowl,

The trails at Caw Caw follow canals carved for rice-growing operations.

songbirds, and wading birds that call Caw Caw home. This place is a birder's paradise, and along the trail you are going to encounter an ample number of observation
decks and viewing platforms in key spots within the park where you can have the
best opportunity to spot that bird you've been searching for and finally check it off
your bird bucket list.

This route combines many of the park's most popular routes to take the hiker on
an adventure past the park's greatest highlights. The trail starts behind the interpretive
center at Kiosk 2. A connector trail leads to the right and to the Upland Forest Trail,
keeping the bird-feeding garden in front of you. You hike through a short section of
bottomland forest and quickly arrive at the edge of an expansive marsh. In the 1700s
and 1800s, slaves carved canals and dikes out of the marsh to create rice fields. The
trail circles around the marsh and passes several observation decks, an observation
platform, and a large eagle's nest that is elevated on a long pole on the right side of
the trail. The trail abruptly leaves the marsh and returns to the forest. Along the next
section of forested trail, you pass through a section of woods containing impressively
large live oaks with Spanish moss hanging from the canopy.

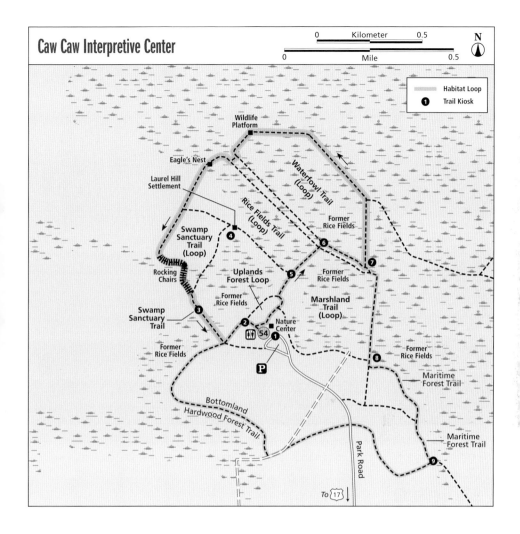

0   Kilometer   0.5

0   Mile   0.5

N

Habitat Loop

① Trail Kiosk

Wildlife
Platform

Eagle's Nest

Laurel Hill
Settlement

Waterfowl Trail (Loop)

Rice Fields Trail (Loop)

Swamp
Sanctuary
Trail
(Loop)

④

Former
Rice Fields

⑥

⑦

Rocking
Chairs

Uplands
Forest Loop

⑤

Former
Rice Fields

Swamp
Sanctuary
Trail

③

Former
Rice Fields

②

Nature
Center

Marshland
Trail
(Loop)

54 ①

Former
Rice Fields

P

⑧

Former
Rice Fields

Maritime
Forest Trail

Bottomland
Hardwood Forest Trail

Maritime
Forest Trail

Park Road

⑨

To 17

In 0.2 mile you reach the start of a wide boardwalk that zigzags through a quiet and tranquil cypress swamp. Walk slowly and quietly and you may be able to keep from spooking the alligators and herons that are commonly spotted wading in the inky-black waters of the still swamp. After 0.1 mile on the boardwalk, you reach my favorite part of the trail. In the shade of the cypress trees, you arrive at an observation deck lined with rocking chairs where you can kick back, relax, and enjoy an incredible view of the swamp around you. After a hot day of hiking around the park, if you had a glass of sweet iced tea and a plate of homemade shrimp-and-grits with a side of fried okra, this would be heaven on earth. Take your time and rock your worries away before following the trail back to the interpretive center where you started.

You are likely to see alligators along the canals at Caw Caw.

Miles and Directions

0.0 Start from the connector trail behind the Nature Center marked by Kiosk 2. The bird-feeder garden is in front of you. Turn right and follow the paved trail until it ends and becomes a gravel path, enters into the forest, then leads to the Maritime Forest Trail.

0.1 Arrive at a trail junction. The Maritime Forest Trail is to the right. Stay straight and join the Upland Forest Trail. In 250 feet you reach another trail junction. The Upland Forest Trail continues straight ahead. Turn right onto the Rice Fields Trail.

0.2 A dirt road crosses the trail. Turn left onto the dirt road and follow the trail toward the marsh. In 100 feet you reach a split in the trail at Kiosk 5. The Laurel Hill Settlement is to the left. Stay to the right on the grassy path that cuts through the marsh and leads to the Waterfowl Overlook.

0.3 At a four-way junction, the Marshland Trail is to the right and the rice fields are to the left. Stay straight and cross over the wooden bridge. In 100 feet you reach a T junction. The rice fields are to the right. The observation deck is straight ahead. Turn right onto the Marshland Trail.

0.5 At the T junction turn to the left onto the Waterfowl Trail.

1.1 A wildlife-viewing platform that looks like a lifeguard stand is on the right side of trail. The trail curves to the left.

1.2 Arrive at a trail junction. The Marsh Trail is straight ahead. Turn right onto the Rice Field Trail and cross the boardwalk. In 100 feet you arrive at another junction. The rice fields are to the left. Turn right and stay on the Rice Field Trail.

1.3 The eagle's nest is to the right, on top of the long pole.

1.4 The trail splits. The Laurel Hill Settlement is to the left. Stay straight and join the Swamp Sanctuary Trail that leads past the large live oak to your left and heads toward the interpretive center.

1.6 Arrive at the start of an elevated boardwalk through a cypress swamp.

1.7 An observation deck with rocking chairs looks out over the picturesque swamp.

1.8 Arrive at a T junction and the end of the boardwalk. The Laurel Hill Settlement is to the right. Turn right toward the interpretive center.

2.0 At the T junction, turn left toward the interpretive center onto the dirt-path connector trail that is blazed with pink markers. Do not go straight on the dirt road.

2.1 Reach a split in the trail. The Upland Forest Trail is to the left. Stay straight toward the interpretive center. In 300 feet you arrive back at the interpretive center where you started.

Hike Information

Local Information: Charleston County Chamber of Commerce, 4500 Leeds Avenue #100, North Charleston, SC 29405; (843) 577-2510

Local Events/Attractions: Cooper River Bridge Run, (843) 856-1949; bridgerun.com. This 10K across the Cooper River Bridge into downtown Charleston takes place in late March/early April.

Middleton Place Plantation and Gardens, 4300 Ashley River Rd., Charleston; (843) 556-6020. Middleton features a museum, an inn, gardens, and a restaurant.

Lodging: Shem Creek Inn, 1401 Shrimp Boat Ln., Mount Pleasant; (843) 881-1000; shemcreek inn.com

Mills House Hotel Charleston, 115 Meeting St., Charleston; (843) 577-2400; mills house.com

Restaurants: Coast Bar and Grill, 39 Rue de Jean St., Charleston; (843) 722-8838; coastbarandgrill.com. Open at 4 p.m. daily

Bowens Island Restaurant, 1870 Bowens Island Rd., Charleston; (843) 795-2757; bowensislandrestaurant.com. Open Tues–Sat 5 to 10 p.m.

Organizations: Charleston County Parks and Recreation Commission, (843) 795-4386

55 I'on Swamp

This short and easy hike just outside of Charleston explores the dikes and canals of an old rice-growing operation. A popular place for bird watching, the canals of the swamp are also home to an abundant number of alligators, blue herons, and turtles. A few sections of slightly elevated boardwalks keep your feet dry while crossing through extremely low-lying bog crossings, but much of this trail follows dirt paths across the tops of canal berms, giving you an up-close-and-personal swamp hike experience.

Start: Gravel parking lot on the left side of FS 228
Distance: 1.8-mile lollipop
Hiking time: About 1 hour
Difficulty: Easy due to length and level walking
Trail surface: Forested trail, boardwalk, old roadbed
Best seasons: Early spring and late fall for cooler temperatures and bird watching
Other trail users: Hikers only
Canine compatibility: Leashed dogs permitted

Fees and permits: None
Schedule: Dawn to dusk daily
Maps: TOPO! CD: South Carolina-North Carolina; USGS maps: Ocean Bay, South Carolina; USFS maps: Francis Marion National Forest Map, Seewee Visitor Center and Francis Marion Ranger Stations
Trail contacts: Francis Marion National Forest, Sewee Visitor and Environmental Education Center, 5821 US 17 N., Awendaw, SC 29429; (843) 928-3368

Finding the trailhead: From the I-526 junction in Mount Pleasant, drive approximately 15 miles and turn left onto I'on Swamp Road (FR 228). Drive 2.5 miles to the parking area on the left (south). GPS: N33 00.281'/W79 40.957'

The Hike

Have you ever wanted to get up close and personal with alligators and other swamp wildlife? I mean, really close? Well, here's your chance. On the I'on Swamp Trail, you follow alongside canals that were constructed for rice-growing operations in the swamp. Today, the old rice fields have been overtaken by beautiful cypress trees, alligators, and the turtles that keep the alligators fed. You may also encounter deer, blue herons, and a variety of other birds. The swamp, like many swamps and wetlands around Charleston, is very popular with birders. During the spring and fall migrations, expect to see a variety of warblers, blue herons, and my favorite, the occasional osprey hunting in larger bodies of water along the trail.

The network of canals and dikes that crisscross through the swamp were once a part of the larger rice-growing operations on the Whitheywood Plantation. From the parking lot a thin path passes a kiosk on the right side of the trail and enters into

A view of an old roadbed along the I'on Swamp Trail

Look for alligators in the canals that cut through I'on Swamp.

a dense and tangled forest of low-lying shrubs, vines, and scrub oak. After 200 feet you reach a junction with an old road that is now grown over with grass. To the left the old road leads back to FR 228. Turn right and follow the old road for 0.2 mile until you reach the first canal. This will be your first opportunity to spot birds and alligators wading in the dark swamp waters that often appear to be pitch black. For someone who is unfamiliar with this type of swamp terrain, walking on these trails can be unnerving, and rightfully so. Exercise extreme caution when walking on these canal trails. While alligator attacks are extremely rare, especially when you are not swimming in the water, do not harass or otherwise attempt to touch or approach these usually docile alligators. Also watch for poisonous water moccasins along the canal trails.

One hundred feet from the first canal is a trail junction and the start of the loop trail through the swamp. Turn left and follow the trail alongside the canal system, passing over several wooden bridges. At the first bridge you cross, you are offered excellent views of the surrounding canals. The viewpoint from this first bridge is an excellent spot to sit and quietly enjoy the tranquillity of the swamp, listen to the

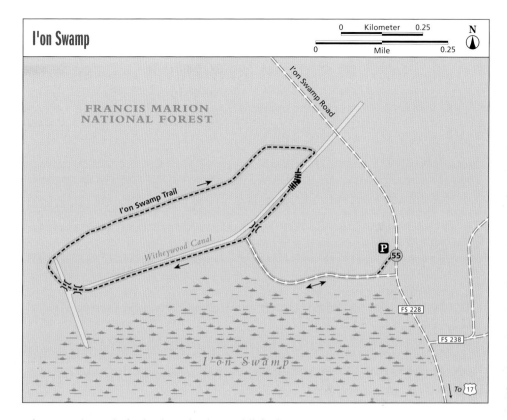

0   Kilometer   0.25

0   Mile   0.25

N

FRANCIS MARION
NATIONAL FOREST

I'on Swamp Road

I'on Swamp Trail

Witheywood Canal

P 55

FS 228

FS 238

I-o-n S-w-a-m-p

To 17

forest, and watch for birds and other wildlife that may move into the viewing area. This is also an excellent place to spot an impressive number of alligators, especially when the water is high. From the first bridge the trail veers sharply to the right and follows along a canal on the northern edge of the loop trail. After the trail turns sharply to the south and begins to head back toward the parking area, you arrive at a very low-lying area of trail. An elevated, single-board walkway has been constructed along this boggy section of trail to keep your feet dry in the cooler months, especially during the early spring season when a larger amount of rainwater flows into the swamp and floods much of this section of trail.

In 0.1 mile you cross another wooden bridge that spans a canal and then quickly arrive at the junction with the old road and then the end of the loop trail through the swamp. Turn right onto the old road and follow the trail back to the parking area where you started.

Miles and Directions

0.0   Start from the trailhead at the gravel parking lot on the left side of FS 228. Follow the trail 200 feet to a trail junction. Turn right onto the old roadbed.

0.3   The trail reaches the canal. Stay straight on the forested path. After 100 feet you reach a T junction. Turn left.

0.7 Cross the wooden bridge. There is a canal on both sides of the trail.

1.4 Cross the single-board, wooden walkways through a 150-foot-long area of the trail that is low lying and boggy during the cooler, high-water months.

1.5 Cross the wooden bridge spanning the canal. In 150 feet reach the junction with the old roadbed that leads back to the parking lot where started. Turn left onto the old road.

1.8 Arrive at the parking lot where you started.

Hike Information

Local Information: Charleston County Chamber of Commerce, 4500 Leeds Ave. #100, North Charleston, SC 29405; (843) 577-2510

Local Events/Attractions: Cooper River Bridge Run, (843) 856-1949; www.bridgerun.com. This 10K across the Cooper River Bridge into downtown Charleston takes place in late March / early April.

Middleton Place Plantation and Gardens, 4300 Ashley River Rd., Charleston; (843) 556-6020. Middleton features a museum, an inn, gardens, and a restaurant.

Lodging: Buck Hall Recreation Area (camping), Buckhall Landing Road, McClellanville; (843) 887-3412

Inn at Middleton Place, 4300 Ashley River Rd., Charleston; (843) 556-6020; middletonplace.org

Restaurants: 39 Rue de Jean, 39 John St., Charleston; (843) 722-8881; 39ruedejean.com. Open daily at 11 a.m.

Fleet Landing, 186 Concord St., Charleston; (843) 722-8100; fleetlanding.net. Open daily at 11 a.m.

Paisano's Pizza, 1246 Camp Rd., Charleston; (843) 762-1135; paisanosji.com. Open daily at 11 a.m.

Organizations: Francis Marion National Forest, Sewee Visitor and Environmental Education Center, 5821 US 17 N., Awendaw, SC 29429; (843) 928-3368

56 Palmetto Trail: Awendaw Passage

Hike the southern terminus of the Palmetto Trail from Buck Hall Recreation Area to the US 17 trailhead on the west side of Murrell. Trek across well-constructed boardwalks, as well as simple, rustic, log-width bog walks along this excellent day hike that explores low-lying marshlands as well as a variety of forests dotted with palm trees.

Start: From the Palmetto Trailhead at Buck Hall Recreation Area

Distance: 7.0-mile shuttle

Hiking time: About 3–5 hours

Difficulty: Easy

Trail surface: Boardwalk, forested trail, old roadbed

Best season: Year-round

Other trail users: Mountain bikers

Canine compatibility: Leashed dogs permitted

Fees and permits: Small per-vehicle fee

Schedule: Daily 6 a.m. to 10 p.m.

Maps: TOPO! CD: North Carolina–South Carolina; USGS maps: Awendaw; South Carolina; USFS maps: Francis Marion National Forest Trail Map at the Witherbee Ranger District Office and online

Trail contacts: Sewee Visitor & Environmental Education Center, 5821 Highway 17 N., Awendaw, SC 29429; (843) 928-3368

Finding the trailhead: *To the eastern trailhead:* From Awendaw drive north approximately 3 miles on US 17 and turn at the Buck Hall Recreation Area sign. Drive to the end of the road and the trailhead is at the small parking area on the left. GPS: N33 02.425' / W79 33.768'

To leave a car at the western trailhead: From Awendaw drive south approximately 0.25 mile on US 17. The trailhead parking lot will be on the right side of the road. GPS: N33 02.254' / W79 37.068'

The Hike

This section of the Palmetto Trail is also popular with bikers so use caution when hiking on this segment of the trail. During times of high rain, the trail can become quite flooded. I highly recommend calling the Witherbee Ranger District Office before hiking on this trail because it can become impassable when the water levels are exceptionally high. Mosquitoes and heat are two other concerns to consider before embarking on your Awendaw Passage adventure. Mosquitoes can become intolerable during the late spring and summer. At the very least be sure to bring some potent bug spray and appropriate long-sleeve clothing and long pants that are lightweight enough to handle the hot weather well during the summer.

This trail can be approached as a day hike or an easy overnight backpacking trip. There are several good campsites along the route. Camping is also available at the start of the trail at Buck Hall Recreation Area, where you will find a collection of great campsites suitable for tents and RVs set directly on the Intracoastal Waterway. This is where the Palmetto Trail meets the ocean, making this a spectacular choice for anglers who want to integrate some reel time into their backpacking trip. Including

A trailhead for the Awendaw Passage

all the fishing around Buck Hall Recreation Area, the trail follows along Steed Creek for much of the way, offering excellent fishing opportunities at several docks and overlooks along the trail. If you're into fishing, be sure to pack the pole on this trek.

There are really two separate trailheads for this segment of the Palmetto Trail. If you are parking a vehicle at the trailhead, it is best to start from the fee parking lot on the east side of the recreation area. When you drive into Buck Hall and reach the junction at the large parking lot, the campground is to your right and the boat ramp straight ahead. Turn left to arrive at the trailhead and parking area for hikers.

The trail follows a boardwalk toward a large palm tree and then turns sharply to the left, crossing a marsh area before crossing Buck Hall Road. You walk through a large grassy field before reaching the other trailhead and the official start of this section of trail.

The trail enters into a dense forest of pine and heads north, then turning back to the south and returning to an arm of the Intracoastal Waterway one more time before leaving the waterway behind and paralleling Awendaw Creek. There are several excellent benches, decks, and overlooks along the next section of trail that make excellent spots to rest, picnic, and fish. The trail turns sharply to the north and crosses US 17. Exercise extreme caution when crossing the busy highway. The trail parallels the highway for a short distance before following Whitestone Road for 0.3 mile. You leave Whitestone Road and continue on an old roadbed to the junction with the Swamp Fox Trail that continues straight ahead toward Steed Creek and Steed Creek Road. This is the official end of the Awendaw Passage and the nearest trailhead is the Swamp Fox Trailhead to the south (left) on highway 17. You can either turn around and hike back to Buck Hall or turn left and hike the 0.3 mile to the Swamp Fox Trailhead on US 17, which is an excellent place to leave a second vehicle or to arrange a shuttle back to the trailhead where you started.

A palm provides shade along the Awendaw Passage.

Miles and Directions

0.0 Start from the parking lot at the Buck Hall Recreation Area. Follow the boardwalk toward the large palm tree and follow the trail as it bears to the left. In 100 feet you cross FR 242, or Buck Hall Landing Road, which leads to the Buck Hall Recreation Area. Cross the road and follow the path through the large field. At the back of the field, you will see a kiosk that marks the start of this trail that leads into the forest.

0.5 Cross the old dirt road and follow the trail as it veers to the left (southwest). In 150 feet the trail turns again to the right (north).

0.6 The trail takes a sharp turn to the left. Watch the blazes closely along this section.

0.7 Cross the wooden footbridges over an often marshy section of trail.

0.9 Cross Reverend Perry Road.

1.0 Reach a long clearing and power lines. The trail veers to the right and then reenters the forest on the other side of the clearing.

1.6 Arrive at the edge of the Intracoastal Waterway, where the trail veers sharply to the right. Along this next section you have wonderful views of the marsh and the waterway.

Palmetto Trail: Awendaw Passage

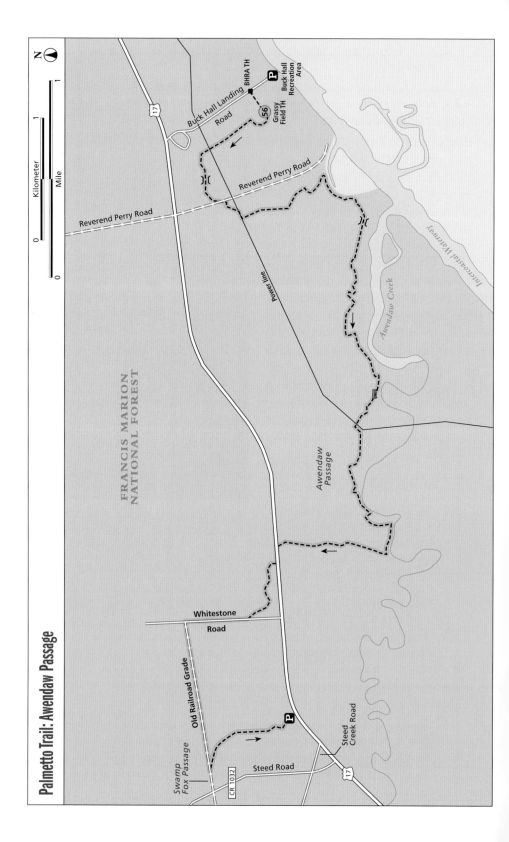

2.0 Cross the footbridge and enjoy a spectacular view of the marsh and surrounding waterways.

2.6 Arrive at a T junction. Turn left and then cross the bridge straight ahead.

3.1 Arrive at a bench overlooking Awendaw Creek. This is a great spot for a rest.

4.2 The trail turns sharply to the right (north) and away from Awendaw Creek.

4.8 Reach US 17. Cross the road and continue on the Awendaw Passage on the other side of road. This is also a good spot to turn around or to arrange a shuttle back to Buck Hall Recreation Area.

5.3 Reach a T junction with Whitestone Road. Turn right and follow the road to the north.

5.6 The trail turns sharply to the left and leaves Whitestone Road following an old railroad bed.

6.3 Reach a trail junction. Straight ahead the trail turns into the Swamp Fox Trail. Turn left and follow the Swamp Fox Trail toward the parking lot on US 17.

6.8 Arrive at the western parking lot for the Awendaw Trail and the end of this hike.

Hike Information

Local Information: Awendaw Town Hall, 6971 Doar Rd., Awendaw, SC 29429; (843) 928-3100; awendawsc.org

Local Events/Attractions: Center for Birds of Prey, 4872 Seewee Rd., Awendaw; (843) 971-7474. Open Thurs–Sat 10 a.m. to 5 p.m. Admission fee; discount for kids 6–18

Blue Crab Festival, Camp Sewee, 7407 Doar Rd., Awendaw; (843) 928-3100. This festival occurs annually in October.

Lodging: Camping at Buck Hall Recreation Area, Buckhalll Landing Rd., McClellanville; (843) 887-3412

Restaurants: Seewee Restaurant, 4804 N. Highway 17, Awendaw; (843) 928-3609

Organizations: Palmetto Conservation, 722 King St., Columbia, SC 29205; (803) 771-0870; palmettoconservation.org

57 South Tibwin Hiking Trail

Trek through a collection of habitats that include hardwood bottomlands, pine uplands, tidal marsh, freshwater ponds, and managed wetlands on this short day hike that introduces hikers to the extensive trail and road system open to hikers and bikers at the South Tibwin Trail complex. A bird blind on the edge of Tibwin Creek lets you unobtrusively observe the expansive marshland that is the highlight of this easily accessible coastal habitat.

Start: From the South Tibwin parking area on US 17
Distance: 2.3-mile lollipop
Hiking time: About 1–2 hours
Difficulty: Easy
Trail surface: Forested trail, boardwalk, old roadbed
Best seasons: Winter, early spring, late fall
Other trail users: Mountain bikers
Canine compatibility: Leashed dogs permitted
Fees and permits: None

Schedule: Daily dawn to dusk
Maps: TOPO! CD: North Carolina–South Carolina; USGS maps: Awendaw; South Carolina; USFS maps: Francis Marion Hiking Trails Map available at the Francis Marion Ranger District office and at the Sewee Environmental Education Center
Trail contacts: Francis Marion National Forest, Sewee Visitor Center, 5821 Highway 17 N., Awendaw, SC 29429; (843) 928-3368

Finding the trailhead: From Charleston drive northeast on US 17 to Awendaw. Continue on US 17 for approximately 7.5 miles. The trail entrance is on the right, marked by a small State Forest sign. GPS: N33 04.221'/W79 31.199'

The Hike

Drive along US 17, pass Awendaw, and keep your eyes open for the small parking lot on the right side of the road. About the only times that you won't see cars parked at the trailhead for the South Tibwin Hiking Trail are during the heat of the summer when the mosquitoes are particularly annoying and bothersome or after a heavy rain when the trails are flooded and often impassable. Closer to McClellanville to the east, you will find the North Tibwin Entrance, which also contains a complex network of hiking trails and dirt roads that are open to hikers and mountain bikers. This is a very popular area with folks looking for a trail to walk, run, hike, or bike for Charlestonians and residents of the Awendaw and McClellanville areas. The trail outlined in this book starts from the South Tibwin parking area. **Note:** Don't get this confused with the north entrance.

A pond along the South Tibwin Hiking Trail

A hunting blind along the South Tibwin Trail

The Intracoastal borders the southern end of the 600-acre South Tibwin Recreation Area. With a proper map and a decent sense of direction, the trails and roads in this area are usually approached in a casual way, randomly selecting roads and trails to explore and heading back to the trailhead whenever you are ready to end the trek. However, while it is fairly easy to become disoriented while you're out on the trail because not all the narrow, old roadbeds are mapped, it's just as easy to find your way out of the hiking area by heading back toward US 17, which can nearly always be heard throughout the area. The Intracoastal and Tibwin Creek serve as excellent points of reference while traveling through the area. Regardless, a compass is highly recommended. With this in mind the route featured in this book is meant to serve as an introduction to the larger area, and I highly recommend that you explore South Tibwin further.

The area is occasionally closed for seasonal hunts. You will see signs stating this at the trailhead when you arrive. However, I recommend that you call in advance and check to make sure that the trails are indeed open for hiking and biking. Also, while the trails are generally well maintained, if you are hiking in this area during the peak

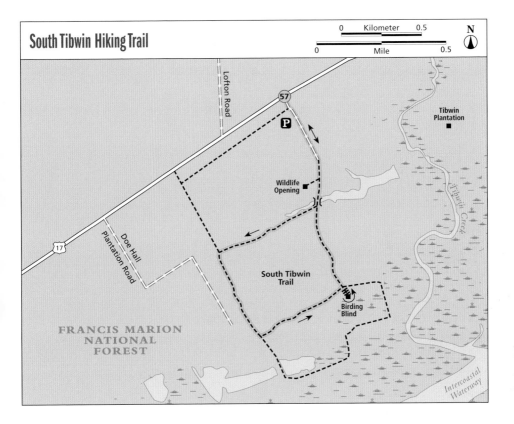

South Tibwin Hiking Trail

of summer the grass along the trails grows very fast and will occasionally grow quite tall, making it slightly difficult to follow the trail and providing plenty of excellent hiding spots for snakes. Take extra caution when hiking along these trails when the grass is high.

Along the trail you may see alligators, mottled ducks, river otters, turtles, and a variety of snakes and fish in the wetlands, tidal areas, and ponds, as well as ospreys and bald eagles soaring above the forest and marshes. The area is particularly popular with birders. Red-shouldered hawks, painted buntings, egrets, herons, and many other species of birds can be seen in the area. A highlight of this route for hikers who flock to forests where they can find their favorite flying fowl is the birding blind that offers expansive and impressive views of the marshland surrounding Tibwin Creek.

The trail starts from the parking area and follows a series of old roadbeds to Tibwin Creek. You cross a bridge spanning the creek before turning to the west and hiking to the western edge of the South Tibwin. The trail turns southward and parallels the border of the hiking area before reaching a marshy area and turning left (east) toward the birding blind. You arrive at a boardwalk that leads to the well-constructed birding blind, which makes an excellent spot to rest and enjoy the views of the expansive marsh. Regardless of whether birds are present, the view is incredibly beautiful, especially in late spring when the grass is at its greenest and the heat has not arrived in full force and killed the enjoyment of the place to a certain degree.

The trail turns to the left (north), crosses another arm of Tibwin Creek, and completes a hiking loop before crossing the Tibwin one last time and returning to the trailhead where you started this hike.

Miles and Directions

0.0 Start from the trailhead for the Tibwin Trail just off US 17. The trail starts from the south end of the parking lot and leads into the forest.

0.3 You reach a split in the trail. Stay to the right.

0.4 Cross the bridge spanning Tibwin Creek. After 141 feet you reach a four-way junction in the trail. Turn right.

0.8 You reach a T junction in the trail. Turn left (south).

1.2 You reach a split in the trail. Turn left toward the birding blind.

1.6 You arrive at another four-way junction. Turn right and take the short spur trail that leads to a boardwalk and the birding blind. After enjoying the view of the marsh and the Tibwin Creek tributary, turn around. When you reach the trail junction again, stay straight and head north back toward the parking lot where you started.

1.9 You arrive at a trail junction and complete the loop. Stay straight and follow the way you came in to return to the parking lot.

2.3 You arrive back at the parking lot where you started and at the end of this hike.

Hike Information

Local Information: Awendaw Town Hall, 6971 Doar Rd., Awendaw, SC 29429; (843) 928-3100; awendawsc.org

Local Events/Attractions: Center for Birds of Prey, 4872 Seewee Rd., Awendaw; (843) 971-7474. Open Thurs–Sat 10 a.m. to 5 p.m. Admission fee; discount for kids 6–18

Blue Crab Festival, Camp Seewee, 7407 Doar Rd., Awendaw; (843) 928-3100. The festival occurs annually in October.

Lodging: The Palms Hotel, 1126 Ocean Blvd., Isle of Palms; (843) 886-3003; thepalms hotel.us

Seaside Inn, 1004 Ocean Blvd., Isle of Palms; (843) 886-7000; seasideinniop.com

Restaurants: Seewee Restaurant, 4804 N. Highway 17, Awendaw; (843) 928-3609

58 Santee Coastal Reserve

Trek through the 24,000-acre Santee Coastal Reserve on this hike that loops through an interesting and dynamic mix of freshwater and saltwater ecosystems. Highlights of the trail, located just south of Georgetown along the state's central coast, include splendid marshland bordering the South Santee River, maritime forest, rice-field wetlands, and a boardwalk over the Washo Reserve. A popular trail with twitchers and birdophiles, this often-overlooked trail and the surrounding reserve should definitely not be missed.

Start: From the trailhead just off Santee Gun Club Road
Distance: 2.2-mile loop
Hiking time: About 1-2 hours
Difficulty: Easy
Trail surface: Forested trail, boardwalk, gravel road, old roadbed
Best seasons: Winter, early spring, late fall
Other trail users: Mountain bikers
Canine compatibility: Leashed dogs permitted
Fees and permits: Admission free; permits required for hunting and camping
Schedule: Dawn to dusk daily
Maps: TOPO! CD: North Carolina-South Carolina; USGS maps: Minim Island and Cape Romain; South Carolina; USFS maps: Santee Coastal Reserve Trail Map available at the reserve office
Trail contacts: Santee Coastal Reserve, 210 Santee Gun Club Rd., McClellanville, SC 29458; (843) 546-6062

Finding the trailhead: From McClellanville travel north on US 17 toward Georgetown. Approximately 3 miles out of McClellanville, turn right onto South Santee Road. Travel for about 3 miles and then turn right onto Santee Gun Club Road adjacent to the St. James Community Center, which is a dirt road that leads into Santee Coastal Reserve. Proceed 2.5 miles to the kiosk for more information. GPS: N33 09.226'/W79 22.011'

The Hike

The Santee Coastal Reserve is located on the huge Santee River Delta. The 24,000-acre reserve features a complex of trails and roads that are open to hikers and bikers. Occasionally the park is closed for special hunts, and during times of heavy rainfall, the hiking trails may be impassable. I highly recommend calling the Santee Coastal Reserve office in advance of your hike to check on current trail conditions. The first impression you will likely have of the park are the impressive and massive oak trees that arch across Santee Gun Club Road. The canopy of these old-growth oaks creates a visually stunning and serene tunnel of trees. Keep your eyes open for a small parking lot on the left side of the road that offers parking for hikers on the Marshland Loop and Bike/Hike Loop trails.

The Santee Reserve is a former rice-field plantation. Throughout much of the past century, the land
was utilized by a local hunting club. In 1974 the land
was purchased by the Nature Conservancy, which
eventually turned the land over to the South Carolina Department of Natural Resources, which man-
ages the land today. The reserve has been recognized
as an important bird area in South Carolina. For the
absolutely best ornithological opportunities, organize
your outing during the late winter or early spring to
observe a large variety of migratory songbirds, wad-

ing birds, and waterfowl. A highlight for hard-core birders is the boardwalk in the
1,000-acre Washo Reserve near the beginning of the trail, which leads to a large
swamp filled with cypress trees. The Washo Reserve is the only portion of the original
land in this area that is still owned by the Nature Conservancy and it supports one of
the largest wood-stork rookeries on the East Coast. Alligators are commonly seen in
the cypress pond and wetlands along the trail. You may also see a variety of wildlife
including white-tailed deer, feral hogs, bobcats, squirrels, bobwhite quail, and other
small game.

The trail starts from the trailhead to the Marshland Loop just off Santee Gun
Club Road. You follow a forested path to the boardwalk, which extends into the
Washo Reserve and out to the edge of the cypress pond. A small observation deck at
the end of the boardwalk offers an excellent resting spot. The views are wonderful.
Continue on the path and cross a small bridge over an outlet of the pond. The trail
is easy to follow as it loops around through a mix of marshland, maritime forest, and
agricultural wetlands cut with old rice-growing canals. In the spring you will find
plants such as blue-flag iris as well as swamp dogwood, cattails, lizard's tail, and water
willow. The forested areas are filled with Spanish-moss-draped live oaks, holly, ferns,
bull-bay, sparkleberry, and sweet gum. The canals are favorite spots for herons and
egrets fishing in the shallow and aquatic-life rich waters. If you approach the canals
quietly, you may get an up-close look at one of these magnificent birds. However,
they often hear you long before you approach the canals and all you see are the quick
flash of feathers and the spectacular view of the large birds gliding over the marshland.

The trail circles around to the north and parallels a long canal before arriving back
at a gravel park road that leads back to the trailhead where you started. For a longer
hike, the bike/hike loop is a 5.1-mile trail that loops to the Intracoastal Waterway,
parallels the waterway as it travels toward the South Santee River, and then parallels
the river on the return to the junction with the Marshland Loop for a total hike of
more than 7 miles.

◀ *Spanish moss decorates the trees in the wetland of
the Santee Coastal Reserve.*

The oak groves of the Santee Coastal Reserve are stunningly beautiful.

Miles and Directions

0.0 Start from the parking lot for the Marshland Trail just across from the large wooden kiosk that marks the trailhead. Cross Santee Gun Club Road to the kiosk, and then follow the path directly behind the kiosk into the forest.

0.2 Reach the trail junction with the boardwalk. Turn right onto the boardwalk that leads out to a small marsh pond.

0.3 Arrive at the end of the boardwalk, and enjoy the excellent views of the pond. Turn around and return to the start of the boardwalk.

0.4 Reach the main trail, turn right and head south on the Marshland Loop toward the small bridge over the seasonal stream. Cross the bridge.

0.5 Arrive at a trail junction. Follow the Marshland Loop to the right. After 220 feet you reach another trail junction with a dirt road. Turn left and follow the Marshland Loop.

1.0 Reach a split in the trail. Stay to the left and follow the Marshland Loop.

1.5 Reach a T junction. The bike/hike trail is to the right. Turn left and continue on the Marshland Loop.

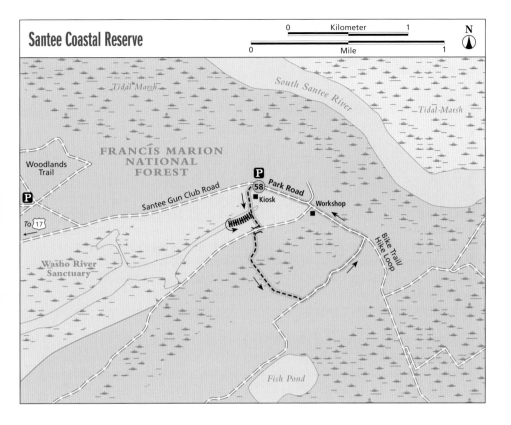

Santee Coastal Reserve

1.8 Arrive at the back of the workshop. Follow the doubletrack trail past the workshop and out toward Santee Gun Club Road. In 350 feet you will reach a dirt road. Stay straight and follow the dirt road back to the parking lot and trailhead where you started.

2.2 Arrive at the kiosk and parking area where you started.

Hike Information

Local Information: Georgetown Chamber of Commerce, 531 Front St., Georgetown, SC 29440; (843) 546-8436; visitgeorge.com

Local Events/Attractions: Hampton Plantation State Historic Site, 1950 Rutledge Rd., George-town; (843) 527-4995. Guided tours Sat–Tues at 1, 2, and 3 p.m. Fee is discounted for seniors and kids 6–15.

Winyah Bay Festival, Georgetown. The fes-tival celebrates the Lowcountry heritage and takes place annually in March.

Lodging: Mansfield Plantation B&B, 1776 Mansfield Rd., Georgetown; (843) 546-6961; mansfieldplantation.com

The Shaw House B&B, 613 Cypress Ct., Georgetown; (843) 546-9663

Restaurants: Limpin' Jane's, 713 Front St., Georgetown; (843) 485-4953; limpinjanes.com. Open daily 11 a.m. to 10 p.m.

River Room, 801 Front St., Georgetown; (843) 527-4110; riverroomgeorgetown.com. Open Mon–Sat 11 a.m. to 2:30 p.m. and 5 to 10 p.m.

59 Santee Coastal Reserve Roadway Walk

Travel just south of Georgetown to discover a network of trails and roads that navigates through one of the best examples of longleaf-pine forest in the state. This easy day hike combines several of the reserve's roads to create a loop of level trekking. Highlights include excellent opportunities for bird and wildlife viewing and an introduction to the wildlife-management techniques found throughout the reserve.

Start: From the Woodlands Trail parking area
Distance: 2.3-mile loop
Hiking time: About 1–2 hours
Difficulty: Easy
Trail surface: Dirt road, old roadbed
Best seasons: Winter, early spring, late fall
Other trail users: Mountain bikers
Canine compatibility: Leashed dogs permitted
Fees and permits: Admission free; permits required for hunting and camping
Schedule: Dawn to dusk daily
Maps: TOPO! CD: North Carolina-South Carolina; USGS maps: Minim Island and Cape Romain; South Carolina; USFS maps: Santee Coastal Reserve Trail Map available at the reserve office
Trail contacts: Santee Coastal Reserve, 210 Santee Gun Club Rd., McClellanville, SC 29458; (843) 546-6062

Finding the trailhead: From McClellanville travel north on US 17 toward Georgetown. Approximately 3 miles out of McClellanville, turn right onto South Santee Road. Travel for about 3 miles and then turn right onto Santee Gun Club Road adjacent to the St. James Community Center, which is a dirt road that leads into Santee Coastal Reserve. Proceed 2.5 miles to the kiosk for more information. GPS: N33 09.151'/W79 23.188'

The Hike

The 24,000-acre Santee Reserve features a variety of trails and roads that are open to hikers and bikers. Occasionally the park is closed for special hunts, and during times of heavy rainfall, the hiking trails may be impassable. I highly recommend calling the Santee Coastal Reserve office in advance of your hike to check on current trail conditions. On this route I would like to introduce you to the opportunities you have for exploring the roadways that crisscross throughout this unique and beautiful park. This route is meant as only an introduction to the miles and miles of roads that you will find in the Santee Reserve and I highly encourage you to get out and explore these roadways further either by foot or bike.

You have a variety of options along this route to create new and longer or shorter loops and out-and-back hikes as you explore the roadways that cut through this complex mix of old-growth pine and hardwood forest. The trail begins at the trailhead for

The Santee Coastal Reserve Woodland Trail ▶

A field along the Santee Coastal Reserve Woodland Trail

the Woodland Trail loop located on the north side of Santee Gun Club Road. While the Woodland Trail loop is an excellent choice for hikers, I encourage the more adventurous to get off the beaten path and walk some of the roads around this trail to introduce hikers to the myriad of possibilities you have to explore this reserve. Also, I find that a more informal approach to this forested section of the reserve is much more enjoyable due to the fact that the Woodland Trail loop is very poorly marked and offers generally the same mix of terrain and opportunities for wildlife viewing as you will find along the roadways throughout the park. Whether you decide to spend an hour on the Woodland Trail or the route in this book, or decide to spend the whole day on a long walkabout around the roadways, is completely up to you. The roads tend to be poorly marked, however, and I highly recommend bringing a compass and picking up a good map from the park office before embarking on any ambitious and far-reaching amblings.

This trail offers a stunning contrast to the wetlands you traverse along the Marshland Loop to the south in the reserve. The roads and trails in this section of the

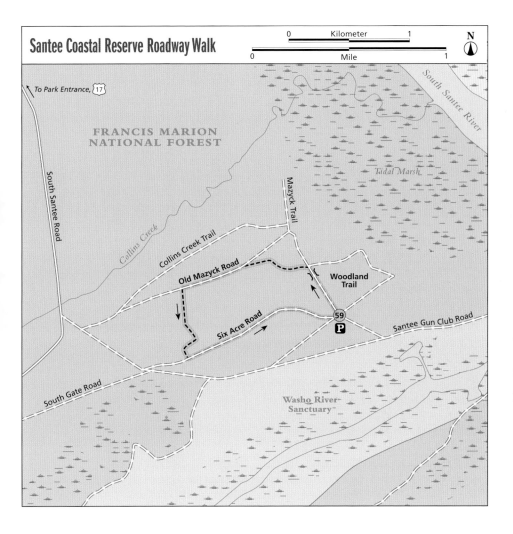

Santee Coastal Reserve Roadway Walk

To Park Entrance, 17

FRANCIS MARION
NATIONAL FOREST

South Santee River

Tidal Marsh

South Santee Road

Mazyck Trail

Collins Creek

Collins Creek Trail

Old Mazyck Road

Woodland
Trail

Six Acre Road

59
P

Santee Gun Club Road

South Gate Road

Washo River
Sanctuary

park trek through much drier forests carpeted in a thick understory of bright-green palmettos. Along the trail you may encounter feral hogs, squirrels, wild turkeys, sparrows, bald eagles, ospreys, turkey buzzards, swallow-tailed kites, and warblers. The pine stands provide refuge for red-cockaded woodpeckers and are considered prime white-tailed-deer habitat.

Start from the trailhead for the Woodland Trail. After parking at the unpaved parking area, walk to the small sign that marks the start of the Woodland Trail. You are facing north and there are roads running in every direction. You really can't go wrong with walking down any of these roads, but to follow the route in the book, go straight on Mazyck's Road, which is also part of the Woodland Trail. After crossing a small footbridge, you arrive at the junction with the Woodland Trail. Stay straight and continue to a split in the road just a few feet ahead. Veer left onto Old Mazyck Road and continue to walk through the stands of tall pine forest, passing several open fields that are used during hunting season. These fields and the surrounding forest are excellent places to spot woodpeckers and deer.

Continue on Old Mazyck Road for 0.7 mile until you reach a junction with an unnamed road that leads toward Six Acre Road. Turn left on this unnamed road. Once you reach Six Acre Road, turn left again and return to the trailhead where you started.

Miles and Directions

0.0 Start from the parking area for the Woodland Trail at the end of the dirt road off Santee Gun Club Road. The trailhead is at the north end of the unpaved parking area. Go straight (north) on Mazyck's Road.

0.2 Cross the wooden bridge.

0.3 Arrive at a trail junction. To the right is the Woodland Trail. Continue straight for 50 feet until you arrive at a split in the dirt road. Straight ahead Mazyck's Road continues. Veer left onto Old Mazyck Road.

1.0 You reach a trail junction with an unnamed dirt road. Turn left onto the dirt road.

1.4 You reach a T junction with Six Acre Road. Turn left and head back toward the trailhead.

2.3 You arrive back at the trailhead where you started your hike.

Hike Information

Local Information: Georgetown Chamber of Commerce, 531 Front St., Georgetown, SC 29440; (843) 546-8436; visitgeorge.com

Local Events/Attractions: Hampton Plantation State Historic Site, 1950 Rutledge Rd., Georgetown; (843) 527-4995. Guided tours Sat–Tues at 1, 2, and 3 p.m. Fee is discounted for seniors and kids 6–15.

Winyah Bay Festival, Georgetown. This festival celebrating Lowcountry heritage occurs annually in March.

Lodging: Mansfield Plantation B&B, 1776 Mansfield Rd., Georgetown; (843) 546-6961; mansfieldplantation.com

The Shaw House B&B, 613 Cypress Ct., Georgetown; (843) 546-9663

Restaurants: Limpin' Jane's, 713 Front St., Georgetown; (843) 485-4953; limpinjanes.com. Open daily 11 a.m. to 10 p.m.

River Room, 801 Front St., Georgetown; (843) 527-4110; riverroomgeorgetown.com. Open Mon–Sat 11 a.m. to 2:30 p.m. and 5 to 10 p.m.

60 Huntington Beach State Park

This easy day hike explores the great diversity of beautiful landscapes that you can traverse within Huntington Beach State Park, just south of Myrtle Beach on the state's upper coast. Discover saltwater and freshwater marshes and pristine maritime forest before enjoying a long walk along the beach on the way back to the trailhead. This is an excellent hike for children and hikers with dogs looking to trek one of the best day hikes on the coast of South Carolina.

Start: The Education Center parking lot

Distance: 3.0-mile lollipop

Hiking time: About 1–2 hours

Difficulty: Easy

Trail surface: Forested path, boardwalk, paved road, beach

Best season: Year-round

Other trail users: Hikers only

Canine compatibility: Leashed dogs permitted

Fees and permits: Free for kids under age 6; small fee for everyone 6 and over; senior discount available

Schedule: Nov 27 to Mar 11 daily 6 a.m. to 6 p.m. Hours extended to 10 p.m. daily during daylight saving time

Maps: TOPO! CD: North Carolina–South Carolina; USGS maps: Brookgreen and Magnolia Beach; South Carolina; USFS maps: Huntington Beach State Park Hiking Trails Map available at the park office and online at southcarolinaparks.com

Trail contacts: Huntington Beach State Park, 16148 Ocean Hwy., Murrells Inlet, SC 29576; (843) 237-4440

Finding the trailhead: *From Georgetown:* Drive 20 miles north on US 17. The park entrance is on the right.

From Myrtle Beach: Drive 17 miles south on US 17. The park entrance is on the left. GPS: N33 30.568'/W79 03.759'

The Hike

Huntington Beach State Park is one of the best state parks in the entire state, especially for outdoors lovers searching for a perfect tent site on the Atlantic Ocean. The park offers plenty of open, sunny campsites designed more for RVs and camper-trailers. However, the best campsites are the primitive campsites nestled in a dense maritime forest. You have to walk your camping gear back to the campsites, but it is no more than 50 feet to the farthest site in the group. A narrow trail connects campers to the coast and to an extensive network of some of the most well-maintained and superbly scenic trails within the entire coastal plain. I highly recommend camping and extensively exploring this wonderful state park. It offers more than 2 miles of trails that traverse through some of the finest examples of maritime forest with a wide diversity of water systems along the trails.

The trail begins at the parking lot of the Nature Center near the campground. Before your hike take the time to explore the 2,500-square-foot center, which houses many examples of the types of native plants, animals, and aquatic life that are found throughout the park. Informative interpretive displays at the center give you insight into the rich history and ecological importance of this dynamic 2,500-acre gem, which is the largest stretch of undeveloped beach along the state's upper coast. The park was named after the American sculptor Anna Hyatt Huntington and her husband, Archer Milton Huntington, who resided in a beach house on this property until 1960 when the land was leased from the Brookgreen Trustees. After enjoying the Nature Center, walk to the end of the boardwalk behind the center and discover sweeping views of the saltwater marsh, which is fed by Oaks Creek. Spartina grass, black pluff-mud crowded with oysters, and a variety of fish can be observed along the boardwalk. At the end of the boardwalk, turn around and return to the parking lot. Right across the street is the trailhead to the Sandpiper Pond Nature Trail. Follow the trail as it traverses through the pristine, dense maritime forest filled with large live and laurel oaks draped in Spanish moss and crowded with loblolly pines and red cedars with a thick understory of wax myrtle, various creeping vines, and abundant palmettos.

The trail winds behind the beautiful, saltwater Sandpiper Pond, and along the way you enjoy several excellent opportunities to enjoy a view of the surrounding complex coastal ecosystem from elevated observation decks. Climb up to the observation platforms and you will be treated to an expansive view of Sandpiper Pond in front of you, the dunes complex rolling behind the pond, and the expansive beach that stretches to the Atlantic Ocean. It is an incredible view and a great place to pull out the binoculars and spot the wide diversity of birds that can be seen in the park, including blue herons, seagulls, osprey, warblers, bald eagles (which have made an incredible comeback in the park), a great variety of ducks, and the endangered piping plover. The park is considered by those with an affinity for avians to be a superior site for bird spotting. So if you go bananas over birds, be sure to bring your binoculars.

The trail emerges from the forest at a parking lot near the north end of the park. Turn right and follow the road and then a paved trail to the boardwalk, which creates a low-impact pathway through the fragile and gorgeous rolling dune ecosystem. The boardwalk leads to a wide, sandy beach stretching in both directions, with the Atlantic Ocean rolling onto the seashell-speckled shore. Turn right and enjoy a leisurely walk on the beach, where you can take your shoes off and enjoy the feeling of sand between your toes as you trek where the water meets the sand and playful seagulls soar overhead. Keep your eyes open for dolphins, stingrays, sea turtles, and other aquatic marine life found in the Atlantic as you make your way back toward the spur trail to the campground, marked by a large metal pole near the dunes.

◀ *One of the top reasons to hike South Carolina is the magnificent coastal views.*

Savor this view from one of several observation decks along the Sandpiper Nature Trail in Huntington Beach State Park.

A boardwalk traverses back over the dunes and leads through a small low-lying marsh area before arriving at the park road through the campground. You can turn right and follow the road and the connector trail back to the nature center and the parking lot where you started. This hike explores a diversity of layers of coastal habitat nestled and protected within the extremely developed and popular Grand Strand of South Carolina's magnificent coast.

Miles and Directions

0.0   Start from the Education Center parking lot. Walk toward the Education Center. In 120 feet you arrive at the start of the boardwalk over the marsh. Enjoy the boardwalk over the saltwater marsh.

0.2   Reach the end of the boardwalk. Turn around and head back toward the education center.

0.4   Cross the park road that runs in front of the education center and reach the trailhead to the Sandpiper Pond Nature Trail. Follow the thin path into the forest. In 300 feet you reach a T junction. A spur trail to the campground is to the right. Turn left and follow the nature trail.

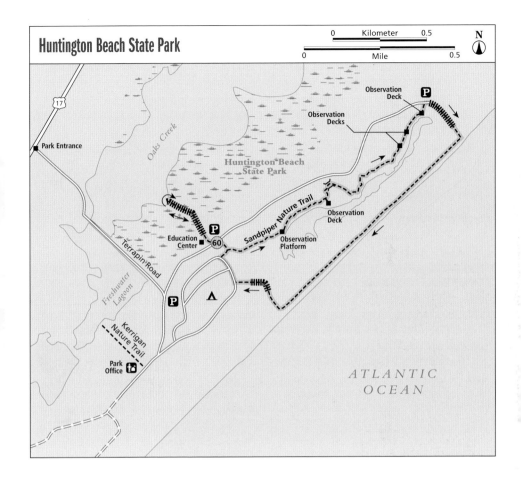

Huntington Beach State Park

0 Kilometer 0.5

0 Mile 0.5

N

Park Entrance

Oaks Creek

17

Observation Deck

Observation Decks

Huntington Beach State Park

Sandpiper Nature Trail

Observation Deck

Observation Platform

Education Center

60

Terrapin Road

Freshwater Lagoon

Kerrigan Nature Trail

Park Office

ATLANTIC OCEAN

0.6 An elevated observation deck to the left of the trail offers impressive views of the pond, dunes habitat, and the Atlantic Ocean beyond.

0.8 Reach a split in the trail. Stay to the right and follow the spur trail to the observation deck 100 feet away. After enjoying the observation deck views, turn around and return to the main trail, then turn right and continue on the Sandpiper Nature Trail.

0.9 Cross the footbridge over a small pond outlet.

1.3 Arrive at an observation deck overlooking the pond to the right of the trail.

1.4 Reach another observation deck overlooking the pond.

1.5 An observation deck to the right of trail offers great views of the pond. In 200 feet you reach the park road. Turn right and follow the road to the Beach Access Trail. In 90 feet follow the paved trail toward the boardwalk.

1.6 Reach the start of the boardwalk that leads over the dune habitat to the beach and the Atlantic Ocean.

1.7 You arrive at the end of the boardwalk. Turn right (southwest) and walk along the beach back toward the campground and park office.

2.6 Turn right at the metal pole that marks the spur trail that leads to the campground.

2.7 A short boardwalk crosses over a small marsh.

2.8 Arrive at the campground road. Turn right to return to the Education Center and the parking lot where you started.

2.9 On the right side of the road, you reach a spur trail that leads to the Sandpiper Nature Trail. Turn right onto this trail. In 150 feet you reach the Nature Trail. Turn left and head toward the Nature Center.

3.0 You arrive back at the trailhead for the Sandpiper Nature Trail. Cross the paved road to return to the Nature Center parking lot where you started this hike.

Hike Information

Local Information: Murrells Inlet Visitors Center, 4124 Business Hwy. 17, Murrells Inlet, SC 29576; (843) 357-2007; www.murrells inletsc.com

Local Events/Attractions: Brookgreen Gardens, 1931 Brookgreen Dr., Murrells Inlet; (843) 235-6000; brookgreen.org. Open daily 9:30 a.m. to 5 p.m. Fee is discounted for seniors 65 and over and kids 4–12.

Marsh Walk, 3979 Business Hwy. 17, Murrells Inlet; marshwalk.com. Enjoy waterfront dining and live music along the saltwater estuary.

Lodging: The Inlet Sports Lodge, 4600 Business Hwy. 17, Murrells Inlet; (877) 585-9360; inletsportslodge.com

Camping at Huntington Beach State Park, 16148 Ocean Hwy., Murrells Inlet; (843) 237-4440. Water and electric sites available

Restaurants: Lee's Inlet Kitchen, 4460 Business Hwy. 17, Murrells Inlet; (843) 651-2881; leesinletkitchen.com. Open Mon–Sat from 4:30 p.m.

Russell's Seafood Grill, 4906 Business Hwy. 17, Murrells Inlet; (843) 651-0553; russells seafoodgrill.com. Open Mon–Sat from 4:30 p.m.

Appendix A: Local Clubs and Organizations

Hiking Clubs

Anderson Hikers and Backpackers
Dennis Mize
608 Blume Rd.
Anderson, SC 29625
(864) 225-4351

Carolina Mountain Club
PO Box 68
Asheville, NC 28802
(828) 738-3395
carolinamountainclub.org

Charlotte Lady Hikers
charlotteladyhikers.com

Palmetto Wanderers
Sandy Best
Richland County Recreation Commission
5819 Shakespeare Rd.
Columbia, SC 29223
(803) 754-PARK (7275)

Conservation Groups

Catawba Riverkeeper
421 Minuet Ln.
Suite 205
Charlotte, NC 28217
(704) 679-9494
catawbariverkeeper.org

Coastal Conservation League
1001 Washington St.
Suite 300
Columbia, SC 29201
(803) 771-7102
coastalconservationleague.org

Foothills Trail Conference
PO Box 3041
Greenville, SC 29602
844-467-9537
foothillstrail.org

Friends of Congaree Swamp
PO Box 7746
Columbia, SC 29202
(803) 331-3366
friendsofcongaree.org

Friends of the Edisto
PO Box 5151
Columbia, SC 29250
edistofriends.org

Friends of Hunting Island State Park
PO Box 844
Saint Helena Island, SC 29920
friends-of-hunting-island-sc.org

Friends of the Reedy River
PO Box 9351
Greenville, SC 29604
friendsofthereedyriver.org

Greenville Natural History Association
PO Box 26892
Greenville, SC 29616
greenvillehiking.com

◀   *A view of the Chattooga River*

The Nature Conservancy South Carolina
2231 Devine St.
Suite 100
Columbia, SC 29205
(803) 254-9049
nature.org

Palmetto Conservation Foundation
722 King St.
Columbia, SC 29205
(803) 771-0870
palmettoconservation.org

SEWEE Association
PO Box 1131
Mount Pleasant, SC 29465
seweeassociation.org

South Carolina Sierra Club
255 Enterprise Blvd.
Greenville, SC 29615
southcarolina.sierraclub.org

The Spartanburg Area Conservancy
100 E. Main St.
Suite 7
Spartanburg, SC 29306
(864) 948-0000
spartanburgconservation.org

Waccamaw Riverkeeper Foundation
PO Box 261954
Conway, SC 29528
(843) 349-4007
winyahrivers.org

The forest along the Winding Stairs Trail. ▶

Appendix B: Further Reading

History Books

Bass, Jack, and W. Scott Poole. *The Palmetto State: The Making of Modern South Carolina.* Columbia, SC: University of South Carolina Press, 2009.

Eastman, Margaret Middleton Rivers and Edward Fitzsimons Good. *Hidden History of Old Charleston.* Charleston, SC: The History Press, 2010.

Edgar, Walter. *South Carolina: A History.* Columbia, SC: University of South Carolina Press, 1998.

Lathan, Robert. *History of South Carolina.* Wings Publishers, 2002.

Rowland, Lawrence S., George C. Rodgers, and Alexander Moore. *The History of Beaufort County, South Carolina: 1514-1861.* Columbia, SC: University of South Carolina Press, 1996.

Weir, Robert M. *Colonial South Carolina: A History.* Columbia, SC: University of South Carolina Press, 1997.

Natural History

Blagden, Tom. *South Carolina's Wetland Wilderness: The Ace Basin.* Westcliff Publishing Inc., 1992.

Brooks, Ben, and Tim Cook. *The Waterfalls of South Carolina.* Columbia, SC: Palmetto Conservation Press, 2007.

Kavanagh, J. M., and Raymond Leung. *South Carolina Wildlife: An Introduction to Familiar Species.* Dunedin, FL: Waterford Press, 2010.

Rosengarten, Dale. *Row Upon Row: Sea Grass Baskets of the South Carolina Lowcountry.* Columbia: McKissick Museum, University of South Carolina Press, 1993.

Schulze, Richard. *Carolina Gold Rice: The Ebb and Flow History of a Lowcountry Cash Crop.* Charleston, SC: History Press 2012.

Stewart, Kevin G. and Mary-Russell Roberson. *Exploring the Geology of the Carolinas: A Field Guide to Favorite Places from Chimney Rock to Charleston.* Chapel Hill: University of North Carolina Press, 2007.

On the Lee Falls Trail, the trail is about as hard to find as a good view of the falls.

The Old Waterwheel Site along the Old Waterwheel Trail

Hiking

Bernstein, Danny. *Hiking the Carolina Mountains.* Almond, NC: Milestone Press Inc., 2007.

Brooks, Ben, and Tim Cook. *The Waterfalls of South Carolina.* Columbia, SC: Palmetto Conservation Press, 2007.

King, Thomas E. *Waterfall Hikes of Upstate South Carolina.* Greenville, SC: Milestone Press, 2009.

Lynch, Scott. *Family Hikes in Upstate South Carolina.* Almond, NC: Milestone Press, 2012.

Molloy, Johnny. *Explorer's Guide 50 Hikes in South Carolina: Walks, Hikes & Backpacking Trips from the Lowcountry Shores to the Midlands to the Mountains & Rivers of the Upstate.* Woodstock, VT: Countryman Press, 2007.

Index

About the Author

Joshua Kinser's passion for travel has led him to work at some of the coolest jobs in the world, which apart from writing hiking guidebooks include exploring national parks as a backcountry wildlife biology tech, working on cruise ships as a musician, and working as a travel writer for magazines and newspapers.

He is the author of several hiking guidebooks to the Southeast including *Five Star Trails: Charlotte, NC* and *Five Star Trails: Raleigh, NC* as well as Moon Handbook's *Florida Gulf Coast,* third and fourth editions. Joshua is also the author of *Following Mowgli: An Appalachian Trail Adventure with the World's Most Hilarious Dog.* This comical book tells the true story of what happens when Joshua attempts to thru-hike the AT with a loveable and eccentric but destructive German shepherd named Mowgli. He is the author of *Chronicles of a Cruise Ship Crew Member: Answers to All the Questions Every Passenger Wants to Ask,* a hilarious look into what it is really like to work on a cruise ship, which draws from his experiences working as a cruise ship drummer for more than five years. The book has spent more than six months as the number-one-selling book about cruise ships on Amazon.com. He has published more than 200 articles online for websites such as Trails.com, eHow, and USA Today Travel. He has worked as a staff writer for Gannet with the *Pensacola News Journal,* and has contributed to publications that include *SAIL Magazine, Bonito and Estero Magazine,* and *Times of the Islands.*

As a backcountry biology tech, Kinser has worked in Florida, Hawaii Volcanoes National Park, Glacier National Park in Montana, and in the national forest lands surrounding Yosemite National Park in California. He also works as a professional drummer, performing with the Chris Crosby Group (www.chriscrosbymusic.com), one of the most popular wedding bands in Charleston, South Carolina. His work as a musician and travel writer have taken him all over the world including the Caribbean, Australia, China, Japan, and New Zealand.

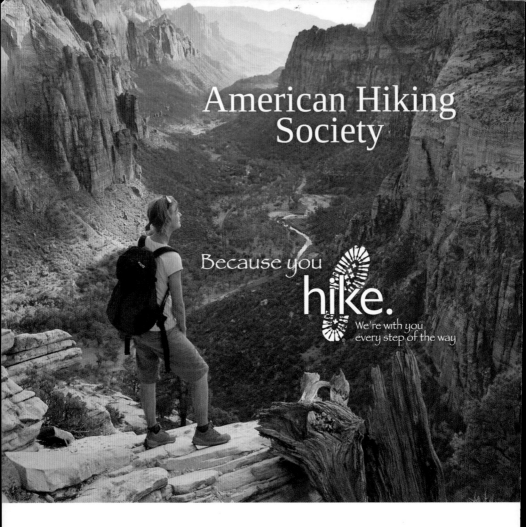

American Hiking Society

Because you hike.
We're with you every step of the way

As a national voice for hikers, **American Hiking Society** works every day:

- Building and maintaining hiking trails
- Educating and supporting hikers by providing information and resources
- Supporting hiking and trail organizations nationwide
- Speaking for hikers in the halls of Congress and with federal land managers

Whether you're a casual hiker or a seasoned backpacker, become a member of American Hiking Society and join the national hiking community! You'll enjoy great member benefits and help preserve the nation's hiking trails, so tomorrow's hike is even better than today's. We invite you to join us now!

American Hiking Society

www.AmericanHiking.org • info@AmericanHiking.org